T0306152

MASCULINITIES AND MANAGEMENT IN AGRICULTURAL ORGANIZATIONS WORLDWIDE

Gender and Organizational Theory Series

Series Editor: Emma Jeanes,
School of Business and Economics,
University of Exeter, UK

The aim of this series is to provide research monographs and edited volumes on all topics within the area of gender and management, broadly defined. The series is intended to encompass different perspectives within feminism (for example liberal, post-structuralist and Marxist) as well as the interplay of feminist perspectives with other forms of identity and discourse. The series also aims to provide books that explore notions of masculinities in an organizational context.

Titles in the series:

The Making of Women Trade Unionists
Gill Kirton
ISBN 978 0 7546 4569 6

Gender and Communication at Work
Edited by Mary Barrett and Marilyn J. Davidson
ISBN 978 0 7546 3840 7

Masculinities and Management in Agricultural Organizations Worldwide

BARBARA PINI
Curtin University of Technology, Australia

Routledge
Taylor & Francis Group
LONDON AND NEW YORK

First published 2008 by Ashgate Publishing

Reissued 2018 by Routledge
2 Park Square, Milton Park, Abingdon, Oxon, OX14 4RN
605 Third Avenue, New York, NY 10017

First issued in paperback 2021

Routledge is an imprint of the Taylor & Francis Group, an informa business

A Library of Congress record exists under LC control number: 2008014373

Notice:
Product or corporate names may be trademarks or registered trademarks, and are used
only for identification and explanation without intent to infringe.

Publisher's Note
The publisher has gone to great lengths to ensure the quality of this reprint but points out
that some imperfections in the original copies may be apparent.

Disclaimer
The publisher has made every effort to trace copyright holders and welcomes
correspondence from those they have been unable to contact.

ISBN 13: 978-0-815-39046-6 (hbk)
ISBN 13: 978-1-351-15324-9 (ebk)
ISBN 13: 978-1-138-35839-3 (pbk)

DOI: 10.4324/9781351153249

Contents

For my parents
Agnes and Albert Pini

Acknowledgements

Having my name, and mine alone on the cover of this book seems somewhat duplicitous when I consider the many people who have helped shape what lies between these covers.

My interest in the research addressed in this book, emerged from my work as a government policy officer working with rural women, and particularly, women involved in agricultural industries. My interest also developed through previous academic studies I had pursued in the areas relating to women and management, gender and organisations and feminist theory. However, the subject matter was with me, albeit in a less structured way, from an age which preceded both paid work and academic study. I grew up on a farm in the town of Proserpine in the northern area of the state of Queensland in Australia. All my father's family were farmers in the district. Like many other Italian migrants, they were drawn to agriculture with the promise of work and eventually became farmers in their own right. Thus, this book is located within my personal experience, emerging as it did from my own background in an agricultural industry. The questions I address in the book as an academic are similar to those which plagued me while growing up and in my roles as granddaughter, niece, sister and daughter to farmers. While returning to such questions as an adult and in the role of scholar has been rewarding, it has also been challenging.

In dealing with these challenges I was fortunate to have the supervisory team of Margaret Grace, Leonie Daws and Jillian Brannock. They provided valuable guidance. Margaret assisted me in applying for a grant for the research. I remain indebted to her for giving me a start in academia.

Ian Ballantyne acted as an industry supervisor for the study. His extensive knowledge of agri-politics and his keen intelligence were of immense value throughout the course of the study. Pam Poggio, was also particularly generous in sharing her time and insights. Pam Bol gave much in terms of administrative support as well as encouragement and friendship.

I developed the book while first working in the School of Management, Faculty of Business at QUT where my former Head of School, Professor Neal Ryan was a key mentor. At this time Stacy Ridge provided expert research assistance and Susan Leggett editorial help.

Friends and family have been important in demonstrating interest in this book. Josephine Previte, Trish Knight and my sister Judith have offered feedback on drafts of work as well as engaged in discussions with me about much of what I have written. I am very grateful.

I am fortunate to be part of a wider national and international community of scholars interested in gender and rurality whose work has invigorated this book. I am thankful to them for this and for the support they have given to my own work. My Australian colleagues, Lia Bryant, Ruth Panelli, Ruth Beilin, Alison Sheridan and Lou Conway deserve special thanks.

Overall, I am very thankful to the farming men and women who so kindly participated in this study. I hope I have done justice to the stories they have shared with me.

Chapter 3 has been adapted from Pini, B. 2005, 'Interviewing men: Gender and the collection and interpretation of qualitative data' *Sociology* 41(2) 1–16. This has been reprinted with the permission Sage Publications (Copyright TASA The Australian Sociological Association 2005). Chapter 4 has been adapted from Pini, B. 2004, 'Paternalism and managerial masculinities in the Australian sugar industry' *Rural Society* 14(1): 22–35. Chapter 6 has been adapted from Pini, B. 2005, 'The third sex: Women in leadership in Australian agriculture' *Gender, Work and Organisation* 12(1): 73–88. This has been reprinted with the permission of Blackwell Publications.

Chapter 1

Introduction

To say that women are poorly represented in positions of leadership in agri-politics is not particularly ground-breaking or profound. In Australia, for example, the major farm group, the National Farmers' Federation, has just one woman member on its seven person board. Across a selection of similar Australian agricultural organizations, the average percentage of women involved sits at just 13 per cent (DoTARS 2005). Studies demonstrate that this type of gender inequality is, unfortunately, replicated internationally in farming groups across the United States, Norway, Canada, Denmark, Northern Ireland, France, New Zealand, Iceland, Sweden, Finland, Italy and Egypt (see Barbic 1993; Bock and de Haan 2004; Demossier 2004; El-Tobshy 2005; Jodahl 1994; Liepins 1998; 2000; Sachs 1996; Shortall 1999; 2001; Silvasti 2003; Verstad 1998; Wells 1998). In fact, in reflecting on men's quantitative dominance of decision-making positions across a range of nation states, rural sociologist Sally Shortall (1999, 96) has contended, 'there is no country where women are well represented in farming organizations. Indeed, farming organizations could accurately be called men's organizations'.

Shortall's (1999) observation provides a useful starting point for this book because it raises the question of what it means for an organization to be tagged with the descriptor 'men's'. Suggesting that agricultural groups are 'men's groups' because of men's numerical hold on leadership positions does not take us very far. For example, it does this not explain why, throughout history, decision-making positions in agricultural groups have been monopolized by men despite farm women's political activism and interests (Meyer and Lobao 1994; Neth 1988), nor why, despite attempts to address gender inequity in agricultural groups, there has been little change in men's disproportionate hold on leadership positions (Panelli and Pini 2005; Pini and Brown 2004; Pini, Panelli, Dale-Hallett and the Women on Farms Heritage Group 2007). Clearly, critiquing agricultural groups as 'men's organizations' (Shortall 1999, 96) requires a more complex analysis than a numerical assessment.

Working from a similar (albeit broader) starting point over a decade ago, Collinson and Hearn (1994, 2) observed that 'in most organizations most managers are men'. They asserted that understanding why this was so required more than a simple body count and advocated research which focused on the enactment and replication of managerial masculinities in organizations. Since this time, numerous gender and organizational scholars have taken Collinson and Hearn's (1994) advice and produced a rich and dynamic literature that has demonstrated that the interconnections between management and masculinities are both plentiful and prevalent (for example, Kerfoot 2002; Kerfoot and Knights 1993; Whitehead 1998). In utilising such a paradigm, the focus of investigation is shifted from women's disadvantage to the typically less studied question of men's advantage, and the actions, practices and discourses by which men seek to retain this advantage (Eveline 1994, 129–54).

Despite the theoretical efficacy of a focus on masculinities as enumerated by writers such as Collinson and Hearn (1994), this type of approach has been little used in studies of rural and agricultural organizations. In part, this is reflective of the ongoing urban bias of much organizational and management scholarship (Pini 2002a). It is also illustrative of the fact that second wave rural studies scholars have been largely preoccupied with the position of agricultural women behind the farm gate rather than in the public domain of farming organizations. Thus, while we have significant evidence of men's numerical dominance of farmers' unions worldwide, we know little about the processes and practices that have produced and continue to reproduce this dominance.

The key purpose of this book is to address this gap in the literature. In doing so, it takes up and elaborates upon Shortall's (1999, 96) claim that agricultural groups could legitimately be labelled 'men's organizations' not simply by quantification, but through reporting on a three year case study of an Australian farmers' union as well as interviews with women leaders from different agricultural sectors. The organization that was the focus for the ethnographic investigation is one of the nation's largest, looking after the interests of over 6,000 farming families. There are two types of managers in the organization – elected leaders and staff. At the time of the study, there were 181 positions of elected leadership in the organization. None was held by a woman.[1] A similar picture exists in relation to the gender ratio of staff management positions in the Farmers' Union. There are 19 district offices in rural and regional areas as well as a major city based central office. Only one of the 19 district offices has a female manager and in the city office only one of the six managers is female. Thus, in order to gain an understanding of women's experiences of agri-political groups as 'men's organizations' (Shortall 1999, 96), further interviews were undertaken with 20 female leaders from different farmers' unions in Australia. In attempting to elucidate the connections between management and masculinities in the Farmers' Union, West and Zimmerman's (1987) notion of 'doing gender' is utilized. This conceptualization of 'gender as a verb' (Fitzsimons 2002) is enumerated more fully in the latter part of this chapter. First though, before turning to theory, the following section provides some preliminary background to the study of gender and agricultural organizations.

Background

Over the latter decades of the twentieth century, a small group of feminist rural scholars engaged in work which, as one described it, had the 'aura of detective stories' (Lyson 1990, 59): its aim was to re-examine the 'facts' related to agriculture and make visible what had been lost or overlooked in androcentric accounts of farmers and farming.[2] The title of Carolyn Sachs' 1983 book, *The Invisible Farmers*, represents both the theme and subject matter of the early work on women and farming. Thematically,

---

1 There are now two women elected leaders in the Farmers' Union.

2 Reviews of the literature on gender and farming have been undertaken by Brandth (2002a), Friedland (1991), Little (2006), Little and Panelli (2003), Panelli (2006), Shortall (2006) and Whatmore (1994).

research by Sachs (1983) and other feminist rural scholars drew attention to the way in which farming had been constructed as a masculine enterprise, and the subject was therefore the documenting of women's contributions to agriculture. In Sachs' (1983) case, this required drawing on in-depth interviews with women in the states of Kentucky, Ohio and Indiana – as well as historical data dating back to seventeenth and eighteenth century New England – to argue that women have been, and continue to be, active participants in agricultural production. A plethora of international literature subsequently emerged during the 1980s and early 1990s which echoed this conclusion. Cumulatively, this literature described the substantial work women undertake on agricultural enterprises as well documented women's secondary status within farming (for example, Boulding 1980; Bouquet 1982; Effland, Rogers and Grim 1993; First-Dilic 1978; Gasson 1980; Gasson and Winter 1992; Gourdomichalis 1991; Haugen 1994; 1998; James 1990; Repassy 1991; Scott 1996; Shortall 1999; Symes 1991; Symes and Marsden 1983; Whatmore 1991).

While the focus of this wave of scholarship, and indeed much subsequent rural feminist scholarship,[3] was largely on gender relations behind the farm gate, questions relating to the gendered nature of agricultural organizations began to emerge. This literature was associated with work that had examined women's marginal position in other agricultural sites besides the farm. These sites included the law (Voyce 1993), the media (Morris and Evans 2001), agricultural training colleges (Schmitt 1998), government agencies (Duffield 1996), and extension services (Leckie 1996). Over this time, gender relations in farmers' unions did not go unnoticed by researchers who began to use the knowledge that had been produced on women's contributions to agriculture to highlight the anomaly of women's lack of presence in agricultural organizations (Alston 1995; James 1989; O'Hara 1998: Sheridan 1994). In complementary work, researchers also began to write women back into the history of agri-politics by noting the important role women played in establishing early farm organizations (Meyer and Lobao 1994), uncovering the way in which mainstream farming groups marginalized important contributions to policy and politics by their affiliated women's groups (Gunn 1997) and detailing the political activities farm women undertook outside of traditional male dominated farm groups (Sachs 1996). Collectively, this scholarship began to challenge the construction of farm women as 'static', 'backward' and 'traditional', and instead emphasized their political agency and interests (Jones 2002, 2). This theme was taken up in another significant body of work that has recorded the so called 'rural women's movement' which occurred across western nations late last century (Panelli 2002; 2007). A central feature of this movement was the formation of new farm women's groups. These groups

---

3 Scholarship on farming women continued throughout the latter part of the twentieth century just as it does today. It has reflected the changes in agriculture in industrialized nations, documenting women's new entrepreneurial roles in farming (Bock 2004; Garcia-Ramon, Canoves and Valdovinos 1995), women's involvement in organic agriculture (Pedersen and Kjaergard 2004; Trauger 2004), the impact of rural restructuring on farming women (Heather, Skillen, Young and Vladicka 2005; Shortall 2001), women's off-farm work (Jervell 1999; Oldrup 1999; Pini 2004b), farming women's emotional health (Price and Evans 2005) and farming women's involvement in new communication technologies (Bryant 1999; Pini 2004c).

initiated annual gatherings of farm women, established online forums for women's networking and convened meetings with leaders of industry, politics and business in order to agitate for equality in farmers' unions (Dale-Hallett, Panelli, Diffey, May, Pini and the members of the Women on Farms Heritage Group 2006; Pini, Brown and Simpson 2003; Pini, Brown and Previte 2004; Pini, Panelli and Sawer 2008).

Despite the growth of the 'rural women's movement' it has largely failed to translate into increasing women's representation in mainstream farmers' unions. At the same time the movement did precipitate government and farming groups sponsoring research on the subject of gender inequity in agricultural organizations (for example, Aslin, Webb and Fisher 2000; Buchy 2001; Elix and Lambert 1998a; 1998b; Fulton and McGowan 2005; Grace 1997). This type of work has been important in a number of respects. It has increased awareness of women's marginal position in farmers' unions, as well as provided a rationale for the introduction of a number of strategies to address the paucity of women in farming groups. These strategies have included the establishment of a database for potential women board appointees, the mentoring of aspiring women agricultural managers and the conducting of management training for women (Panelli and Pini 2005; Pini and Shortall 2006).

Nevertheless, much of the government and industry sponsored research has tended to characterize gender relations in farming groups in a reductionist and simplistic manner (Pini 2003b). That is, as a list of stable and singular barriers that, with appropriate liberal feminist interventions, could be overcome. This work has left little room for interrogating the relationship between men and managerial masculinities in farming organizations or for exploring questions of agency and resistance. The next parts of the chapter outline the type of theoretical framework that has been found to be conducive to such an analysis and which will be utilized in this book.

Theorizing Gender

Despite Diamond and Quinby's (1988, ix) early attempt to rationalize a 'friendship between feminism and Foucault', a number of feminist theorists have remained wary of, ambivalent about, or antagonistic towards an engagement between feminism and poststructural theorists and theories (Benhabib 1994; Cacoullos 2000; Gubar 1998; Hekman 2000; Maynard 1995; Nussbaum 1999; Smyth 1992). In contrast, others have argued that the tools of poststructuralism present feminism with new possibilities and potential. A number of the criticisms different feminists have levelled against poststructuralism, including Foucault's now infamous neglect of gender and feminist theory (see Nash 1994), deserve to be taken seriously. Nevertheless poststructuralism can be conceptually and politically useful to feminism. As a consequence, this book adopts a feminist poststructural theoretical framework, in order to examine masculinities and management in agricultural organizations (Brooks 1997; Davies 2004; Kenway, Willis, Blackmore and Rennie 1994; McLaren 2004; Sawicki 1991; Weedon 1987; Zalewski 2000).

Feminist Poststructuralism

In her seminal work *Feminist Practice and Poststructuralist Theory*, Chris Weedon (1987, 20) argued that while 'different forms of poststructuralism vary both in their practice and in their political implications, they share certain fundamental assumptions'. Of these, perhaps what is the most central and arguably the most provocative is that subjectivity is not immutable, coherent, stable or singular but conditional, fractured, multiple and partial. As Davies and Harre (1990, 46) evocatively contend, poststructuralists understand that 'one is always an open question mark with a shifting answer'. The theorization of the subject as slippery and shifting rather than known and taken-for-granted has understandably seen the subject become 'a contested site in social scientific research' (Davies, Flemmen, Gannon, Laws and Watson 2002, 291), given that the belief in a fixed, coherent self was central to Enlightenment thought (Flax 1990, 41) and political projects such as feminism (Probyn 1993).

Of those poststructural theorists associated with challenging the long held common-sense view of the humanist subject is French philosopher Michel Foucault who posited that the subject 'is not a substance. It is a form' (1997, 290). In articulating a rationale for this radical reconceptualization of the subject, Foucault (1987, 121) explained that because his interest was in 'how the subject constituted himself', whether it be as 'a mad subject or as a normal subject, through a certain number of practices', it was necessary to reject 'a priori theory of the subject'. It was thus the pursuit of uncovering and understanding the way in which certain historical subjects came to be constituted and known – and viewed as true and self-evident – that led Foucault (1980) to challenge as fiction the notion of a pre-given, fixed subject.

In suggesting a means of understanding the ways in which a subject may come into being, Foucault (1980) proposed the notion of 'discourses'. Discourses is a term which has subsequently become, as O'Farrell (2005, 78) writes in her lucid introduction to the work of the author, 'indissolubly linked with Foucault' and has simultaneously 'generated a number of misunderstandings'.[4] Foucault (1980, 93) himself defined the term as 'historically variable ways of specifying knowledge and truth – what it is possible to speak at a given moment'. It is discourses, sets of organized, regulated and historically and socially specific statements, beliefs, meanings, practices, values, language and knowledge, that make subject positions available to people and, thus, it is through discourses that subjectivities are constituted (Scott 1988, 35). In this sense, poststructuralists insist that language is not a transparent mirror to the world. There is no immediate and clear correspondence between a word, an object or an identity. St Pierre (2000, 483) elaborates on this assumption stating, 'In other words, we word the world. The "way it is" is not "natural". We have constructed the world as it is through language and cultural practice'.

Alsop, Fitzsimmons and Lennon (2002, 82) explain that there are two crucial aspects to Foucault's (1980) notion of discourse. The first is that discourses are historically variable. They are not static and nor are they singular. They are, in

---

4 Bacchi (2005) argues that this has been particularly the case within feminist theorizing.

contrast, multiple and conflicting; there are numerous ways of giving meaning to the world and constructing the world. These are themes at the core of Foucault's (1981) *The History of Sexuality* which details historical differences in the ways sexuality has been known, constructed, spoken about and understood over time. The second key aspect of Foucault's (1980) concept of discourses, according to Alsop et al. (2002, 82), is that discourses are intricately connected to power and knowledge. That is, they define a means of thinking, talking, feeling and acting about a subject at particular moments and places in time. They mark out what can be legitimately said as well as what can legitimately not be said. They influence and regulate, and when they come to be viewed as natural, normal and 'true', it becomes difficult to challenge them or operate outside them. As Foucault (1977, 199) explained, 'Discursive practices are characterized by the delimitation of a field of objects, the definition of a legitimate perspective for the agent of knowledge, and the fixing of norms for the elaboration of concepts and theories'.

What is foregrounded in Foucault's (1981, 83) conceptualization of discourse is that power is 'not an institution not a structure; neither is it a certain strength we are endowed with'. In explaining Foucault's (1980) notion of power, St Pierre (2000, 489) notes that the philosopher himself 'rarely uses the word "power" but speaks of "power relations" or "relations of power"' as a means of explicating the view that power is not monolithic, unitary or fixed and nor is it something that is held by one group over another. Power in Foucauldian terms is mobile, plural, capillary-like and dynamic. We are thus unable to exempt or absolve ourselves from the relations of power. This is, importantly, not equivalent to saying that power is absolute and unremitting, for if one is not outside power one is not outside the possibilities for freedom. In Foucault's (1978, 101) terms, 'discourse transmits and produces power; it reinforces it, but also undermines and exposes it, renders it fragile and makes it possible to thwart it'. In this respect resistance is implicit in Foucault's notion of power (Ramazanoglu 1993). As Foucault (1980, 142) notes, 'there are no relations of power without resistance; the latter are all the more real and effective because they are formed right at the point where relations of power are exercised'.

As a theoretical perspective, poststructuralism is, of course, not inherently feminist. However, as the following section will demonstrate, the assumptions overviewed are central to the work of those feminists who have enthusiastically embraced poststructural theory.

Gender as Performative

Numerous contemporary feminist scholars have sought to utilize, appropriate and extend poststructural theory in order to theorize gender and gendered power relations. One such writer whose work contributes significantly to the analytical framework adopted in this book is Judith Butler. At the centre of Butler's (1990) controversial and complex *Gender Trouble: Feminism and the Subversion of Identity* is the Foucauldian critique of the subject.[5]

---

5 This is not to suggest that Butler's (1990) work is free of criticism of Foucault, nor that she unequivocally accepts all of his claims. See, for example, Butler (1990, 128–34).

Butler (1990) begins the book by noting that this critique runs counter to a key assumption about identity in much feminist theory. That is, that 'there is some existing identity, understood through the category of women, who not only initiates feminist interests and goals within discourse, but constitutes the subject for whom political representation is pursued' (Butler 1990, 3). It is this assumption which Butler (1990) seeks to 'trouble' in arguing that the gendered subject is socially and discursively constituted. However, as Alsop et al. (2002), note, Butler's (1990) polemic takes us far beyond distinguishing between sex and gender because she maintains that neither sex nor gender are natural categories. The widely held view that sex is to nature as gender is to culture is not subscribed to by Butler (1990; 1993), for she views sex to be as culturally constructed and as fabricated as gender. As she explains, 'gender is not to culture as sex is to nature; gender is also the discursive/cultural means by which "sexed nature" or a "natural sex" is produced and established as "prediscursive", prior to culture, a politically neutral surface on which culture acts' (Butler 1990, 7). For Butler (1990; 1993), the sexed binary male/female does not exist outside the discourses of gender that bring these sexed bodies into being. In this process some bodies come to 'matter' – that is, to be 'intelligible', 'human' and 'livable' – while others do not (Butler 1999, xxii).

Butler's (1990; 1993) proposal is that sexed and gendered identities can be understood as 'performed'. So, rather than viewing gender as a stable set of traits or a dualistic category of behaviours she advocates that:

> Gender is performative insofar as it is the effect of a regulatory regime of gender differences in which genders are divided and hierarchized under constraint. Social constraints, taboos, prohibitions, threats of punishment operate in the ritualized repetition of norms, and this repetition constitutes the temporalized scene of gender construction and destabilization…Performativity is a matter of reiterating or repeating the norms by which one is constituted; it is not a radical fabrication of a gendered self. It is a compulsory repetition of prior and subjectivating norms, ones which cannot be thrown off at will, but which work, animate, and constrain the gendered subject, and which are also the resources from which resistance, subversion, displacement are to be forged. (Butler 1993, 21–2)

There are a number of key theoretical insights in the above quotation. The first is that gender is relational and interactional. Gender is not 'a noun', as Butler (1990, 24) explained so succinctly. Rather it is something that West and Zimmerman (1987, 125) claim is 'done'.[6] In order to exemplify this argument in *Gender Trouble*, Butler (1990) used the example of female impersonators or drag queens. As well as illustrating gender as performative, the example of the drag queens also works to unsettle and denaturalize notions of what is real and true in terms of gender. We have a man's body but it is dressed and acting as a woman, so displacing and disturbing categorizations of gender. The fact that, as Butler (2004, 213) reflected more recently, 'some of those men could do femininity much better than I ever could, ever would want to, ever would', undermines the taken-for-granted binary masculine/male and feminine/female.

---

6 For a discussion of the synergies between the work of Butler (1990) and West and Zimmerman (2002) see Maloney and Fenstermaker (2002).

The second point of relevance in the above quotation from Butler (1990) is that gender is not about a singular performance or a number of performances, but an ongoing performance. In this respect gender is constantly deferred rather than ever fully achieved. Gender is, like all identities, as Hall (1996, 2) tells us, 'never arrived at'. In order to illustrate this process in *Bodies that Matter*, Butler (1993, 8) describes what occurs when a child is first born or seen on an ultrasound and the statement is made 'It's a girl'. She writes that 'in that naming the girl is "girled" brought into the domain of language and kinship through interpellation of gender'. The words do not just describe the identity of 'girl' but bring her identity into being. The baby will not just be 'girled' as she is born or seen on an ultrasound. She will be 'girled' throughout her life. This 'girling' or naming, Butler (1993) explains, is repeated and reiterated so that gender appears to be naturalized and normalized. It is this observation which makes Butler's (1990; 1993) work so useful for feminist scholarship, as she illuminates why essential and immutable physical and biological differences between men and women may appear to be so real and taken-for-granted rather than a fiction: it is because gender is something we do every day in every way, often automatically, without questioning and with a very limited degree of reflexivity. Over time these repeated performances then solidify, giving the appearance that they are natural, fixed and pre-determined.

In the aftermath of the publication of *Gender Trouble* (1990), significant criticism was directed at Butler for 'overarching with her term "performative"' (Roden 2005, 29). For example, in her contribution to a volume of radical feminist responses to poststructuralism, Jeffreys (1996, 359) rails against those feminist theorists who have proposed 'a harmless version of gender as an idea which lesbians and gay men can endlessly play with and be revolutionary at the same time'. Jeffrey's (1996) criticism fails to acknowledge that Butler (1990) was not proposing a theory of performativity which was entirely voluntary. As the quotation cited indicates, Butler (1990) noted that gender performances are circumscribed by power or what is referred to above as the 'regulatory regime of gender differences'. This is the third crucial point of relevance to glean from her quotation. That is, gender performances do not occur in the absence of power relations. It is not a matter, as Butler (1993, x) is at pains to point out, of waking up each morning and selecting what gender one may like to perform from the closet. This is because gender performances are policed by ourselves as well as by others (West and Fenstermaker 1993, 157). As we take up different gendered subjectivities, we will be called to account (and call ourselves to account) according to dominant discourses, those regimes of truth and knowledge dictating what it means 'to be a man', 'to be a woman', 'to be masculine' or 'to be feminine'. Normative gendered identities are regulated by these discourses, thus limiting what performances may be possible (Butler 1990, 42).

The final note to highlight in the quotation from Butler (1993) is her emphasis on the potential for change, resistance and agency. Again, this is a crucial point given the extensive criticism that has been directed at the philosopher for what has been seen as her denial of human agency (see Benhabib 1994, 80). Butler (1993, 15) emphasizes that her critique of an essential subject does not 'foreclose the possibility of agency', but it 'does locate agency as a reiterative or rearticulatory practice, immanent to power, and not a relation of external opposition to power.' Further, while social norms and practices may constrain our performance of gender, we are not determined by them. She states explicitly that 'the subject is not determined by the rules through which it is generated because signification is not a founding act, but rather a regulated process of repetition' (Butler 1990, 145). The potential for change and agency and 'gender transformation' are to be found, Butler (1990, 179) says, in the subject's failure to repeat those 'acts that seek to approximate the ideal of a substantial ground of identity'. Thus, for Butler (1990), transformative change is located within the discursive field, as subjects reject/resist orthodox acts of gender repetition and thereby resignify what it means to be woman/man/feminine/masculine.

Butler's (1990) notion of gender as performative has been highly influential and widely adopted by gender scholars, including pro-feminist writers interested in masculinities. Originally, pro-feminist scholars of masculinities typically relied heavily upon sex-role theory.[7] Today, however, this has changed. The following section traces the significant shifts in conceptualizing masculinities that have occurred over recent decades and the debates that have accompanied these shifts.

Theorizing Masculinities

In his book *Contemporary Perspectives on Masculinity*, Clatterbaugh (1990) identifies six ways in which masculinity has been approached and understood. These are: conservative, men's rights, spiritual, socialist, group-specific and pro-feminist (see also Connell 2001; Hearn 1992; 1998; Lingard and Douglas 1999; Messner 1997). It is perhaps understandable that there is no consensus in this literature on a definition of masculinity. Instead, writers have pointed out that definitions of masculinity are confused and contradictory (MacInnes 1998; Nilan 1995). Clatterbaugh (1998, 27) comments wryly that 'it may well be the best kept secret of the literature on masculinities that we have an extremely ill-defined idea of what we are talking about'. Imms (2000) says that the notion 'multiple masculinities' is problematic as we do not have sufficient data to further our understanding of the myriad ways in which masculinities may be enacted. Reflecting on this issue, Hearn (1996; 2004) even questions whether there is any usefulness in attempting to define a term that appears to encompass so many disparate practices, processes and discourses. He suggests that it may be more advantageous to use terms such as 'men's practices', 'men's social relations' or 'hegemony of men' rather than 'masculinities', given the imprecision of the latter term. Clatterbaugh (1998, 41) supports this assertion, claiming that since 'talking about men seems to be what we want to do', why obfuscate matters by using the concept masculinities?

Thankfully, some conceptual clarification arises when one seeks to define masculinities using the framework identified by Clatterbaugh (1990). In terms of the perspective of most importance to this book, that of pro-feminism, he says that masculinity is typically viewed as socially and culturally constructed, related to power and, in certain manifestations, requiring critique and deconstruction. He notes that

---

7 Feminist and pro-feminist rural social science was also heavily reliant on sex-role theory as work began in the 1970s examining the position of farming women relative to men (for example, Cooper 1989; Kohl 1977; Pearson 1979; Rosenfeld 1985).

today feminist and pro-feminist scholars are more likely to theorize masculinities in this way than through sex role theory. This latter theorization suggests that women's disadvantage is a result of girls and boys 'learning' to act in certain stereotypical ways and internalizing these behavioural regimes through processes of socialization. Biological difference is thus negated. It is thought that as girls and boys exhibit different traits and characteristics associated with 'femininity' and 'masculinity' respectively, they are rewarded, while deviations are sanctioned. Ultimately, these processes reinforce particular ways of being in the world as a 'girl/woman' or 'boy/ man'. The liberal feminist premise of sex-role/socialization theory is that because 'sex' is learned, we can 'unlearn' it through appropriate education or training.

Hegemonic Masculinity

While sex-role/socialization theory dominated early studies of men, it came under significant attack in what has become a seminal article in gender studies published in *Theory and Society* and written by Carrigan, Connell and Lee (1985). In this paper, the writers argued that sex roles did not actually describe the reality of many men's lives. 'Let us be blunt about it,' they asserted, 'the "male sex role" does not exist' (Carrigan et al. 1985, 581). They claimed that sex-role theory was overly simplistic in presenting a static and uniform picture of masculinity when there was great variety and diversity in masculinities and many differences between groups of men. In terms of the latter, Carrigan et al (1985) highlighted the differences in the position of heterosexual and homosexual men in society. They noted that in any hierarchical ranking of masculinities, heterosexuality was always given precedence over homosexuality and, further, that sex-role theory was inadequate in explaining why this was the case. In order to understand the differential ranking afforded to heterosexual and homosexual masculinities the authors suggested appropriating the notion of hegemony from Italian Marxist, Antonio Gramsci. Gramsci's interest was in questioning how a dominant economic class comes to legitimate its control of other, subordinate classes. For Carrigan et al. (1985), the terms of the question were the same, but the focus was on gender. That is, how is it that some men come to legitimate their power over some other men and over women? The answer, they suggested, was via 'hegemonic masculinity'. Hegemonic masculinity, they argued, is a particular variety of masculinity that is 'culturally exalted' compared with other 'subordinated' masculinities such as homosexual masculinity and in relation to women (Carrigan et al. 1985, 179). It is, according to masculinities scholar Bob Pease (2000, 33), a 'dominant discourse' defined in opposition and/or complimentary terms to femininity and other forms of masculinity.

In this early theorization of hegemonic masculinity, Carrigan et al. (1985) made three further definitional assertions about the term. The first was that the configuration of masculinity viewed as hegemonic will not necessarily be the most common form of masculinity. Hegemonic masculinity, they wrote, 'may actually correspond to the actual characters of a small number of men' as it may not be the most easily displayed of masculinities (Carrigan et al. 1985). As Connell (2006, 21) has elaborated more recently, this is often seen in peer groups where just a small number of boys enjoy influence and prestige amongst a much larger group who actually cannot display the same mode of masculinity. At the same time, while few men may enact hegemonic masculinity, they all benefit from it, according to Carrigan et al. (1985) and Connell (1995). This 'patriarchal dividend' is the advantage all men – even those who may not be 'the frontline troops of patriarchy' (Connell 1995, 79) – gain as a result of women's subordination.

The second feature of hegemonic masculinity emphasized by Carrigan, et al. (1985) is that it is subject to change. As an example they explained that in Renaissance Europe a passion for beautiful young boys was compatible with hegemonic masculinity, but that this association had shifted by the end of the nineteenth century and hegemonic masculinity came to be far more closely connected with displays of heterosexuality. As Connell has elaborated on the concept of hegemonic masculinities in subsequent writing, and particularly in the books *Gender and Power* (1987), *Masculinities* (1995) and *The Men and the Boys* (2000), the shifting nature of hegemonic masculinity has continued to be stressed. Such an objective is evident in Connell's (1995, 77) text where hegemonic masculinities is defined as 'the configuration of gender practice which embodies the currently accepted answer to the problem of legitimacy of patriarchy'. Before concluding the page on which this definition is penned, Connell (ibid.) writes, 'I stress that hegemonic masculinity embodies a "currently accepted" strategy'.

The insistence of the temporal nature of hegemonic masculinity gestures towards the third aspect of defining hegemonic masculinity identified by Carrigan et al. (1985). That is, there is no singular hegemonic masculinity, just as there is no singular masculinity. It is, as Beynon (2002, 2) succinctly states, a 'singular-plural' in that there are different masculinities which are hegemonic in different times, places and contexts. It certainly may appear that hegemonic masculinities are fixed and given, but this is not the case. It is part of the power of hegemonic masculinities that they appear natural, stable and given (Gardiner 2002).

Criticisms of Hegemonic Masculinity

Despite its widespread use, Connell's (1987; 1995; 2000) notion of hegemonic masculinity has not escaped criticism from other gender theorists (Clatterbaugh 1998; Collinson and Hearn 2005; Demetriou 2001; Francis 2000; Hearn 2000; 2004; Hooper 2001; Jefferson 2002; Kerfoot and Whitehead 1998; Lorber 1998; Martin 1998; McMahon 1993; Miller 1998; Phoenix and Frosh 2001; Wetherell and Edley 1999; Whitehead 1999b; 2002). Some of these criticisms are related to the broader problems associated with the notion of 'masculinities'. There is, for example, the question of the abstract and ill-defined nature of hegemonic masculinities and the issue of how we can study what we cannot necessarily isolate and identify. For example, in an early critique Donaldson (1993) emphasizes the plural and contradictory nature of hegemonic masculinities. As an example he cites the case of Australian rugby league player Wally 'The King' Lewis who would seem to have embodied hegemonic masculinity throughout his career. But, Donaldson (1993) asks, what of Lewis' decision to retire prematurely from football because of his baby daughter's diagnosis as hearing impaired? Is Wally Lewis still representative of hegemonic masculinity? Drawing on similar examples, the author argues that hegemonic masculinity may not be a useful theoretical apparatus, given it is surrounded by such mystification.

A further criticism levelled against utilizing the term hegemonic masculinities is what Connell and Messerschmidt (2005, 839) summarize as 'the problem of reification'. This is at the centre of Jefferson's (2002, 70) critique which notes that for all Connell's (1995) emphasis on the relational and contingent nature of hegemonic masculinities, 'it is still common to see masculinity used attributionally'. Jefferson (2002, 71) objects to the fact that Connell (1995; 2000) always uses hegemonic masculinity in the singular. In a similar vein, Collier (1998) protests at the way hegemonic masculinity has come to be used as shorthand to refer to a categorical set of traits and behaviours (for example, aggression, competitiveness). This is a trend that Connell (1998c, 476) also observes: that hegemonic masculinity has come to be seen as the 'once famous "Type A personality"'. Collier (1998), like Martin (1998), also opposes the way in which hegemonic masculinities are typically portrayed as negative, as well as routinely and unquestioningly associated with men, when, as he suggests, many women could also be associated with hegemonic masculinity. This latter argument is also made by Kerfoot and Whitehead (1998, 440), who write that 'hegemonic masculine-type behaviour is not the sole prerogative of men' but it is often presented as such in the literature.

An associated critique of the notion of hegemonic masculinity is that it is over-simplified. This is a concern of Demetriou (2001) who worries that Connell's (1995; 2000) notion establishes a false dualism between hegemonic and non-hegemonic masculinities. He posits that these are not necessarily always in opposition because different modes of hegemonic masculinity may appropriate/subsume/extend practices of non-hegemonic masculinity. This creates what he labels an 'hybrid masculine bloc' which, by its very 'heterogeneity is able to render the patriarchal dividend invisible and legitimate patriarchal domination' (Demetriou 2001, 354). Whitehead (2002, 93) also finds fault with hegemonic masculinities and what he believes to be the simplistic and reductionist assumptions about power inherent in the term which suggests that 'men are the winners' and 'women the losers'. For Collinson and Hearn (2005), concerns about hegemonic masculinity being oversimplified are evidenced by the fact that we occupy multiple social locations which position us in complicated, differentiated ways. Someone may be positioned within discourses of hegemonic masculinity by virtue of their gender or sexuality, but may simultaneously be positioned within discourses of subordinate masculinity as a result of their ethnic or class background.

The criticisms of the term 'hegemonic masculinity' are not unfamiliar to Connell (1998a; 1998c; 2003; 2006) who has also raised questions about the cogency and usefulness of the notion. However, the author posits that it is necessary to differentiate between whether it is the term itself or the usage of the term which is problematic. This point is also made by Christine Skelton (2001) in her fascinating study of 'masculinity making' in primary education, *Schooling the Boys*. She acknowledges that there are problems with hegemonic masculinities, but asserts 'much of the cause for criticism lies with the way in which it is often loosely used' (Skelton 2001, 52). This is a salient point given the widespread use of the term and one also highlighted by Connell

(1998a; 1998c; 2003; 2006).[8] In a detailed response to these criticisms, Connell joins Messerschmidt (2005) in identifying what is useful about the term hegemonic masculinity, what is not useful, and what requires re-working. What is important to hold on to, claim Connell and Messerschmidt (2005), are the concepts of masculinities as multiple and as hierarchical. However, what should be disregarded is the suggestion that links hegemonic masculinities to men's 'global power over women' (Connell 1987, 183). This, they claim, does not fully represent the nuanced and contested nature of gendered power as it manifests between different groups of men and women. Further to this, Connell and Messerschmidt (2005, 847) posit that there is still more work to be done on the notion of hegemonic masculinities. In particular, they argue for the need to incorporate into the concept of hegemonic masculinities a focus on agency, difference and embodiment. They also call for increased acknowledgement of the contradictions and complexities in hegemonic masculinities.

I find many of the arguments Connell (1987; 1998a; 1998b; 1998c; 2003; 2006) has made about hegemonic masculinities over the years very persuasive. Indeed, the analysis offered by Connell and Messerschmidt (2005) reveals that, despite criticisms, the term still has much to offer as we seek to understand gendered power relations. Hegemonic masculinities will thus be engaged in this book as a key analytical device to understand why there are so few women managers in farming organizations worldwide. Important questions to be addressed will also include what masculinities are currently hegemonic in farmers' groups and what masculinities are subordinated. Also of interest will be understanding any shifts in hegemonic masculinities in farmers' groups and the implications of these shifts.

Overview

This book comprises eight chapters. Following this introduction, the still scant literature that has considered masculinities and rurality is reviewed. Of course, there is a large and compelling feminist rural social science literature which has never been solely about women. Indeed, subjects such as the coterminous relationship between men and the identity of farmer, men's dominance of land ownership in agriculture and men's hold on certain agricultural tasks have been of considerable concern to feminist researchers who have produced, over more than 30 years, a vigorous critique of rural and agricultural men's power. However, little of this work has problematized masculinities utilizing the type of theoretical framework outlined in this chapter. Attention is thus focused on detailing the types of rural and agricultural studies that have emerged in recent years which could be classified as 'explicit, critical and gendered studies of men' (Hearn 1997, 49). The chapter begins by examining the broader literature on rurality and masculinities before turning to the more specific sub-category of studies on agriculture and masculinities. The few investigations that have considered men, masculinities and management in agricultural organizations are afforded particular attention.

8 Connell and Messerschmidt (2005, 830) note that a recent database search revealed more than 200 papers that used the exact term in titles or abstracts, while papers that used a variant of the term in the title or referred to hegemonic masculinity in their text ran into the many hundreds.

Chapter 3 focuses on methodologies and the study of agricultural masculinities. The specific task is to explore the ways in which the elected members of the Farmers' Union engaged particular performances of masculinity in interviews. These were as heterosexual men, powerful men and knowledgeable men. In seeking to understand these performances, I argue that we need to critique interviews as gendered interactions by asking 'who is asking who about what and where'. That is, we need to be reflexive about the subjectivities of the researcher and researched, critique the extent to which the research questions focus on gender, and identify ways in which the research environment is gendered. Before concluding the chapter, I highlight the types of methodological, epistemological and ontological questions that have yet to be explored by researchers investigating rurality and masculinities.

Chapters 4, 5 and 6 present the qualitative data obtained throughout the ethnography of the Farmers' Union which collectively demonstrate that agricultural organizations are infused with hegemonic masculinity.

Chapter 4 begins by reference to the typology of managerial masculinities outlined by Collinson and Hearn (1994). In this typology, the authors identify five dominant types of managerial masculinity in organizations: paternalism, authoritarianism, entrepreneurialism, informalism and careerism. It is argued that the most common form of managerial masculinity practised by male elected members in the Farmers' Union is that of paternalism. When this style of management is ineffective, male leaders deploy a more authoritarian form of managerial masculinity. In order to render these 'highly abstract notions of managerial masculinity concrete', some of the 'everyday practices' of the Farmers' Union such as meetings, the franchise system and staff-constituent interactions are examined (see Kronsell 2005, 283). The chapter also explores the emergence of a 'new' form of managerial masculinity evident in the discourses of members of a Young Farmers' Group established as an addendum to the mainstream Farmers' Union.

In an illuminating account of poststructuralist feminism, St Pierre (2000, 503) asserts that some of the most significant questions raised when one views the world through this theoretical lens are: 'Who gets to be a subject in a particular discourse, in a particular set of practices? Who is allowed a subject position and who is not?'. These questions are addressed in Chapter 5 in relation to agricultural politics and leadership. That is, who gets to be the leaders and how, and who is excluded and how? In addressing these questions, I continue to demonstrate the potency of paternalism as a mode of managerial masculinity within the Farmers' Union. It is argued that elected members draw on a dual discursive process to establish their identities as men in management. In the first of these discourses, the managerial men's similarity to farming men is emphasized. Farming and management require toughness, strength and knowledge. Women are 'the other' in this discourse. They can be neither farmer nor manager. In the second of the discourses, managerial men in the Farmers' Union further their claim to legitimacy by emphasizing their particular organizational knowledge, expertise and experience. The elected members differentiate themselves from 'farmers' who are positioned as lacking the professionalism and capacity for leadership. Of course, some farmers may one day become elected leaders but, according to the elected leaders, this will only be a select group and they will require considerable grooming and training from established older patriarchs.

One of the key concerns of feminist poststructuralists has been to expose the way in which women can alter, critique, disrupt and subvert dominant gender discourses (Alcoff 1988). This theme is taken up in Chapter 6. Here, attention turns to one of the most common ways in which the paucity of women in agricultural management has been addressed, that is through the establishment of women-specific networks. Two women's networks in district locations were investigated as part of the ethnography. These networks have been highly successful in a multitude of respects, as they have provided leadership opportunities for women as well as facilitated the circulation of new and alternative gender and farming discourses (Teather 1997; 1998; Fincher and Panelli 2001; Panelli 2007). It is, however, not with such benefits that this chapter is concerned. In keeping with the study's interest in masculinities, the chapter asks how men in the mainstream Farmers' Union have responded to this gender equity strategy. Focus group interviews with women involved in the networks provide rich data on the types of derogatory discourses by which agricultural men have sought to discredit the networks and the women involved in them. It is argued that collectively these discourses represent a 'mobilization of masculinity' by the elected members (Martin 2001), as they re-inscribe normative definitions of femininity and masculinity and act in powerful ways to regulate and contain women's involvement in agricultural management.

Women's experiences as leaders in agriculture are explored in Chapter 7. Given that very few women have stood for election in the Farmers' Union under investigation, and even fewer have been successful in achieving a decision-making position, opportunities to hear women's voices on this issue were necessarily limited. Twenty women leaders from other farmers' unions were therefore interviewed in order to understand the ways in which women in agricultural leadership resist, negotiate and/or accommodate the discourses of masculinity which dominate in the organizations of which they are part. As the women explain, this requires a delicate balancing act as they attempt to position themselves both as 'woman' and 'manager'. Many of the women's experiences of the balancing act are characterized by the metaphor of 'the third sex' used by one of the interviewees. This metaphor reveals the challenges of taking up the subject position 'woman manager' when normative notions of management and femininity are so conflicting.

Chapter 8 summarizes the key findings of this study. In light of these findings the chapter questions whether change is possible, and if a more equitable and inclusive public agricultural arena may emerge in the future. Following this, suggestions for future research are canvassed. Given that this is the first book length study of masculinities in farmers' unions, this study should only be seen as the very beginning of what needs to be a much more extensive investigation. In this regard, particular attention is given to the reconfiguring of agricultural governance as a result of globalization, and importantly, the gendered dimensions of such a shift.

Conclusion

This chapter has introduced the subject under investigation in this book, that is, managerial masculinities in agricultural organizations. It has established that gender inequality in agricultural groups is a world-wide phenomenon, but explained that despite this, little attention has been afforded to making explicit men and masculinities in the farming arena. This is understandable given that feminist rural social science scholars have had to concentrate so much attention on understanding and documenting the gendered dimensions of family farming. It is also not surprising given the 'somewhat half-hearted' attention rural studies scholars have afforded to feminist perspectives and concerns (Little 2002a, 665). However, it means we know little about why it is that in farmers' unions internationally women are so poorly represented in positions of leadership. Thus, the central aim of this book is to document and critique the discourses by which managerial farming men legitimate and reproduce their organizational power. To achieve this aim I draw upon feminist poststructural theory, and particularly Judith Butler's (1990) notion of gender as performative. Also critical to theorizing masculinities in the farming organization under investigation will be Connell's (1995; 2000) notion of hegemonic masculinities. The type of framework outlined has been widely used by gender and organizational scholars, but most of this work has been centred on metropolitan organizations. In contrast, this book places discourses of masculinity *and* discourses of rurality/agriculture at the centre of its inquiry. To begin this task, the following chapter introduces the emerging research which has begun to examine the intersections between these two discursive fields.

Chapter 2

Rural and Agricultural Masculinities

After five years of academic writing I have filled a large folder with referee reports on journal articles I have written. Together they could be read in a number of different ways – as a commentary on my writing strengths and weaknesses, as a reflection of the trajectories my work has taken, or as an indication of shifts in my own views and perspectives. An alternative narrative could also be told from these reports about the preoccupations and dominant traditions of different academic disciplines, as well as the place of gender and feminist theory in such disciplines. The potential for the latter reading was clearly conveyed to me last year on receipt of referee reports concerning an article I had sent to an international journal of rural studies. Of the three reports two were favourable. One was not. This negative report contained barely two lines which read: 'This is a political economy journal. Not a gender studies journal'.

These comments provide a useful entry point for this chapter as they clearly signpost the prevailing orthodoxies of rural social science. It is indeed a field where the place of political economy has been viewed as foundational (Morris and Evans 2004) and that of feminist theory little more than fragile (Pini 2003a). It is also a discipline in which, as Chris Philo (1992) first argued in what is now recognized as a seminal article in rural social science,[1] the subject has been very narrowly defined. Philo's (1992) contention was that traditionally the subject of rural studies has been 'Mr Average', which has meant the marginalizing of 'other' perspectives and experiences of rurality. 'Mr Average' masqueraded successfully as the universal subject of rural studies as he was the unnamed norm. He was thus omnipresent in terms of marginalizing and excluding, but paradoxically invisible and therefore not able to be called to account.

Thus, the study of rural and agricultural masculinities is not in itself novel or atypical. Men and masculinities have always been the central protagonists in the discipline. The critical distinction is that today (some) rural social scientists have begun to talk about and write about men and masculinities differently. In this scholarship, 'Mr Average' has shifted from being 'taken-for-granted, implicit and untheorized', to being named and critiqued. This chapter reviews this still scant literature, beginning with work which has focused on the broader subject of rural masculinities and then turning to the more specific body of scholarship that has considered agricultural masculinities. Included in this latter body of research are studies in which rural social scientists have asked the 'man question' (Zalewski and Parpart 1998) in the context of agricultural organizations. These studies are examined in the final part of the chapter.

---

1 See Little (2006, 365) and Cloke (2006, 448).

Rural Masculinities

In responding to Philo's (1992) critique of the narrowness of the conventional subject of rural social science, writers first sought to attend to those 'others' whose experiences had been hidden, neglected or excluded in past accounts of the rural (see Cloke and Little 1997). While this work[2] was critically important in bringing new voices to rural research and unsettling 'Mr Average's' centrality in narratives of rurality, it also gestured to the need for more nuanced and critical work on questions of power and subjectivity in rural studies. As Cloke and Little (1997, 275) reflected in concluding their edited book *Contested Countryside Cultures: Otherness, Marginality and Rurality*, marginality is 'relational' and thus understanding 'otherness' necessitates an understanding of how and why some identities have come to be seen as legitimate, stable and natural in rural areas while 'other' identities are not.

In the decade since Cloke and Little's (1997) book, as feminist rural scholars have sought to address these challenging questions, they have found inspiration and guidance in the 'cultural turn' in agricultural and rural studies. This theoretical shift and its attendant emphasis on difference, representation and meaning have unsettled the notion of 'the rural' as a self-evident, stable and universal category (for example, Halfacree 1995; Jones 1995; Phillips, Fish and Agg 2001). As writers have begun to detail the different ways in which rurality is socially and culturally constructed, gender has emerged as a key theme.

It is this notion, that there is an inter-relationship between discourses of rurality and gender, which is at the centre of Campbell and Bell's (2000, 544) editorial in a special edition of *Rural Sociology* on the subject of masculinities. In introducing the edition, the authors draw a useful distinction between 'the masculine in the rural' and 'the rural in the masculine'. They delineate the former as being the different ways in which masculinity is constituted in those spaces and sites rural social scientists would deem 'rural'. In contrast, 'the rural in the masculine', they suggest, refers to the engagement of 'the rural' symbolically to constitute masculinities. In this instance, rurality may be performed in both rural and urban spaces.

In many respects – and as Campbell and Bell (2000) themselves recognize – the differentiation of 'the masculine in the rural' and 'the rural in the masculine' is somewhat artificial as they tend to collapse together on so many occasions. Indeed, as the literature reviewed below will demonstrate, the discourses of masculinity and rurality often appear to feed off each other, becoming almost indistinguishable. Nevertheless, as Brandth and Haugen (2005c) claim, the categorization provides a useful entry point into the literature as it signals the multiple ways in which notions of gender and rurality intersect. In light of this, the following sections provide a brief introduction to recent work pertaining to the 'masculine in the rural' and to the 'rural in the masculine'.

---

2 Such work continues (see Cloke 2006).

The Masculine in the Rural

A key focus of work on the 'masculine in the rural' has been rural young men, as evidenced in studies by writers such as Kenway, Kraak and Hickey-Moody (2006) Bye (2003), Leyshon (2005), Alloway and Gilbert (2004) and Bye (2003). Three key themes underpin this work. The first is that different discourses of hegemonic masculinity circulate in 'the rural' and that these discourses are undergoing change. While this is evident in all of the studies it is particularly highlighted in Kenway et al.'s (2006) book *Masculinity Beyond the Metropolis*. The context and backdrop for the book is globalization. Indeed, as the writers argue, it is their drawing together of the literature on globalization and masculinity that marks the book as particularly significant. In bringing these burgeoning fields of research into dialogue, they note that globalization has brought economic, cultural and geographic change to rural spaces, but that the consequences of this in terms of male identity/ies have not been examined. In order to do so, the authors undertake what they label 'place-based global ethnographies' of four rural towns in Australia. Data for the study are obtained from a range of sources including semi-structured interviews with young people (aged 13–16), focus groups with senior male and female students, parents, community members and teachers, participant observation and documentary material relevant to each of the towns. The study's findings on the impact of globalization on masculinity can be illustrated in relation to the theme of paid work. In one of the rural towns studied, the authors identify the existence of what they label a 'melancholic masculinity' experienced by those young men who remain bound to traditional notions of masculinity and to the type of heavy industrial work that was previously easy to find in the town. In other towns, new industries such as tourism are seeing the emergence of new employment opportunities and the opening up of new ways of being a man, drawing on discourses of entrepreneurship and business acumen. The message is that globalization is influencing masculine identities and the lives of young men in rural Australia in complex and uneven ways so that there is no singular identity 'rural young man' or unitary notion of hegemonic rural masculinity.

The second of the themes emerging from the literature on the 'masculine in the rural' is that the practice of hegemonic masculinities in rural spaces occurs at the expense and exclusion of 'others'. Leyshon's (2005) ethnographic study of the gender identity work of young men in pubs in rural Ireland provides insight into this process of 'othering'. Both in this site and in the New Zealand rural pubs studied by Campbell (2000) there are invisible but strongly guarded codes and norms that govern who may drink, where they may drink and how they may drink (see also Campbell and Phillips 1995). Most obviously, Leyshon (2005, 166) writes that the rural pub is 'no place for a girl', but also marginalized in this space are youth who are non-locals, young men who do not want to drink copious amounts and young men who do not want to engage in obscenities. Campbell's (2000) study of pub drinking, which did not focus solely on youth, reveals that such exclusions may continue into middle and old age for men and women in rural communities. In two pub sites in rural New Zealand, the author noted that recently arrived residents, white collar workers and women are rarely present. Besides gender, localness and labour are critical entry requirements for pub drinking. Once permitted entry, men must continue to confirm their masculinity by engaging in competitive conversational practices and by drinking substantial amounts of alcohol while showing no side effects. Importantly, Campbell (2000) notes that the men who do monopolize the public drinking space of the rural pub are those who are also influential men in the wider community as leaders of business, council and clubs. The practice of pub drinking thus acts as an expression – as well as a source – of power for certain men in the community.

What is evident in the above readings of the 'masculine in the rural' in non-metropolitan pubs is a final theme in the literature. That is, that discourses of rurality and masculinity constantly intertwine. This is a key finding in a study of the declining participation of rural young men at university by Australian scholars Alloway and Gilbert (2004) as well as an investigation of young men and hunting in Norway undertaken by Bye (2003). In the Australian study the authors examine interview narratives, identifying dominant storylines of what it means to be a 'real young man' and a 'real country boy'. One such storyline is 'boys want the practical'. To be a 'real young man/real country boy' is to be one who eschews formal education and learning and the (imagined) restraints of the indoors classroom. The discourses of masculinity and rurality thus coalesce, producing particular futures for the rural young men that involve the rejection of university. The young rural men's denunciation of theory and education and their privileging of the body over mind are not just tied to their need to be seen as sufficiently 'masculine'. They are equally tied to their need to be seen as sufficiently rural or 'real country boys'. This need to differentiate oneself from what is 'urban' and what is the 'urban masculine' is also articulated by the young rural men interviewed by Bye (2003). City based hunters are portrayed as incompetent, uncontrolled and self-indulgent. They are ridiculed for caring more about the type of clothes they are wearing than the hunt itself. In contrast, the rural young men present themselves as authentic hunters, patient, focused and skilful. Bye (2003, 152) notes that the young rural men's discourses about hunting 'reinforce the traditional rural masculinity' while their discourses about rural women and hunting actually open up masculinity for 'redefinition' in that they acknowledge women can play a role (albeit a marginal one) in hunting. She hypothesizes that this may be because urban masculinity may be a more significant threat to rural masculinity than is rural femininity. Overall, in both the research of Alloway and Gilbert (2004) and that of Bye (2003) we are given rich examples of the 'masculine in the rural' and the ways in which gendered identities are shaped, not just by discourses of masculinity or femininity, but also by discourses of urbanity and rurality.

The Rural in the Masculine

In introducing their edited collection entitled *Country Boys: Masculinity and Rural Life*, Campbell, Bell and Finney (2006, 1) demonstrate the potency of 'the rural in the masculine' by reference to politicians in the United States noting how leaders such as George Bush have drawn upon the imagery of 'the rural' to demonstrate and reinforce their 'masculine' identity (see also, Connell 1993; Kimmel 1996). This type of exploitation of the symbolic resources of rurality will not be foreign to observers outside the United States. In my own country of Australia campaign images of the former Prime Minister John Howard (1996–2007) invariably presented him as engaged in rurality – pictured in some country location with broadbrimmed Akubra hat donned and sleeves rolled up. This is because, like the United States, despite our high level of urbanization, images of rurality and agriculture remain dominant in the Australian consciousness. Traditional hegemonic notions of masculinity play a central role in these images. At centre stage is the determined, practical, independent, strong-willed individual – the 'man on the land' – heroically, aggressively and stoically fighting the vicissitudes of nature and ever loyal to his mates. This image, which Russel Ward called *The Australian Legend* (1958), has understandably been attacked by Australian feminist writers who have noted the absence of 'women', 'sexuality' and 'family' in the mythologizing about 'the rural in the masculine' (Murrie 1998). They have pointed out that, if present at all, women are the peripheral figure in this landscape – important more as supporters of men and admirers of masculinity than for their own sake (Poiner 1990; Dempsey 1992). Despite this, conventional discourses of rurality and masculinity continue to enjoy privileged status in many cultural representations of the Australian nation such as in poems, books, songs and films (Coad 2002; Lucas 2006; Connell 2006).

Beyond Australia, writers have noted a similar mythologizing of 'the rural in the masculine' in a range of texts. These have included children's stories (Jones 1999), advertisements (Campbell and Kraack 1998), men's movement blockbusters (Bonnett 1996), military training materials and paperbacks (Woodward 1998; 2000), films (Bell 1997; 2000a) and contemporary government policy (Anahita and Mix 2006). Despite their disparate data sources the studies all note a constant interplay in the texts between discourses of masculinity and discourses of rurality. For example, Campbell and Kraack (1998) explain that it is no mistake that the New Zealand beer advertisements they investigate are filmed in rural landscapes. This is a landscape that is seen as the polar opposite of the urban. It is problem free, friendly, clean, egalitarian and peaceful. Concurrently, this natural environment is tough, rough and rugged and needs to be tamed. The symmetries between social constructions of rurality and masculinity are thus exploited by the beer advertisers. The same cross-over is evident in the military texts examined by Woodward (1998; 2000). Woodward (1998; 2000) explains that it does not matter that most British military operations are 'far removed from the uplands and heathlands' which feature so prominently in textual representations of the military, for these rural images powerfully convey a masculinity of independence, strength and adventure. Bell (2000b) reads a similar conflation between 'the natural' rural environment and 'masculinity' in texts he examines, such as the literature on the myothetic men's movement and film representations of gay men. He does, however, note a degree of complexity: on one hand, there is evidence of a conflation of men/masculinity/heterosexuality/nature, while on the other hand (sometimes) a conflation of men/masculinity/homosexuality/ nature. This latter characterization is typically associated with particular forms of same-sex activity such as 'hillbilly priapism or rustic sodomy' (Bell 2000b, 559). Collectively, the literature on 'the rural in the masculine' counters the normative belief that it is femininity rather than masculinity that is most closely associated with nature. As Jones (1999, 132) comments, it would be expected that it would be 'female children rather than male children who should be at home in nature' in textual representations of childhood, but this is not the case. Instead it is the male child who is associated with nature and who is thus presented as the embodiment of what is a 'natural' childhood.

Rurality/Masculinity/Management

While scholars have now examined the interplay between discourses of masculinity and rurality in a number of different sites, little work has focused on leadership, and specifically, the way in which managerial masculinities are deployed and circulated in rural organizations. As will be demonstrated later in this chapter, some work has emerged on the more specific subject of masculinities in agricultural organizations. However, there is little known about how management may be undertaken by men in non-metropolitan organizations not connected with farming.

There is, however, some very beginning work that provides insight into the relationship between management, masculinity and rurality. Representative of this work is a study by Charles and Davies (2000). What is of principal concern to these authors is 'the significance of place' and the fact that this has been largely ignored in studies examining women's under-representation in management (Charles and Davies 2000, 545). The 'place' of interest to them is Wales. Here, as in Scotland and the north of England, women are much less likely to be in senior management positions than they are in London. Drawing on a comprehensive range of data, the authors conclude that place matters in terms of how men manage and women's level of involvement in management. The dominant mode of managerial masculinity amongst Welsh men is paternalism. Charles and Davies (2000) suggest that paternalism is commonly practised by male Welsh managers because of place-specific material and discursive features. Material conditions in Wales include the legacy of male dominated engineering, agricultural and extractive industries, which has negatively impacted on women's progress to senior management as well as women's participation in employment more generally. In terms of discourses which have legitimated paternalism, Charles and Davies (2000) note the prevalence of notions of 'the ideal' Welsh man and woman, particularly in rural areas. These are discourses which emphasize women's roles as mother and wife and men's roles as patriarch and breadwinner.

The particular form of managerial masculinity dominant in the Welsh organizations, that of paternalism, is also the variant of managerial masculinity hegemonic in the discourses of the rural American businessmen interviewed by Bird (2006). These small business owners express this paternalism by positioning themselves as embodying the role of 'Father' in relation to their wives, families, employees and broader rural communities. Like Charles and Davies (2000), Bird (2006) refers to literature which has suggested that paternalism is typically viewed as anachronistic in contemporary organizations (for example, Kerfoot and Knights 1993; Brueggemann 2000), and thus questions why it is the case that this mode of managerial masculinity dominates in the rural business context. Importantly, like Charles and Davies (20000), she suggests that 'place' may matter when it comes to management and the type of managerial masculinity enacted by men managers because discourses of rurality, as well as the material conditions of rural living, are conducive to paternalism. Bird (2006) highlights how notions of rurality and manhood that centre on gentlemanly behaviour and care and protection provide a buttress for the deployment of paternalistic managerial masculinity. Material factors that sanction and shore up paternalism are also evident in the rural communities studied by Bird (2006) as they are in the Welsh communities researched by Charles and Davies (2000). In 'Madison Town', for example, Bird (2006) suggests that paternalism has been fostered by the declining number of small businesses in rural communities and the limited opportunities for employment. These factors have elevated the position of male business owners in the rural community as well as enmeshed relationships between employers and employees.

Clearly, scholarship on masculinities, rurality and management is still at an embryonic stage. In seeking to further work on the subject, management and organizational scholars could gain much inspiration by turning to the work of feminist and pro-feminist geographers who have, over past decades, produced an important body of literature demonstrating the gendered nature of place (for example, McDowell 1992; Rose 1993; Massey 1994; McDowell 1999). This work has recognized the plurality of masculinities and the need to afford attention to the way in which masculinities are enacted 'in specific contexts, in different organizations and in different places' (McDowell 1999, 137).

Agricultural Masculinities

To date, the literature on rural masculinities has largely focused on masculinities in the farming sector, reflecting the traditional dominance of the study of agriculture within rural social science (Garkovich and Bell 1995), as well as the tendency of feminist scholars to concern themselves with gender and farming rather than gender and rurality more broadly (Little 2002a). This is not to suggest, however, that there is a plethora of literature on the subject. As Brandth (2002) notes in an analysis of the literature on European family farming, studies of men and masculinities in agriculture are also still scarce. In the following sections I provide an overview of this literature around the key subject areas that have thus far been explored by writers. These are masculinities and farming technologies, masculinities and the identity of farmer, masculinities and sustainable agriculture, masculinities and the crisis in agriculture, masculinities, farming and sexualities, masculinities, age and farming and masculinities and agricultural organizations.

Masculinities and Farming Technologies

The first work explicitly examining the relationship between masculinities and farming was undertaken by Berit Brandth in 1995. This was foregrounded by an earlier study by Brandth (1994) in which the author examined how women who farm in their own right construct their identities when normalized discourses of farming and femininity are so contradictory. In this work she noted the critical importance of 'the tractor' as a boundary marker distinguishing men and women's work and observed that women who did drive tractors and use heavy machinery transgressed a long established gender norm on farms (see also, Pini 2005d). In this article, as was her intent, Brandth (1994) examined the tractor as a potent symbol of masculinity from the perspective of the women's gendered identities.

In a follow-up paper in 1995 examining tractor advertisements in the Norwegian forestry press, Brandth's intention again was to focus on women farmers and femininities. However, the complete absence of women in the tractor advertisements shifted her focus. Rather than producing further evidence of what had already been well established in the literature – that is, that women are absent from the agricultural media (for example, Bell and Pandey 1989; Sheridan 1994) – she asked what tractor advertisements can tell us about the construction of masculinity in farming. The image presented in the advertisements is of man (as singular) battling, controlling and ultimately conquering nature. The tractor is portrayed in pictures and texts as strong, physical and powerful. By using a tractor the male farmer embodies these traits. As Brandth (1995) reads the images over the period from 1984 to 1994, she witnesses a shift in the representation of the tractor and wonders if this is suggestive of agricultural masculinity evolving into a new form. By the end of the twentieth century, tractors had become increasingly technically sophisticated as well as increasingly comfortable. Structural changes in farming also saw new discourses emerge within farming as business skills and entrepreneurial drive came to be accentuated over physical strength and hard work. Collectively, Brandth (1995) supposes that this may lead to, and be indicative of, a shift in farming masculinities towards a more managerial/business discourse. Regardless of these shifting discourses, she emphasizes that the conflation between man/masculinity/machine remain intact and the absence of woman/femininity a constant.

The veracity of this claim is evidenced in more recent work on the subject by Saugeres (2002a). In this study, the author draws on interview data with 36 French farming men and women to examine the place of the tractor in constructions of agricultural masculinity. Saugeres (2002a) argues that the tractor is used by men as a symbol of masculine power and acts to produce and reproduce patriarchal ideologies which exclude women. Men's monopoly over the tractor is legitimized by 'common sense' discourses, which suppose that men are more innately technically competent and more naturally predisposed to utilising technology. The fact that so few women drive tractors is also invoked as a legitimising 'common sense' discourse to support gendered constructions of farming and technological competence. Clearly, the meanings attributed to farming technologies such as a tractor are not uniform or fixed (Brandth 2006; Bryant and Pini 2006). Further, as Saugeres (2002a) demonstrates, such technologies may be a key site for contesting inequitable gendered power relations. However, it is clear that tractors are a critical symbolic and material resource for enacting the masculine identity of 'farmer'.

Masculinities and the Identity of Farmer

Since Brandth's (1995) pioneering work, a number of studies have sought to further enunciate the ways in which masculinities are constituted in farming. Liepins (1998; 2000), for example, has undertaken a study of the rural media in Australia and New Zealand identifying as hegemonic a discourse she entitles 'tough men farm' which denotes farming as involving battles with nature, physical strength and rugged individualism. Alongside this dominant discourse the author identifies the emergence of a new farming identity she labels 'sensitive-new age' men in farming. Farmers who enact this identity place emphasis on business over physical skills, demonstrate a commitment to alternative agriculture practices and advocate more egalitarian on-farm gender relations.

In similar work, Brandth and Haugen (1998; 2005a; 2005b; 2005c) engage in a textual analysis of the magazine of the Norwegian Forest Owners' Federation, *The Forest Owner*, in order to identify gendered representations of farming identities. To assist their analysis the authors examine representations of gender in the magazine in four historical moments: 1976, 1986, 1996 and 2002. This provides a rich description of the ways in which gendered images, symbols and discourses of farming have changed, and indeed not changed, over time. In their analysis of the early period, the authors identify the centrality of the discourse Liepins (1998; 2000) labelled 'tough men farm'. However, in the 1980s a shift emerges as the Norwegian farm foresters are depicted as battling machines more than nature. A particularly 'macho' portrayal of the forest worker is evident in 1986 as images are presented of strong, athletic and dynamic young men brandishing power saws and tools (Brandth and Haugen 2005b, 155). At the same time, the writers note some destabilization occurring in the representation of masculine farmer identities. Computer technology starts to be highlighted and discourses of entrepreneurialism and business development come to prominence. By 2002, further change is evident in the masculine farm identities portrayed in the rural media. Logging is much less central and 'new' forms of income generation are highlighted. In sum, the 'forest owners' and now 'property owners.'

Despite other changes, one constant across the decades of the analysis undertaken by Brandth and Haugen (1998, 435) is that women are seldom represented as forest farmers (see also Reed 2003). When they are depicted, the authors claim, it is as an 'exceptional' woman against the unnamed, unmarked masculine norm. Insight into how this textual exclusion is normalized and legitimized in the everyday discourses of farm men and women is provided by Saugeres (2002c) in her work based in rural France. Saugeres (2002c) first identifies the way in which a number of the farming men in her study describe themselves as 'paysan' which is suggestive of a traditional farmer working closely with the land. The definition of the 'good farmer' is a 'natural' farmer. The progression of this argument is that men have an inherent predisposition to farm the land and an innate knowledge of how to farm the land. The land is feminized by the farming men – depicted as nurturing mother or sexualised as potentially threatening and destructive. Saugeres (2002c) emphasizes that not all of the farming men she interviewed had the same imagined relationship with the land. However, even in those cases where male farmers did not claim to have a natural affiliation to the land they still identified themselves as legitimate farmers in their own right. This was not the case with women. Women cannot be 'good' farmers for they have no embodied relationship with the land. This positioning of women is solidified by discourses that suggest that, compared with men, women's bodies are deficient and lack the capacity for the physical and technical work of farming. When women do farm alone they are dismissed as not 'real' farmers for utilizing male help and/or for failing to subscribe to normative definitions of femininity.

The dynamic nature of farming identities, and the relationship between identity change and broader material and discursive shifts in society, are themes also worked through by Australian rural sociologist Lia Bryant (1999). While Bryant's (1999) focus is broader than an examination of masculine subjectivities in farming, her findings still provide a useful addition to the literature. Interviews with 22 men reveal that some participants continue to position themselves within traditional discourses of agricultural masculinity. However, they demonstrate what the author says are 'detraditionalized identities' mobilizing around the notions of 'manager' and 'entrepreneur'. Sitting in between the traditional and detraditional identities is a further subject position adopted by some farming men in the study. This is 'the new traditional farmer' who shares some of the meanings of farming held by the traditional farmer but is open to change in other respects such as in relation to gender roles. Bryant's (1999) analysis is particularly useful in linking the shifts in farm men's identities with a multitude of changes such as those evident in the nature of farming, agricultural policy and global farming regimes. For example, she sees the shift to an entrepreneurial/managerial identity among male farmers as intricately connected to the discourses of neo-liberalism and managerialism dominant in Australia's agricultural policy throughout the late 1980s and the decade of the 1990s.

Masculinities and Sustainable Agriculture

While Bryant's (1999) research focuses on the relationship between agricultural masculinities and numerous intersecting changes affecting farming, studies by Peter, Bell, Jarnagin and Bauer (2000) and Barlett and Conger (2004) take a more specific approach and examine the way in which masculinities are being (re)shaped through one particular change in farming: the shift to organic agriculture. In the first of these studies Peter et al. (2000) examine the differences in the beliefs, practices and discourses of members of the sustainable agriculture group, Practical Farmers of Iowa (PFI), and their non-PFI neighbours. In distinguishing between the gendered performances of the men, Peter et al. (2000) use the terms monologic and dialogic masculinity. They argue that the men who are engaged in sustainable farming display a dialogic masculinity in that they have a 'broader understanding of what it is to be a man' (Peter et al. 2000, 216). Unlike the conventional farmers, these men are more open about revealing their mistakes and emotions as well as less intent on controlling and dominating nature. The discourses of individualism, physicality and toughness are less central to the sustainable farming males. In contrast, those men continuing to farm utilizing traditional productionist methods define their masculinity in terms of a battle with the land which is contained and managed via large machines. Men involved in mainstream farming are not only intent on controlling nature; this patriarchal performance also entails the control of emotions and women. These men are defined by the authors as exhibiting a monologic orientation in that they subscribe to rigid gender roles and boundaries and are not open to change.

Like Peter et al. (2000), Barlett and Conger (2004, 221) and Barlett (2006) argue that the shift to sustainable and organic farming is heralding a 'new masculinity' in farming. They suggest that this masculinity is the antithesis of two dominant traditional male identities in farming: agrarian masculinity and industrial masculinity.

In the latter, public and private are enmeshed, farming is presented as a way of life rather than a business and emphasis is given to the farm continuing in the family name. In contrast to this is an 'industrial' farming discourse. This positions the farm as a business, emphasizes profit and efficiency and maintains a separation between the family and farm. The 'new masculinity' discourse the authors see emerging is one that is in opposition to conventional discourses of farming masculinity. Barlett (2006, 63) explains that the men involved in sustainable agriculture construct their identities 'through private relations with nature, orientation to the divine, and stewardship of resources'. In doing so they face pressure from peer groups and family, but gain support from other spheres such as sustainable farming organizations.

Masculinities and the Crisis in Agriculture

Shifting agricultural masculinities is a theme developed by Irish scholar Caitriona Ni Laoire (1999; 2001) in work on the impact of rural restructuring on young farming men's masculine identities (see also, Ni Laoire and Fielding 2006). Ni Laoire (1999; 2001) paints a bleak picture of life for a young Irish farming male. He may inherit the farm but this is associated with a sense of duty and responsibility. It also requires 'staying behind' when others, typically women and those with a higher education, are leaving rural areas in large numbers. Even the language of 'staying behind', Ni Laoire (1999; 2001) contends, connotes a sense of failure and exclusion. This is especially so, she suggests, in the current context of rural restructuring, which has seen a significant decrease in the number of family farms and a consequent loss of community life and support networks. While careful not to posit any simplistic connection between high rates of suicide amongst rural young men and rural/agricultural change, she points out that as the foundational ground upon which male farmers have traditionally based their identities shifts, some may struggle to adjust. She also recognizes the continued masculine hegemony of rural areas, but rightly questions the 'apparent disparity' between this and the high levels of suicide amongst rural young men.

Connell's (2000) contention that hegemonic masculinity may not be the most easily practised, nor the most beneficial to men's health and well-being, is implicit in Ni Laoire's (1999; 2001) nuanced reading of young Irish farming men's lives. In *Troubled Fields: Men, Emotions and the Crisis in American Farming* by medical anthropologist Ramirez-Ferrero (2005) it is explicit. In this book, the author uses data from an extensive ethnographic study of male farmers in Oklahoma to identify the discourses through which men construct their identities as masculine farmers, and to explore the relationship between these constructions and increasing mental and physical health problems amongst this population. As his introductory chapter explains, farmers have a suicide rate three times that of the general population. Why, he asks, is this the case? In addressing this question he deconstructs the notion of 'pride', which he says is at the centre of farming men's identities. Pride is not simply a psychological or biological phenomenon, Ramirez-Ferrero (2005) claims. It is, in fact, embedded in culture and involves a complex web of practices, beliefs and discourses pertaining to family, survival, control, self-reliance, hardship, endeavour, independence, connection to the land and Christianity.

In his examination of 'pride', Ramirez-Ferrero (2005) describes conflicting discourses of what it is to be a farmer that resonate with the work of Barlett and Conger (2004), Barlett (2006) and Ni Laoire (2002; 2004). That is, the 'family' farming discourse (agrarian) and the 'industrial' farming discourse. Ramirez-Ferrero (2005) argues that, for farming men in crisis, there are negative implications – regardless of which discourse they adopt. Those farmers who subscribe to a traditional discourse are likely to be labelled as 'bad' farmers, seen as out-of-date and lacking contemporary know-how. Those farmers who do take up the industrial discourse will be seen as 'bad managers', having created their own fate through poor business decisions. The men in his study are 'conversant in a language of pride and much less so in a language of vulnerability' (Ramirez-Ferrero 2005, 99). Thus, in the face of vulnerability they will have few resources and are likely to withdraw from family and community.

Masculinities, Farming, Sexualities

The intersection between discourses of farming, masculinity and sexuality has only just begun to be examined in the literature (Little and Leyshon 2003). This is despite the fact that the conjugal heterosexual relationship is central to family farming. It is this 'ubiquitous uncontested nature of heterosexuality' within rural communities which is the focus of work undertaken by Jo Little (2003, 406) in a rich analysis of two campaigns – 'The Farmer Wants a Wife' conducted by the British magazine *Country Living* and a 'Singles' Ball' held in the rural New Zealand community of Middlemarch. Little (2003; 2006; 2007) argues that heterosexuality is largely unacknowledged or named in rural spaces. It is thus that 'other' sexualities become deviant, different and unnatural. Her view is that to understand more about divisions and exclusions within rural communities made on the basis of gender and sexuality we need to interrogate how discourses of heterosexuality circulate and become legitimated in rural areas. The rationale for the campaigns is 'the problem' of the lack of sustainability of many rural communities, and more particularly, the decline in farming in rural areas.[3] The 'solution' to this problem is the nuclear family. Heterosexuality is the natural choice for the farming men, but they are lacking women to fulfil this choice. However, it is not women per se who are required for the farming men. It is a particular type of woman – stable, traditional, practical and tolerant of farming life – since the ultimate goal as inscribed in the campaigns is marriage. Most interestingly, Little (2003; 2006; 2007) claims that 'masculinity as portrayed in the schemes is unthreatening, lacking in aggression and generally a bit hopeless'. This, she notes, is quite different from representations of the masculine farmer as powerful, strong and independent. What is different between the farming men represented in the campaigns and those depicted in more traditional images is the absence/presence of a wife. This is the message of campaign organisers who stress that with the assistance of a suitable female partner these male farmers can be transformed.

---

3 Such campaigns have been undertaken in Australia as well (see Pini 2007).

The privileging of heterosexuality in rural/agricultural spaces identified by Little (2003; 2006; 2007) is a theme also explored in work by Bryant (2006). However, this is a 'raw heterosexual masculinity' rather than a benign and inept heterosexual masculinity. Bryant's (2006) focus is on younger men (aged 18–30) enrolled as undergraduates in agricultural related degrees in an Australian university and their perceptions of gender relations on the campus and within the agricultural sector more broadly. Importantly, Bryant (2006, 70) notes that the 'raw heterosexual masculinity' must be 'publicly observable' and thus the male students engage in such practices as the public objectification of women, public boasting of heterosexual activities and public drinking to excess. Bodily strength and capacity are reified and seen as naturally occurring attributes of masculinity, and essential to the identity of the (male) farmer. Women studying and working in agriculture are seen as lacking in femininity and not appropriate heterosexual partners.

While discourses of homosexuality are absent in the agricultural training environment described by Bryant (2006), they are central to the 75 gay farming men's narratives documented by Will Fellows (1996). In the collection *Farm Boys*, the author details aspects of the men's childhoods, the attitudes and values of their families, their experiences of coming out and their lives subsequent to coming out. Fellows (1996, 18) notes that many of the men in the study reported that while they were growing up homosexuality was depicted as an 'unnatural phenomenon of the city'. This silence surrounding homosexuality is, as the author explains, not unique to farming communities, but felt acutely by his informants due to other aspects of the culture of rurality (for example, conservatism) and the geographic isolation. Many also report the stringent enforcement of rigid and traditional gender roles on their farms and the attendant tensions this produces for those who act outside these norms. At the same time Fellows (1996, xvi), like Bell (2006), reports that there are contradictions in the interplay between homosexuality, masculinity and nature in that 'the rural' is also imagined as a space of homosexual desire in terms of the 'farm-boy fantasy'.

The complexity of the relationship between nature, sexuality and gender is a theme further explored by Little and Panelli (2007) in a reading of an Australian television series entitled 'Desperately Seeking Sheila.' The programme maps the experiences of four Australian 'bush bachelors' as they spend a three week period with a 'sheila' they have selected from a group of single women from the United Kingdom and Perth, Australia. Little and Panelli (2007) find further evidence of heteronormativity in the rural. They note that the very nomenclature 'bachelor' positions the men as heterosexual. It is not that these men are not interested in sex; it is just that their 'outback' location has made meeting a partner problematic. They also find further evidence of the characteristics of hegemonic discourses of rural masculinity in that footage of the men presents them as strong and macho; a notion amplified as the women in the series view any sensitivity they display as unexpected and atypical. However, the depiction of nature in the series, and the relationship of nature to sexuality is, the authors suggest multifaceted. In part, nature – the Australian outback – is presented as uncompromising and tough, and is engaged as a source for testing and determining a woman's suitability as a potential (marriage) partner for the men. At the same nature is depicted as romantic and gentle and a source for nurturing and supporting the relationships.

Masculinities, Age and Farmers

Despite being differently situated in Ireland, the findings from a study of young farming men by Ni Laoire (2002) echo those of Bryant (1999), Liepins (1998; 2000) and Brandth and Haugen (1998: 2005a; 2005b; 2005c). In this work, Ni Laoire uses interviews with 11 male full time farmers to explore questions of occupational subjectivity. Ni Laoire (2002; 2004) finds evidence of both the 'tough men farm' discourse and the newer 'farm men are businessmen' discourse in her analysis of the transcripts. Self-reliance, independence, hardship and strength emerge as key themes in the men's description of farming but so do entrepreneurship, business acumen and technological competence. By embedding the discussion of the more recent 'farm as business' discourse within the broader gender and organizational literature on entrepreneurship, Ni Laoire (2002, 22) departs from other writers who have noted the emergence of this 'new' discourse by highlighting that it too, like its predecessor, is 'highly gendered'. Moreover, Ni Laoire (2002) notes that, in the interview narratives, this new discourse exists alongside the more conventional 'tough men farm' discourse rather than supersedes it. Thus, much of the traditional hegemonic masculine definition of farming as an occupation remains intact for the young farming men. Possible change exists in another of the alternative farming discourses evident in the data. This is a discourse that is connected to agrarian values, but focuses on environmental protection, greater emotional openness and an ethic of care.

The question of what discourses of masculinity are engaged by young farming men is taken up in an Australian study by Coldwell (2007a; 2007b). In this study the author finds that young male farmers distance themselves from traditional gender ideologies, and argue that there has been substantial change in ideas and beliefs about gender. The young men also demonstrate an interest in environmental care and sustainability. However, the discourses many deploy to describe being a farmer, and particularly a 'real' farmer, demonstrate that normative discourses about gender continue to enjoy currency in agricultural arenas (for example, he is strong and physical).While the young men suggest that women are 'awesome managers', their inability to 'lump bags' disqualifies them from being a 'real farmer.' In this respect, Coldwell (2007a; 2007b) makes links with earlier work by Saugeres (2002b) that focused on how women's bodies are constituted as inferior and lacking in capacity for farm work. As Saugeres (2002b, 646) claims, what is important is not whether men or women are physically stronger, but that the definition of masculinity which is seen as central to farming mobilizes around physical strength. As an occupation, then, farming gives bodily expression to hegemonic masculinity, while acting to exclude women.

According to a study by Gullifer and Thompson (2006) the view that farming is strongly connected to physicality is not just held by young farming men. Interview data with eight farming men ranging in age from 65 to 80 demonstrate the further potency of what Liepins (1998) described as the 'tough men farm' narrative. For these men the discourse provides a source of pride and self-worth in their old age. Three other themes are identified in the interviews by the authors. These are the emphasis on the physical aspects of aging, the attachment to place and the value given to feeling productive. What is suggested in the data is that tensions emerge for older farming men as their physical body no longer performs according to the dominant prescriptions of what it means to be a 'farming man'.

Masculinities and Agricultural Organizations

Since Collinson and Hearn's (1994, 2) initial plea to 'name men as men' in management and organizations and their further invocation for scholars to 'break the silence' on men, masculinity and management (1996, 1), a rich literature has emerged on the subject. Unfortunately, however, the men who have been 'named' in this to date have been largely urban based, and the masculinities on which 'silence' has been broken typically constructed in metropolitan organizations. Thus, there is little literature that speaks to the relationship/s between discourses of management, masculinity and rurality/agriculture. Three key exceptions are studies by Liepins (1998; 2000), Brandth and Haugen (1998; 2000) and Harter (2004). This work is outlined below.

The research by Liepins (1998; 2000) and Brandth and Haugen (1998; 2000; 2005a; 2005b; 2005c) relies upon textual data from agricultural media in Australia/ New Zealand and Norway respectively. Of interest to the authors is identifying the dominant discourses of gender and agriculture on farms and within farmers' unions. In terms of the latter, the authors arrive at some very similar conclusions, despite their different geographical locations. Three issues are relevant.

First, like their Antipodean counterparts, the Norwegian agricultural leaders draw on a managerial discourse of power, decisiveness, control and authority. This is what Liepins (1998) called the 'powerful men lead' discourse. She contends that the 'over-riding features of a hegemonic masculinity in agricultural politics' revolve around a notion of 'pinnacle leadership' which gives emphasis to importance, rationality, credibility and aggression (Liepins 1998, 382). It is a discourse associated with a range of symbols including business suits, immediate and easy access to business and government leaders, and long working hours. Importantly, the historical reading undertaken by Brandth and Haugen (2000; 2005a; 2005b; 2005c) enables them to identify changes in the representations of agricultural masculinity over a 20 year period. What they notice is that in the most recent publications there is greater emphasis on the masculinities associated with organizational and managerial spaces rather than on-farm spaces. It is the agri-political group which is now, the authors suggest, a key site for displaying masculinities within the agricultural sector.

The second common finding between the authors is that there is slippage – or what Brandth and Haugen call 'spill-over' (2000, 21) – between depictions of hegemonic on-farm masculinities and agri-political masculinities. While the textual references to the objects and symbols of the environments of archetypal 'farmer' and 'agri-political leader' differ, connections are made between what they 'do'. They both 'do gender' by displaying the characteristics of 'fighters' and demonstrate strength, power and toughness. In both studies the writers suggest that the tough and powerful masculinities embedded in on-farm constructions of agriculture permeate the construction of masculinities in agri-politics because the former still occupies a dominant position in the sector. Those managers operating in the public world of agriculture can therefore gain greater credibility by aligning themselves with a similar construction of masculinity, despite the disparity in the contexts in which these are displayed.

The third point of similarity between the findings of Liepins (1998; 2000) and Brandth and Haugen (2000; 2005a) is that the hegemonic constructions of managerial masculinities in agricultural groups render particular groups within the sector invisible or marginal. For example, there is limited discursive space given to representing the masculinities of younger and unskilled male workers. Furthermore, women and femininities are typically absent. In examining her Australian and New Zealand data, Liepins (1998) identifies the appearance of an alternative discourse of femininity in agri-politics, which favours communication, networking and relationships over aggression, hierarchy and control. Importantly, however, she notes that this subject position is only apparent in women's farming groups and not the traditional producer groups.[4] Indeed, in the male dominated producer groups in New Zealand and Australia, women participants in agri-politics are represented in terms that approximate those of hegemonic masculinity or, as Liepins (1998, 384) labels them, 'woman as masculine'. The 20 year period of Brandth and Haugen's (2000; 2005a) study demonstrates this exclusion of women/femininities from discourses of agriculture to be a constant. In the texts examined, women enter as elected members at a local scale, and, in 1996, one woman is elected to the main central governing board of the Federation, but these are anomalies. On other occasions, women enter as elected members, but the authors witness them 'dropping out' soon after as they choose not to stand for re-election or are voted out after a single term. Further, Brandth and Haugen (1998, 439) conclude that if women are presented at all they tend to be portrayed 'as women and as tokens in a "man's world"'. Men's gender is not an issue because it is the norm that 'powerful' men lead.

In another study of masculinities and agricultural organizations, Harter (2004) takes as her focus the Nebraska Co-perative Council (NCC) and its 108 constitutive producer co-peratives. As a theorist of organizational communication Harter (2004) works from a different disciplinary framework than the above authors, but reaches surprisingly similar conclusions about particular manifestations of masculinity dominant in agricultural organizations. The study of the organizations is established against the background of a gendered critique of agrarianism (see also, Fink 1991). That is, the image of the farmer is characterized by a masculine subjectivity. He is practical, self-reliant, resilient, independent and physically active. Despite the fact that discourses of agrarianism first emerged in a past that is now long forgotten, Harter (2004) contends that they retain currency in informing the gendered organizing of the Co-operative. Like the authors above, she notes that agricultural leaders have a propensity to engage discourses of battle and war to describe their activities. For the men of the NCC, the key opponents are multinationals and bureaucracies. What is of particular interest to Harter (2004) is the disjuncture between the masculine discourses mobilizing around agrarianism (for example, independence, self-reliance) and the feminine discourses associated with co-operative forms of organizing (for example, interdependence, collectivity). She argues that the process of navigating between and across conflicting gender discourses leads to a range of paradoxes in organizational culture and practice. One of these she labels the 'paradox of agency' (2004, 108). This is evident in the fact that so few Co-operative members

---

4 See also, Shortall (1994), Grace (1997) and Mackenzie (1994).

demonstrate involvement in the activities of their Council, preferring to abrogate their responsibilities to their elected leadership. She writes:

> Ultimately, by abdicating personal agency within a participatory community many members enact roles that privilege certain definitions of masculinity over others – definitions that emphasize technocratic rationalities rather than interdependence. Such hegemonic constructions of masculinity emerge from and are reinforced by the mythic belief system of agrarianism. The frontier has always been a patriarchal myth in which men dominated other men, women, and nature. (Harter 2004, 109)

Harter's (2004) analysis is particularly useful as she highlights the way in which different discourses of masculinity may be present in agricultural organizations, but not enjoy equal power. For example, she argues that masculine discourses of efficiency and managerialism have become prevalent and powerful. These sit in opposition to the discourses of participation and equality that have traditionally been important in the Co-operative, but are today less privileged. Harter's (2004) study also reveals that identifying the discourses by which men construct their subjectivities in agricultural organizations cannot be done without reference to broader discursive influences. These may be on-farm gender discourses such as those mobilizing around the occupational identity of 'farmer'. Alternatively, they may be off-farm gender discourses circulating in rural communities such as those which assign particular roles and traits to the subject 'rural woman'. Conversely, they may be gendered discourses informing men's sense of themselves as masculine leaders in farmers' unions (such as those associated with new modes and practices of management).

Conclusion

This chapter has reviewed the literature on rural and agricultural masculinities. It has drawn attention to the fact that within rural social science men and masculinities have been everywhere but nowhere, omnipresent yet invisible. That is, while they have been the principal categories for investigation and analysis, they have also traditionally been unexamined as the taken-for-granted norm. In recent years this paradox has begun to be recognized by rural studies scholars. Thus, there is now a growing body of literature that has not just emphasized the hegemony of men and masculinities in agricultural and rural spaces, but also attempted to critique and interrogate the implications of this in terms of gender equality. Such work has been invigorated by the turn to culture in rural studies and the associated focus on 'rurality' as a social and cultural construct. What has emerged most strongly from studies of 'the masculine in the rural' and the 'rural in the masculine' is that there is a complex interconnection between dominant discourses of masculinity and those of rurality/agriculture. The 'country boy' thus has what has been described as a 'double-barrelled' legitimacy, situated as he is within the discourses of hegemonic masculinity and rurality (Finney, Campbell and Bell 2004).

While still scant, the literature on agricultural masculinities highlights four themes of relevance to this book. The first is that while gendered identities are varied and fluid, and no singular discourse constructs gender in agriculture, there has traditionally been a dominant discourse of farming masculinity which has mobilized around physical strength, control of nature, tenacity, hardship, toughness, independence and individualism. The tractor has been a key marker of hegemonic masculinity in farming and the physical body critical to its performance. The second theme of importance emerging from this review of the literature is that it is evident that challenges to hegemonic masculinity in agriculture are emerging. For example, farmers involved in sustainable agriculture are less likely to constitute their subjectivities in terms of physicality and control, while new discourses of entrepreneurialism, business and management are also coming to occupy a prominent place in the identities of farming men. Whether or not these 'new' discourses of farming will lead to more egalitarian gender relations is, however, questionable. The third notable theme in the literature is that the shifts in men's farming identities cannot be separated from broader structural and discursive changes occurring at the local, state, national and global levels. Factors such as rural restructuring, the emergence of more progressive notions about gender equity, and increased out-migration from rural communities have all been shown to influence the shaping of farming men's identities. As Bryant (1999, 256) notes, these are collectively 'chipping away' at traditional occupational identities in farming. Finally, just as there is an intersection between the discourses of rurality and masculinity there is also an intersection between the discourses of agriculture and masculinity. Being a 'real farmer', a 'real agricultural leader' and a 'real man' are often constructed as synonymous. How this was enacted in interviews with agricultural managerial men is the subject of the following chapter.

Chapter 3

Researching Managerial Masculinities in Agricultural Organizations: Methodological Reflections

There is a glaring omission from the work reviewed in the last chapter on the subject of rural masculinities and more specifically agricultural masculinities: that is, any commentary on the process of undertaking research. We have been afforded no insights by rural researchers into the dilemmas and complexities of undertaking scholarship on masculinities. Thus we have 'findings' – the empirical results that are beginning to tell us the 'what' about rurality and masculinity – but no discussion or critique of the 'how' involved in coming to these findings. This may be related to the broader scholarly context in which writers about masculinity/rurality are operating. There has been very little methodological rumination in the discipline of critical men's studies (Haywood and Mac an Ghaill 2003, 111) or in rural studies (Pini 2002b; 2003a). As a consequence, when I began this study I had little to guide me as I wrestled with a number of methodological and epistemological conundrums. These included questions such as: How do we study what has not been named and known (Kronsell 2005)? And, what is the role of women in the study of masculinities (Davies 1995)? Moreover, what is the place of a feminist in the study of masculinities (Gardiner 2002)? And is it possible to engage a feminist methodology in undertaking a study of masculinities (Campbell 2003)?

While I found little of assistance in the rural and men's studies literature there has been, fortunately, decades of feminist scholarship which speaks to some of the concerns I had. Such work is embedded in the feminist commitments to reflexivity and political change (Fonow and Cook 2005; Letherby 2003; Pini 2003a; Ramazanoglu and Holland 2002). This literature has traced the trajectories of feminist scholarship including the critical debates which have surrounded the subject of the study of men and masculinities. Illustrative of early work was Tania Modleski's *Feminism Without Women* (1991) which worried that the semiotic shift away from 'women's studies' to 'gender studies', and the associated emerging focus on masculinities, would lead to the evacuation of scholarship on women and the end of any project of gender reform. Just over a decade later, writers in Judith Kegan Gardiner's edited collection *Masculinity Studies and Feminist Theory* (2002) were arguing that masculinity studies had enriched feminist theory and vice versa, and that there was considerable scope for further conversation between the two. The move within feminist thinking from a sense of suspicion and sometimes hostility towards masculinity studies to a sense of consensus and collaboration was due, in part, to the theoretical ground shifting as a result of insights gained from poststructuralism. This led to the destabilization of gender categories and profoundly countered the assumptions about a shared universal identity 'women' and a fixed coherent enemy 'men' which had underpinned much of the early debate about the relationship between studies of masculinity and feminism.

Thus today feminists have moved beyond asking whether we should study men and masculinities, as they define 'masculinity studies within and not against feminism as an intellectual and political project' (Wiegman 2002, 37).[1] They are, however, still resolving questions of how this may be done. As Campbell (2003) has argued, while feminists have a rich tradition of documenting methodological issues, much of this has been related to the study of women. We know little about what occurs when women, and particularly feminist women, research masculinities.

In light of this neglect, the purpose of this chapter is to reflect on my experiences as a feminist researcher interviewing male managers. The chapter is divided into five main sections. To begin, I outline the literature on women researchers interviewing men. Following this, I begin the conversation that will continue throughout this book describing the gendered context of the Farmers' Union. This is a very brief discussion simply to set the scene for the interviews. In the next section I introduce the 15 male elected members I interviewed, before turning to explore their performance of masculinity in the interview process. I then detail the men's display of heterosexuality, power and knowledge throughout the interviews. This serves a two-fold purpose. First, it provides a preliminary picture of how managerial men in agriculture constitute their identities as 'masculine men'. Second, it gives emphasis to the usefulness of examining gendered performances in the research process itself. In the final section of the chapter, I examine why the male interview participants performed these versions of masculinity. I argue that in order to examine the way in which gender may shape an interview, we need to go beyond a simple focus on the gender of the researcher and the researched, because the gender focus of the research and the gendered context of the research environment are also critical factors in mediating the relationship between an interviewer and interviewee. The questions relevant to an understanding of gender and interviewing are thus, 'who, whom, what and where'.

Interviewing Men

Increasingly interviews are seen as far more than straightforward and self-evident interactions in which a researcher extracts information from an informant by asking a series of questions and obtaining replies. Rather, the interview is today more likely to be seen as a shifting space in which knowledge is co-created inter-subjectively between a differently situated researcher and participant. In this conceptualization of the interview, the identities of the interviewer and interviewee are seen as important in shaping the interview process, and ultimately, the data gathered or not gathered. Illustrative of this more nuanced definition of the interview is Schwalbe and Wolkomir's paper 'Interviewing Men' (2003, 56). The authors understand gender

---

1 The same could be said of the questions of 'can men do feminist research?'; again, we have moved to asking how men can do feminist research. For an excellent discussion of this issue see Butz and Berg (2002).

and particularly masculinities as a 'dramaturgical task', and argue that a research interview may be used by men as a means of performing this task. They claim that when interviewed by a female researcher, men may attempt to signify their masculine identity by seeking to control the interview, by demonstrating knowledge and expertise, or by sexualizing the researcher. This was certainly the case for Terry Arendell (1997) who provides particular insight into the interview as a gendered conversation by comparing her experiences of studying divorced mothers and divorced fathers. Unlike the women participants, the men asserted dominance by critiquing her interviewing skills, assisting her with the set up of the tape recorder and lecturing her on the study topic. She notes that these men saw themselves as 'collaborators if not conductors of the research' (Arendell 1997, 350). Also proving difficult for Arendell (1997) was listening empathically while some informants made sexist and derogatory comments about women. This was also an issue for Winchester (1996) in her study of lone fathers. She noted that a female researcher's interviews with men may reinforce stereotypical gender discourses which suggest that women's role in conversations is to be empathic listener and facilitator for men's narratives. This, along with her participants' sexist language and beliefs, placed the men in her study in a position of power in the interviews.

While similar experiences have been documented by other female researchers interviewing men (for example, Gurney 1985), some female researchers have argued that being located in traditional discourses of femininity by male participants can be advantageous for their research as one may be viewed as unthreatening and different. For example, Horn (1997) said that in her study of the police, 'not being one of the boys' proved to have some benefits. She claims she was not viewed with the suspicion and mistrust that other (male) police scholars have reported and that this opened up access to the research site. This is not to discount the fact that being situated as a researcher within these dominant discourses of femininity – or indeed situating oneself within such discourses – raises another set of dilemmas for the woman researcher. Horn (1997) notes, for example, that the flip side of being positioned within normative definitions of femininity means being viewed as in need of care. In this respect, respondents may deliberately withhold information or access, believing a researcher is in need of protection. There are also, clearly, ethical issues of duplicity if one uses 'one's femininity and desirability to manipulate males in a setting for information' (Easterday, Papademus Schorr and Valentine 1977, 345).

As a means of re-dressing the difficulties that may arise from men's gender performance in an interview, Schwalbe and Wolkomir (2003) suggest a number of strategies related to questioning style, dress and non-verbal interactions. While they do not name these as such, much of what they identify as tactics to counter displays of hegemonic masculinity involve the researcher herself engaging in specific types of gender performance. An illustration of this is documented by Lee (1997) who describes consciously choosing not to perform traditional femininity in terms of dress and make-up as a means of avoiding or minimizing the likelihood of sexual advances from her participants. Meanwhile, in her study of men's use of domestic technologies, Lohan (2002, 175) describes a much more multifaceted gender display as she alternatively/simultaneously positions herself as sexual being, friend, feminist and respectful listener.

A further complexity surrounding issues of women interviewing men is raised by Schoenberger (1991) in terms of the fact that other social attributes, besides gender, may mediate the research relationship. In reflecting on interviews undertaken with male corporate elites, Schoenberger (1991, 281) says her 'class' status marked her as 'one of them' despite her position as a woman. Interviewing a similar elite population in three London City banks, McDowell (1998) writes of differently positioning herself according to the interview subject's gender as well as age. She explains that an interview does not simply involve the negotiation of gender but of, in her case, 'the double positionalities', as 'a white, heterosexual, middle-aged woman interviewing a range of younger people, mainly white, and in the main explicitly heterosexual, about power relations in daily interactions in the workplace' (McDowell 1998, 2140). Similarly, while Campbell (2003) believes being a woman made it difficult for her to build rapport with the male police she interviewed, other social categories to which she belonged (or did not belong) also made a difference. She writes:

> I can only speculate that had I been older (or younger maybe), male, a more experienced researcher, a police colleague, white, middle class, a Freemason, or any other combination of social identities, an entirely different set of interviewing relations' would have prevailed. (Campbell 2003, 297)

Schoenberger's (1991) observations counter the second wave feminist assumptions that there is a singular, known and essential identity of 'man' or 'woman' and that this identity would be given priority in any interview situation. It is a position most famously articulated in a 1981 paper by Anne Oakley. Here the author initiated a spirited attack against the 'proper interview', arguing against conventional approaches to interviewing which assert that there must be a split between subject and object, an hierarchical relationship between interviewer and interview and an interviewer who is distant and uninvolved (Oakley 1981, 51). It is not surprising to find that, since this time, Oakley's (1981) claims have been criticized for being based on a simplistic notion of power and for failing to recognize differences between women (for example, Dyck, Lynam and Anderson 1995).[2] More recent work on women interviewing women has demonstrated that power in the research process is multi-dimensional and multi-layered and further, that other social categories besides that of gender may mediate the research relationship and render rapport problematic (Limerick, Burgess-Limerick and Grace 1997; Phoenix 1994).

Thus, it is clear that power is not held exclusively by men over women, just as it is not possessed exclusively by the researcher over the researched. The interaction is much more fluid and contested, and power much more dispersed. This is why Scheurich (2001, 73–5) refers to interviewing in the postmodern as an experience of 'dominance-resistance/chaos-freedom'. He explains that we can:

> Look at the interview and conclude that there is dominance of the interviewee by the researcher, resistance of the interviewee to researcher dominance, and chaos-freedom enacted by both the interviewer and the interviewee. Within this chaos/freedom, there

---

2 It is also a factor recognized by Oakley (2000) herself in later work.

are speech enactments which cannot be encapsulated or captured by the dominance of the researcher or the resistance of the interviewee. (Scheurich 2001, 73)

Missing from the above analysis is any gender critique; gender discourses do not all have equivalent status. Thus, within the interview interaction – in the space of 'chaos-freedom' – masculinity discourses typically confer greater power than discourses of femininity (Connell 2000). This demonstrates why it can be problematic for women to interview men, as the availability to men of masculinity discourses presents them with greater opportunities to exert power when interacting with a female interviewer. What is also absent from the above quotation, when viewed in the context of a gender stratified society, is that any questioning about gender inequity may also shape the interview process. As Schwalbe and Wolkomir (2003, 58) argue, men's displays of masculinity may be 'heightened if it seems that the interviewer is interested in gender, broadly construed, because this makes the subject's identity as a man more salient to the interaction'. It is on this basis that they have postulated that to examine the impact of gender on interviews we need to move beyond 'who is asking whom' to 'who is asking whom about what' (Schwalbe and Wolkomir 2001, 91).

In this chapter I take up this suggestion. I argue, however, that we need to go further and question 'who is asking whom about what and where', because it is also the gendered context of the research environment which informs the interview relationship. In using the term 'where' I do not simply mean the room, building or organization in which an interview takes place, although the physical site of the interview is another factor mediating the enactment of power relations (Elwood and Martin 2000). The 'where' to which I refer is the broader field or context in which the research is taking place. For this research, the context was the agricultural sector in Australia and more specifically, a farmers' union where, as the following section will demonstrate, women are seldom seen, and their invisibility even more rarely questioned.

The Context

As stated in the introductory chapter, women are not represented in any of the 181 positions of elected leadership in the Farmers' Union. This is across a three level hierarchical structure. The first level consists of local groups called Committees, the second level encompass district level groups called the Executive, while the third level is a state wide Board of 26. This male dominance of managerial positions is replicated in the Farmers' Union staff of 100. These 100 staff members are located in 19 district offices across the State of Queensland and in the capital city office. Across the 19 district offices, there is just a single woman manager just as there is in the capital city office where there are six managerial positions. When the female manager began work in the capital city office she was profiled for constituents under a magazine headline 'Farmers' advocate with the feminine touch.' It was clearly unusual and noteworthy to have a female in such a position.

Importantly, the Farmers' Union is only one organizational site within this agricultural industry in which men predominate. For example, across the 20 mills where the crop is processed no woman occupies any senior, middle or lower level management position. Two women have recently been appointed to the eight member Board of the extension and research organization associated with the industry (for the first time in its 100 year history). However, in the majority of forums – and arguably the visible forums – within this industry, women fail to be represented as managers. As the introductory discussion demonstrated, this is not unusual either within Australia or in other international contexts.

Despite the low representation of women in positions of agricultural management, there was a marked absence of discussion about this at the industry forums I attended. One of the few occasions when I witnessed a public discussion about women's representation in the industry was at a forum organized by a women's agricultural network. Some members of the primarily female audience who had raised the issue were chastised by a female staff member of the Farmers' Union whose comments I recorded in my research journal. She stated:

> This whole conversation has been about women. It shouldn't be about women. You need to accept that it is a chauvinistic culture and if you mention women and make it about women then you just get people's backs up. (Research Journal, May 1999)

In summary, women are absent from leadership positions across the whole of the agricultural industry which was at the centre of my study. This has been the case across the 75 year history of the organization I studied. It is in this context – where women are seldom seen and their invisibility rarely questioned – that I undertook this research.

Background to the Interviews

While a range of methods was used to provide data for the case study, this chapter focuses specifically on the 15 interviews undertaken with elected male members of the Farmers' Union. The selection of these particular men from the possible 181 elected members was assisted by the General Manager of the organization. As the organization had committed cash and in-kind support to the study, he acted as a co-supervisor or 'industry supervisor'.[3] In this role he provided assistance in both selecting interview participants and facilitating access to these participants. As well as wanting to elicit the views of elected members from the three levels of leadership, I also wanted to obtain a variety of perspectives on gender relations. With ten years in the organization, the General Manager knew the membership and their views very well, and I therefore used his recommendations to approach participants. Although no one refused, this does not mean that all were equally willing to participate. It is possible that the General Manager met some resistance but ultimately convinced

---

3 The reasons why the agricultural group supported the research will never be fully known. However, at the time of the study government and women's groups were placing considerable pressure on farming groups in Australia to address gender equity. The decision to support the research required a vote from the 26 member state council. While I was not privy to the discussion, two elected members told me that the debate had been 'heated' and the decision to support the study 'very close'.

members to be involved in the research, given that the project had been approved by the highest tier of leadership.

All the 15 members interviewed were married with children and all but two were over 50 years old. The majority were, in fact, over 60 and had been elected members of the agri-political group for extended periods of time ranging from 15 to 27 years. The nature of their duties differed according to the level of their leadership position. The time needed for these duties ranged from two days a week to half a day a week.

After the General Manager had contacted each of the potential interviewees and solicited their involvement in the project, I telephoned each to introduce myself personally. Following this telephone exchange, I wrote to the men thanking them for agreeing to participate in the project, detailing the aims of the project, and outlining the more specific outcomes being sought from the interviews. As the interviews did not take place until half-way through the three year study, I had an opportunity to meet each of the participants face-to-face before we commenced the data gathering. I used these exchanges, as well as the earlier contact, to develop and build rapport with the men. This typically involved disclosing some aspects of my own upbringing, discussing difficulties facing the industry and asking questions about the elected members' farms and families.

Each interview progressed through five stages. The introductory stage centred on my providing information about the interview and research process. The second stage focused on obtaining some background information about the participant and building rapport, as questions were relatively unthreatening. In the third and fourth parts of the interview, I moved to questions about barriers to women's leadership and strategies for change. In the final part of the interview, participants were invited to make further comments or to clarify earlier answers.

The interviews were taped and transcribed in full and coded thematically. In this coding I focused on the dynamics and interaction of the interview process as well as the actual content of what was said. I was assisted in this process through post-interview observation forms I completed. The forms recorded my thoughts on issues such as rapport, any surprises in the data obtained, my own performance as an interviewer, comparisons with other interviews, and so on (Burgess 1984). Through these processes I gained insight into how the elected male members practised masculinity in the interviews.

Male Managers and the Performance of Masculinities in Interviews

Heterosexual Men

Few researchers talk about sex in the field. Certainly, 'coming out' about sex in/and the field is particularly problematic for women scholars given that male academics have recourse to broader gendered power relations which authenticate their sexual encounters/desires – provided, of course, they are heterosexual (Wilson, 1995). Challenging this silence is an article by Cupples (2002, 383) in which the author argues that 'it is impossible to escape our sexuality in the field and therefore it should be acknowledged'; just because we don't mention it doesn't mean it doesn't exist. Caplan (1993, 24) comes to a similar conclusion, arguing that regardless of attempts we may make to disregard or dismiss our sexual identities in research, we may find that in the field participants will often construct these for us.

This was clear to me even before beginning the interviews with the managerial men when I attended a meeting of the 26 member State Board in order to outline the study. Even in this highly formal environment, my gendered identity as 'sexual object' was highlighted. I was providing an interim report on my research and outlined different strategies for increasing the credibility of the research within industry. One strategy I listed was 'nurturing good relationships with key industry figures such as the General Manager'. This was met with laughter, nudging, winking and a range of asides directed at both myself and the General Manager.

I was to become very familiar with this type of sexualizing throughout the study, and more particularly, in the interviews. I typically met the men being interviewed after a meeting they had attended in the main city office, as this was convenient for them. This meant that other men would see me approach and the two of us walk away to conduct the interview. On these occasions a range of sexual comments and innuendos was made by the male observers. When I approached one member to ask if he was ready for the interview he stated, 'I've always got time for a pretty woman'. Another member joked to a participant that he should 'behave himself' with me 'behind closed doors' as we walked away to conduct the interview. Once the interviewee and I walked away from the other males, this overt sexualizing of me did not continue. There was, however, an exception.

What two particular participants did throughout their interviews was to call me 'Karen' – one eleven times and one nine – even after repeated corrections had been made: before the interviews began, such as in telephone conversations arranging the meeting time, and in engaging in small-talk before the interview. The 'Karen' to whom they referred is an Australian actress who shares my surname and became nationally famous as a centrefold in the magazine, *Australian Playboy*. This association was referred to by one of these participants who, when asked a question, replied laughing, 'Well Karen, oh…sorry Barbara. You can see she made a big impression on me'. My post-interview observations note how 'annoyed' and 'frustrated' I was at this apparent mix-up in my identity. Unrecorded is that through identifying themselves as men knowledgeable about and interested in 'Karen', these participants were asserting their masculine heterosexual identities. Further assertion of these identities was gained by associating or 'confusing' me with the *Playboy* centrefold. I was not an educated, intelligent and articulate researcher – but a sexual object.

This type of performance of heterosexuality by the elected members continued, despite my attempts to play down my sexual identity and play up other identities when interacting with them. This deliberate strategy was one I adopted after attending one of my first industry social functions. I was attending as a 'researcher' pleased to have my first opportunity at participant observation, but seen by some – in a crowd consisting almost entirely of men – as an 'available woman', and harassed by one particular attendee. After spending the entire evening attempting to avoid him and being in other situations where gratuitous sexual innuendos were made, I wrote in my research journal:

Should I not have gone? Should I have been less extroverted? Quieter and more reserved? Tried to be more in the background and watch? But then this would mean not being Barbara, but maybe I have to consciously not be me in these social situations if I'm going to go to them. (Research Journal, December 1999)

Following this, I deliberately engaged some strategies to neutralize my identity as 'single young woman' such as arranging to attend an event with a male friend rather than alone, leaving early in the evening and/or finding out who would be in attendance before accepting to determine if other women were likely to be there.

As discussed previously, Liepins (2000) and Brandth and Haugen (2000) suggest that in agri-politics male leaders define their roles by drawing on notions of power, importance, knowledge and expertise. What has not been identified in this previous work as hegemonic in discourses of agricultural leadership is an emphasis on heterosexuality. This does not necessarily indicate that a focus on heterosexuality is absent in how other agricultural leaders perform masculinity. This would seem unlikely, given the importance of heterosexuality to the identities of farming men (Little 2003; 2006; 2007) and the pervasiveness of heterosexuality in discourses of managerial masculinity (Sheppard 1989). It may be that the discourse of heterosexuality is more typically practised by elected members in informal rather than formal discursive sites, and the previous work, which has focused on public texts such as agricultural media and the reporting of interviews with male leaders, may not have revealed the existence of this discourse. My own observations at the Farmers' Union support this assertion. It appears as well that, because the sexual innuendos men made to other men as they prepared for the interview did not continue throughout the interview process, this masculine heterosexual identity is performed most often by men for other men.

Powerful Men

A second way in which elected members performed masculinity in the interview process was by positioning themselves as busy, powerful and important men. I am not suggesting, of course, that they were not busy, powerful or important. Indeed, interview transcripts are littered with references to national and international travel, discussions of meetings with senior managers of other corporate institutions (for example, banks) as well as leading politicians. Media appearances were also highlighted, as was the key role the elected members had in decision-making processes that affected a large population. The participants also had all of the accoutrements of powerful men that were obvious to me even before the interviews began – spacious offices with large teak desks, attentive secretaries who seemed to constantly pre-empt their needs, corporate cars and business attire.

What is critical about these busy and important men is that they ensured that I knew that they were busy and important. One elected member conveyed this clear message by making access particularly difficult. The first interview I began with him, which he had re-scheduled twice because of other commitments, was interrupted when his secretary knocked on the door to say he was wanted on the phone. He explained that he needed to take the call and had been asked to be interrupted because it was an 'important call from Canberra' (the Australian Government). He cancelled two further scheduled interviews at the last moment with similar explanations. I did eventually interview him, but he was an hour and a half late having, he said, 'other business' to attend to, and had to leave soon after apparently to attend other meetings. This was despite the fact that he had selected the time of the interview.

Similar messages of being important, busy and powerful were conveyed during the interviews. Some participants regularly looked at their watches, asked how much longer it would take and/or told me that they had other appointments to which they were committed, even though they were informed in writing prior to the interview that it would take one hour. No interviews went over this time, and in fact, given the reticence of some members to answer questions, some were considerably shorter. Further, all nominated the time that would best suit them for the interviews. Clearly, while these men were busy and concerned with important industry business, considering gender equity was not included in this business.

Knowledgeable Men

Like the display of power and heterosexuality, the display of knowledge/expertise was also evident to me before the interviews with participants began. At two presentations to the Board questions about the methodology of the research and its credibility were subject to considerable debate. As I have reported elsewhere (Pini 2004a), a number of the male leaders were strongly opposed to the qualitative research design, considering it open to bias and prejudice. One in particular who worried that I would attract only 'whingeing women' or those 'with an axe to grind' was dismissive of my attempts to explain the value of a qualitative approach and the strategies I would engage to ensure trustworthiness. He and his supporters were indifferent to my academic training and credentials as they criticized the framework of the study and stressed their own practical, hands-on knowledge of the industry and the industry people they represented. On another occasion at which I presented preliminary findings from the study, a male elected member challenged me with a dossier of material (newspaper clippings, internet articles) about what he saw as the problems of affirmative action. I had not canvassed the take-up of affirmative action strategies so this appeared out of context, but he made his point to me and the male audience that he was 'knowledgeable' about the subject of gender equity and could, like me, quote sources (however dubious) to support his point of view.

When interviews began, all elected members were aware that I had been engaged in the full time study of the organization for nearly 18 months. As well, I had been spending two to three days a week in the city office of the Farmers' Union. Furthermore, they would have been aware that I had grown up on a farm and that my father had been an elected member of the organization. When I first commenced the study, this family background in the industry had been the focus of a story about the research published in the organization's fortnightly magazine sent to all of the 6,600 farming constituents. While over half the elected members asked me the size of my parents' farm (which gives a sense of one's wealth/status in the industry), they made no other reference to my background. There was no recognition in the interviews that I had any knowledge of the industry – gained from life-experience or academic study. I was then treated by some to long descriptions of how the organization and industry were structured and given detailed accounts of such processes as the voting system of the organization, and the processes for planting, harvesting, selling and marketing. These were like mini-lectures which I found difficult to interrupt in order to move the interviewee to a different subject.

In other instances elected members demonstrated their own expert knowledge and their positioning of me as innocent and a little dim by taking on the tone and manner of enlightener/teacher/father, by engaging in non-verbals such as the shaking of the head, and by beginning answers to questions with statements such as, 'What you need to understand is…' or 'What you don't understand is…', rather than simply answering the question I had asked. The message was that the question being asked was irrelevant or silly and I needed to be given guidance about what I should be asking. For example, in one instance I asked an elected member why he thought women were not involved in the industry. He cautioned my need to 'take the script back' and suggested I 'ask other questions first', the most important of which seemed to him to be: 'Are there actually women involved in the industry?' Rather than continue with the line of questioning I had prepared, I used this response to engage the member in a discussion about what he meant by farming, and more specifically, involvement in farming. This provided rich data on the social and gendered construction of agricultural work so it actually proved to be a useful exchange. This does not, however, detract from the fact that the elected member adopted a tone and style in this interview of educator and enlightener.

Elected members reinforced their masculine gendered identities around expert knowledge by excluding me from certain knowledge. They did this by simply refusing to answer questions posed to them in interviews. These silences communicated a lack of interest, disapproval and resistance to the research. The most salient example of silence was in relation to a report on findings from a survey I had administered to women in the industry asking about barriers to their participation and strategies which could facilitate some change. Respondents to the survey had suggested that a lack of support, the conduct, time and location of meetings as well as the masculinist culture of the organization were key factors limiting their participation in the industry (Pini 2002a). Organizational strategies, education and training strategies, remuneration strategies and support strategies were all considered important to women's increased involvement in the producer group (Pini 2003c).

Seven members said they could not comment on the survey findings report as they had not read it. Five others claimed to be in a similar position as they could not recall what was in the report. These responses may be seen as natural and understandable outcomes for what are very busy people. Many of us would relate to being told that someone has simply not had time to read a report they had been given. However, that this lack of comment may have been more manufactured than real was evident from the three interviews where elected members did offer feedback. One of the three talked about the fact that he had concerns with the methodology of the survey, an issue he said he had discussed with others. A second member asked for the tape to be turned off and proceeded to tell me of the negative reaction the report had elicited from the elected membership. The third member adopted a more overtly aggressive masculine identity than I had previously encountered, but also revealed that there had indeed been a great deal of discussion about the survey by the elected leadership:

Interviewer: Can I ask you if you had any comments to make on the survey report I sent you?

Elected member: We had a good laugh about it.

Interviewer: Who's that?

Elected member: Our committee. People thought it was a load of bullshit. Full of bias.

Interviewer: Were there any particular parts?

Elected member: We didn't agree with a lot of it. It's not a boys' club. Our meetings aren't held in pubs. I can see where the perception arises, but if you wait and sit back for them to change you'll never get anywhere. A lot of things in there I see as an excuse.

Interviewer: Can you give me an example?

Elected member: Well, for a start you can't make a meeting dynamic if people don't turn up. (Elected member, Interview 7)

While I was seeking the views of this particular member, he chose to respond by referring to 'we'. Through this slippage in the use of the personal pronoun he made it clear that this is not an individual perspective, but one shared by the committee of men of which he is part. That there were deficiencies in the report was the collective male perspective. Furthermore, these deficiencies were so marked that any discursive niceties which might have been engaged in a formal interview were eliminated. He made it clear that the report was not taken seriously – it was the subject of humour and was trivialized. The use of the word 'bullshit' to describe the report is significant, as a range of field work experiences had revealed to me that men considered such language inappropriate in front of women. For example, on different occasions when I had overheard elected members swearing or attended meetings where swearing occurred, they were apologetic about it. In some interviews as well, men had suggested that the prevalence of swearing at meetings precluded women's involvement. This elected member's decision to describe the report in the way he did may have been to make it clear that I was no longer anchored in the same category as 'most' women and also to emphasize the degree of anger the report had elicited.

Questioning Who is Asking Whom about What and Where

Schwalbe and Wolkomir's (2001) advice for analysing the dynamics of gender interviewing by questioning 'who is asking whom about what' provides a useful framework for beginning to understand the masculinities engaged by the managerial men in interviews for this study. They argue that in any research project where a focus is on gender it is likely that the male participants will engage in more pronounced gender identity work as their masculine selves may be viewed as central to the research. I was, however, not just interested in gender, but in questioning the reasons for women's lack of representation in management and this is likely to have further exaggerated some men's significations of hegemonic masculinity. In such a situation – where masculine identities are seen as being challenged and there is a sense of anxiety about losing power associated with those identities – hegemonic masculinities are likely to become more visible. In McDowell's (1998) case, being an older and more experienced researcher enabled her to circumvent the difficulties a focus on gender could present. As a doctoral student and younger than most of the men I interviewed by 20 to 30 years, I was in a significantly different position as a researcher interested in gender issues.

It is thus clearly important to take up Schwalbe and Wolkomir's (2001) suggestion and to include an analysis of the subject of research in any critique of gender and interviewing. However, I do not think that they take us far enough. My experience at the Farmers' Union reveals that to understand the masculinities performed in the interviews, we need to extend their proposed question for analysing gender and interviewing to 'who is asking whom about what and where'. Gender is, of course, never absent from a site, but some arenas may be more overtly and strongly gendered than others. In such a space, a woman asking men about gender relations is likely to face a high degree of resistance. In this instance, it was not just the research topic but the context in which this topic was being addressed which produced the gendered dynamics of the interviews.

As an organization with no women in any of its 181 positions of elected leadership, the Farmers' Union is a site in which gender has a high degree of salience. However, it is not just men's numerical dominance of these positions which is relevant to the gendered context of the research site. It is also the way in which this numerical dominance is understood by male industry leaders as being natural and right because of, firstly, women's alleged lack of involvement in farming, and secondly, their assumed greater interest in domestic roles. These explanations, which both normalize and legitimize women's lack of participation in industry leadership, are the types of 'gendered images of the workplace' which Herod (1993, 312) found to be so important in shaping the information he received in research examining a United States labour dispute. The male local union president interviewed by Herod (1993) barely acknowledged the existence of a women's support group, and when he did so, he characterized it as little more than a catering service for the male workers who were the central protagonists in his narrative. This was despite other evidence which suggested that the women's support group was actually very actively engaged politically in industrial action against the company which was at the centre of the dispute.

Similar gendered perspectives coloured the interviews I had with male managers, and in part explain the masculinities performed by these men in the interviews. Their having little to say in interviews and/or treating me as someone requiring educating may have been a result of the gendered context of the industry. Why women are not in agricultural management may have been viewed as obvious and self-explanatory. Moreover, to unsettle what is considered to be 'known' and 'true' – as may have occurred when I produced the survey report – is a risky enterprise in terms of a relationship between researcher and researched. It is likely that Herod's (1993) male union leader would have reacted negatively if he had been presented with a similar report which presented a version of events which contradicted his perspective.

In many respects, I saw the Farmers' Union and its elected membership reflected strongly in the union and male union leader described by Herod (1993) and saw parallels between his research focus on women's organizational invisibility and my own. However, the fact that as an interviewer Herod (1993, 312) could say of his interview subject that he was 'a white male, as am I', meant that ultimately my experience of interviewing men was quite different. In my own study, the research topic and my 'positionality' intersected to produce the gendered encounters that I have described in this chapter. This positionality was, as I have explained, multi-dimensional and thus, while my sense is that gender was an important factor in itself in the interviews, it was the combination of my gendered identity and youth which made the interviews particularly problematic for me. This was clear to me on those occasions when my academic supervisor, 'your professor' as she was called by interviewees, attended meetings with me and was treated with a degree of respect by male leaders that I never encountered. Such is the complexity of understanding the influence of gender and interviewing, and the need to move analysis on the subject beyond a simple focus on the gender of interviewer and interviewee to a more sophisticated critique which explores the intersection of the mediating influences of 'who, whom, what and where'.

Conclusion

Given the critical importance of my female identity in the research described in this chapter, it is intriguing to question how having a male interviewer might have made a difference to the research interviews reported in this chapter. Day (2001) asks, for example, if having a male researcher may give a topic higher status. Would a male researcher have been more easily accommodated at informal all male (or largely male) social activities, which are common-place in the organization and which, as I mentioned, I found difficult to participate in and access? (see also Pedersen 1998). At the same time, unable to dismiss him outright on account of his gender, would male agricultural leaders have subjected a male interviewer to more exaggerated displays of power, importance, knowledge and expertise? What of the performances of masculinity by a male researcher? For example, would he have colluded in some of the practices of hegemonic masculinity in order to facilitate access in the manner of McKeganey and Bloor (1991)? These researchers describe going to the pub and playing sport when undertaking fieldwork with male participants in order to build rapport and reciprocity. Would this, however, have led to the type of ethical conundrum described by Schacht (1997) who did not challenge the misogyny he witnessed while undertaking ethnographic work on rugby players? Would a male researcher whose own masculine self was far removed from that of the managerial men feel like an 'alien' as described by Levinson (1998)? Would it therefore have been more difficult for him than it was for me? Would his interest in the subject of gender have rendered him a mystery to the men he was studying and placed him under a cloud of suspicion so that he was assumed to be gay, in the manner described by other male researchers (see Bruni and Gherardi 2002)? Would even his use of qualitative research methods have made him appear as subscribing to a 'softer/effeminate' identity so that his masculinity was questioned (Haywood and Mac an Ghaill 2003, 120)?

These are, of course, speculative questions. The literature provides no further assistance because, while men and masculinities have begun to be named in rural studies, such naming has not extended to male rural social researchers. Campbell and Bell (2000, 532) come close in writing that there is 'something unexpected, faintly disturbing, occasionally humorous and not a little suspicious' about studying masculinities, but end their reflexive journey there. This is not to undermine in any way the work that is being done by male rural social researchers on the subject of masculinities, but to encourage them to take their analysis of gendered identities further. As this chapter has demonstrated, such scholarship will provide us not just with knowledge about the research process, but also with important data about men, masculinities and agriculture.

Chapter 4

Paternalism and Shifting Managerial Masculinities in Agricultural Organizations

Within the literature on managerial masculinities two of the most widely cited scholars are David Collinson and Jeff Hearn (see for example, 1994; 1996b; 1996a; 2005). These authors were early in recognizing the paradox that while management is often conflated with men and masculinity in that it is typically embedded in discourses of instrumentality, rationality, purpose, control, power and prestige, men and masculinity are largely absent as categories for analysis within management scholarship. Seeking to address this anomaly, they presented a typology of five hegemonic forms of managerial masculinity: authoritarianism, careerism, informalism entrepreneurialism and paternalism.

In this chapter, I use Collinson and Hearn's (1994) framework to begin to understand managerial masculinities as they are manifest in agricultural organizations. I argue that the most dominant discourses of masculinity within the Farmers' Union are those of paternalism and, to a lesser degree, authoritarianism. The co-existence of managerial masculinities is not uncommon. Indeed, Collinson and Hearn (1994) emphasize that their categorical groupings are not discrete and that discourses of managerial masculinity often intersect. The multiplicity of masculinities in the Farmers' Union is further demonstrated in the final part of the chapter, which describes the discourses of professionalism and entrepreneurialism in the narratives of men involved in a Young Farmers' Group. In the concluding section of the chapter, I explore the question of why paternal and authoritarian managerial masculinities dominate at the Farmers' Union when the evidence suggests that in the majority of contemporary organizations, other gendered discourses of management have come to ascendancy. The conclusion also notes that while a masculinity focused on professionalism and entrepreneurialism is not hegemonic in the Farmers' Union at present, it is consistent with broader shifts occurring in discourses of farming and management, and may therefore come to precedence in agricultural groups in the near future.

Managerial Masculinities: A Framework for Analysis

The first of the type of dominant managerial masculinity identified by Collinson and Hearn (1994) is that of authoritarianism. This is a form of managerial masculinity associated with the practices of bullying and the creation of fear and coercion. While some scholars have argued that this managerial discourse is most typically mobilized by older men (Collinson and Hearn 1994; McDowell 2001), others have found it equally prevalent amongst some younger male managers (Barrett 2001; Prokos and Padavic 2002). It is this type of dictatorial control and aggressive masculinity that David Wicks (2002) identifies as predominant in the managerial practices and ethos at the Westray mine in Canada prior to a 1992 explosion which killed all 26 men working underground. In a sobering analysis of published documents emanating from the disaster, Wicks (2002) reveals the way in which management fostered a culture of fear and intimidation. Unsafe work concerns were dismissed and trivialized. Those who complained were subjected to harsh and derogatory abuse and found themselves subjected to more punishing work conditions. This is typical of authoritarian management masculinity. That is, those who fail to subscribe to the dominant regime are treated with overt hostility and positioned as weak and inferior. In an environment where authoritarian masculinity is hegemonic, the message to workers from management is, as Wicks (2002, 219) observes, you better do what you 'are told.'

It might be argued that the type of authoritarian managerial masculinity identified by Wicks (2002) is rare and extreme and unlikely to be found in many contemporary organizations. This may be the case. However, the literature suggests that new, less overt, but by no means more benign forms of authoritarian managerial masculinity may be emerging as dominant in organizations. O'Sullivan and Sheridan's (2005) textual reading of episodes of the Thames ITV series *The Bill* provides an illustration of this phenomenon. The author examines episodes documenting a change in management at the fictional inner city London police station, Sun Hill. The 'new' male manager differs from his predecessor in his youth and personal style and in his professed commitment to egalitarianism, communication and teamwork. However, as the plot unravels we see that behind these so-called new 'feminine management' skills is a violent man fuelled by a ruthless, aggressive, career driven masculinity. This 'new' man is not so new for, as O'Sullivan and Sheridan (2005, 316) contend, despite his rhetoric and outward appearance, his managerial masculinity is in fact 'an authoritative style replicating the top-down management style of its predecessors'.

The second dominant form of managerial masculinity identified by Collinson and Hearn (1994) is more contemporary in its origin than authoritarianism. It is entrepreneurial masculinity. Being a workaholic, ruthlessly competitive and single minded are its central tenets. Entrepreneurship is also embedded in notions of creativity, adventurousness, pragmatism and aggression (Bruni, Gherardi and Poggio 2005). Mulholland (1996) provides an evocative portrayal of entrepreneurial masculinity in her detailed reading of two of the 70 interviews she undertook with some of England's richest entrepreneurs. The two men presented themselves as tough, hard-nosed and confident. They minimized or dismissed the contributions others (such as wives and families) made to their success. In their narratives, they were the central and only protagonists, independently achieving wealth and status. Like the two publishing entrepreneurs studied by Reed (1996), these men also emphasized self-sacrifice and workaholism. As such, Reed (1996) suggests that the discourse of entrepreneurial masculinity is closely entwined with the masculine discourse of breadwinner (see also Hodgson 2003). Entrepreneurs do, act, and produce. They work long hours and they work full time. The discourse of entrepreneurial masculinity consequently necessarily precludes those with domestic or familial responsibilities. While this may resonate with our memories of the 1980s and the Gordon Gekko 'lunch is for wimps' discourse, it would be wrong to assume that entrepreneurialism is a discourse of the past. In recent years, marketization, privatization and managerialism have seen entrepreneurial masculinity become ascendant in an arena where it would previously have had little currency: that is, the public sector (see Brewis 2003; Deem 2003; Rasmussen 2004). Now the language of entrepreneurialism identified by Collinson and Hearn (1994, 14) as that of 'performance levels' and 'budget targets' is commonplace in the public realm. Indeed, in the public vocational education sector, Kerfoot and Whitehead (1998, 453) find a 'boys own' culture 'framed in Darwinian narratives of survival and aggression, competition and combativeness'.

In a number of ways, the discourse of entrepreneurial managerial masculinity shares characteristics with the managerial masculinity of careerism except that the end goal of careerism is hierarchical advancement within an organization. While another primary goal of careerist managerial masculinity – providing for wife and family as 'the breadwinner' – echoes that of entrepreneurial masculinity, a careerist may also believe it necessary to sacrifice family and personal relations and outside interests in order to progress up the corporate ladder. They may have to travel extensively, relocate on numerous occasions, forego vacations and work excessive hours in order to meet deadlines and commitments. They may give up sick leave and even annual leave. In her influential Australian study *Doing Leadership Differently*, Amanda Sinclair (1998) refers to this as 'heroic leadership'. The male managers she interviews emphasize that career progress requires physical and emotional toughness, and distance themselves from women and 'other' men who work part time, work from home or care for children. The dominance of the managerial discourse of careerism in organizations may make it problematic for women to have children so they may choose to remain childless (Wood and Newton 2006). Alternatively they may, like the banking women managers in studies by Blair-Loy (2001) and Smithson and Stokoe (2005), have to do 'macho pregnancy' by minimizing any disruption that their maternity leave may cause. As Linstead and Thomas (2002) found in their study of the impact of restructuring on middle-managers in a manufacturing firm in the United Kingdom, managers attached to masculine discourses of careerism may face insecurity about their identities in the face of demotion or termination. This is clear in the story of Terry, who loses a managerial role after 20 years in the position and 39 with the company. His poignant questions of 'what was it all for?' and 'who can I be now?' illustrate the devastation that job loss or demotion may have for the careerist manager (Linstead and Thomas 2002, 16).

A further category of managerial masculinity identified by Collinson and Hearn (1994) is that of informalism. McDowell (2001, 185) contends that this is perhaps the 'least distinctive of the five discourses'. While it certainly may be the case that the different manifestations of this type of managerial masculinity may be difficult to identify, there would be few women (let alone women managers) who would not be conversant with the notion 'the boys' club' (Sinclair 1998, 41) or what Maddock and Parkin (1994, 33) call the 'locker room culture'. As the name suggests, informalism is a discourse which relies on informal networks and interactions between male managers both within and outside their organization.

In organizations where informalism is dominant, humour may be used as a means of unifying men as well as excluding women and some men (Collinson 1988). At its worst, this humour is likely to manifest in sexual harassment or the sexualization of women (DiTomaso 1989). Alternatively, inclusion may be fostered via discussing political or current events, cars or by involving oneself in practices such as sport or drinking. This is a point made by Wajcman (1999, 97) in her book *Managing Like a Man*, wherein she recounts the story of a cartoon posted on the pin board of a woman manager she interviews. The cartoon depicts several men and a woman playing golf, with one of the men instructing the woman that she will need to improve her stroke in order to become a manager. This lampoons the fact that in the case study company 'Chip', where the woman was employed, drinking, socialising, informal networking or being 'one of the boys' were all highly valued (Wajcman 1999, 128). This process of men seeking out informal means of aligning with other men is taken up by McDowell (2001) in her study of masculinities in merchant banking. Like Roper (1996) before her, she contends that the homosocial practices and processes of informal managerial masculinity need to be understood in terms of male desire. She notes the way in which men express their fondness and affection for other men as well as managerial men's high level of awareness of the dress, style and image of other men. Often this very intimate homosocial/homoerotic managerial context is disguised via humour or horseplay, but its potency in creating a boundary to exclude women is no joke. Martin (2001), too, highlights the importance of desire in men's use of what she calls 'affiliating masculinities'.

The final dominant discourse of managerial masculinity identified by Collinson and Hearn (1994) is that of paternalism. This is a mode of management that Knights and McCabe (2001) argue has typically been presented in the literature as gender-neutral. At the most, they say, writers have noted that this form of management resonates with familial images and, particularly, images of fatherhood. While they acknowledge the symbolic and discursive importance of the fatherly motifs of paternalism, they suggest that there is far more to the masculine gendering of managerial paternalism than familial overtones. One crucial feature of paternalism is the basis from which it derives its power. Unlike authoritarian masculinity, which relies upon gaining power through overt and brutal means, paternalistic managerial masculinity derives its power by claiming it as a moral right based on privilege or seniority and justifying it as being for the benefit of those in subordinate positions. Thus, when paternalism is the dominant form of managerial masculinity, as it was in an Argentine company studied by Stobke (2005, 113), women may not be hired because of an 'unwritten' rule that they should be shielded from hard and dirty work or they may be treated as 'child-like' as was the case of the Alberta oil women workers interviewed by Miller (2004). It is not surprising that paternalism has been superseded by other forms of managerial masculinity in many organizations, as its central tenets seem embedded in a world far removed from the twenty-first century. Indeed, Collinson and Hearn (1994, 14) note that this form of managerial masculinity has its historical foundation in nineteenth century middle class conceptions of 'gentlemanly principles', with an emphasis on 'a polite, civilized and exclusive male culture'. Paternalism was, until very recently, common in many financial institutions. It was, for example, evident in the UK bank studied by Knights and

McCabe (2001) as well as the merchant banks investigated by McDowell and Court (1994). In these sites male paternal managers emphasized their fraternal links and connections through attendance at the same high-status schools and universities, involvement in the same prestigious leisure pursuits and even patronage of the same expensive tailors. Entry into their masculine club is carefully monitored and only possible via these established networks. As Collinson and Hearn (1994) note, paternalism is replicated through older men grooming or mentoring younger men into leadership positions. In this respect, the older men provide the role of 'father' to organizational sons.

Paternalistic Managerial Masculinity

Despite the fact that Collinson and Hearn's (1994) framework must be understood as necessarily fluid and not exhaustive, it still provides a useful conceptual tool to critique and analyze masculinities in agri-politics. That it can be engaged as a comparative template is an argument supported by work of McDowell (2001) and Knoppers and Anthonissen (2005). McDowell (2001) uses the typology to re-interrogate data she had collected for a past research project on merchant banking in the City of London. She finds it particularly helpful as a means of identifying the dominant expressions of managerial masculinity within the banks, as well as for highlighting the very different configurations of masculinity enacted across work units within the organizational hierarchy. In contrast, Knoppers and Anthonissen (2005) draw on the typology of masculinities to explore connections between athletic and managerial discourses. They use the categorization to demonstrate the considerable overlap between the two discursive fields of sport and management and to suggest possible future research directions. In the next sections of the chapter, I follow the lead of these other writers and explore the managerial masculinities in the Farmers' Union, drawing on Collinson and Hearn's (1994) typology. To begin, I examine the different manifestations of paternalistic managerial masculinity in the Farmers' Union.

Paternalism and the Organizational Structure of the Farmers' Union

One of the defining features of paternalistic masculine management is its emphasis on hierarchy (Collinson and Hearn 1994, 13). Thus, organizations where paternalism is dominant differ significantly in terms of mode of operation when compared with many contemporary organizational forms referred to as 'horizontally structured', 'team based' or 'flat'. The emphasis on hierarchy in the Farmers' Union is evident in terms of staff as well as elected members. Staffing is organized on a tiered basis. Managers are allocated particular areas of expertise and have responsibility for staff in their areas, but considerable decision-making power is invested in the Chief Executive Officer (CEO). His overall authority was confirmed for me one day when talking with a staff member about assistance I required from the organization. This staff member commented somewhat tongue-in-cheek that if you wanted something done you needed to invoke the name of the CEO. When I laughed she said, 'Haven't you ever noticed how everyone around here starts their sentences with "John[1] said..."". This was an insightful observation and one I came to validate (and indeed use myself) over the course of the research.

The hierarchical nature of staffing arrangements is even more pronounced in district locations. It is the practice, for example, that junior staff in the district offices address managerial staff and elected members by their surnames rather than their first names as is the case in most modern organizations. This practice had gender and age dimensions in that junior staff are typically almost all female and young (in their 20s), while the senior staff and elected members are almost all male (in their 50s and 60s). The practice therefore reinforces the paternalistic positioning of women and younger people as subordinate to older male managerial patriarchs.

As stated, members are elected to three tiers of leadership with a clear chain of command from top to bottom. Changes to policy or procedure are required to move through each of the three levels. Elected members wanting to serve at the highest tier are also expected to have first 'done their time' at lower levels of representation. This is problematic for aspiring women leaders, as well as some men who do not subscribe to these values. This was evident in one district where a female candidate was standing for election to the highest tier despite not having served in the Farmers' Union previously. One elected member explained that in his district there was 'protocol' and 'respect' for older and more senior and long term representatives. He said:

> I respect (female Executive candidate). She knows the industry from top to bottom, but I don't support her for the Executive because I believe in protocol. It's the way we've always worked. Generally, the next guy moves up and people need to know if she goes on to the Executive she will be jumping over two or three guys, who are supposed to be next in line. (Elected member, Interview 9)

Of significance in this extract is the elected member's reference to what is 'supposed' to occur in terms of seniority and protocol. This is not based on any constitutional or legal requirements, but on what is an established cultural norm and practice. These notions of 'seniority, social privilege and birthright' are embedded in the construction of paternalism (Collinson and Hearn 1994, 14). These values also informed how members were expected to behave once elected. That is, once elected there was an expectation that you would defer to more senior and established members, neither challenging their opinions nor broaching any opinions of your own. This was evident as one 'younger' elected member in his forties explained why he believed younger people did not nominate for office:

> Because every time they open their mouth they get told that they're too young to have that sort of opinion which is what I've been told. Every time you talk, you get older guys sitting on their bums shaking their heads. (Elected member, Interview 3)

This elected member went on to give an example of having his views on a controversial issue responded to with, 'You haven't been in this establishment long enough to have

---

1 This is a pseudonym.

an idea like that'. It is notable that this elected member was, at the time, in the middle of his second term. He had thus served the Farmers' Union for five years, but this was still not considered sufficient time to warrant voicing an opinion against the mainstream. Also of note is the fact that this elected member was, at the time of the study, the only Board member of the Farmers' Union with tertiary qualifications in management. These were dismissed by the other board members when compared with the value of their own lived, practical, tacit knowledge. This issue will be taken up further in Chapter 5.

Paternalism and the Gendered Division of Labour in the Farmers' Union

In her seminal article entitled 'Hierarchies, jobs, bodies: A theory of gendered organizations', Acker (1990) argued that gender is implicated in a myriad of organizational processes, practices, symbols and images. Of these, she said that perhaps the most obvious is the gendered division of labour in organizations. This observation certainly rang true for me when first approaching the Farmers' Union to undertake the study. As I walked through the building towards the CEO's office I noted that, with only one exception, men occupied all the stand-alone offices. Women staffed desks outside these offices as well as made up a pool of staff in an open plan area. In this sense the gendered division of labour between secretarial/ administrative staff and managerial staff was, as Acker (1990) says, reinforced by the gendered allocation of organizational resources such as office space. The all female secretarial staff provided the almost all male managerial staff with very traditional secretarial services such as shorthand, typing, diary organising and answering the phone, as well as attending to other personal needs such as bringing them coffee or lunch.

There are two key implications of this in terms of the discursive replication of paternalism. In the first instance, even if the female secretaries had been allocated higher level executive responsibilities, servicing tasks dominated their time, making it difficult for them to take on any higher level administrative work and affording them little career opportunity. They were consequently kept 'firmly in established roles' (Collinson and Hearn 1994, 14). The second issue is that, as Knights and McCabe (2001) found in their study of shifting managerial masculinities in the finance sector in Britain, having a secretary symbolizes authority and status. Male managers in the Farmers' Union could therefore signal their paternal power and prestige through their secretarial staff.

Celebratory office events (for example, to mark birthdays, arrival of new staff, and so on) were also a practice that saw the production and reproduction of paternalistic managerial masculinity. While men may have contributed to these events (with money or as speakers), women secretaries took responsibility for the 'housework' involved in preparing the events and cleaning up after the events. Again, this is indicative of a paternalistic managerial culture resembling family relationships: 'there is no limit to the demands that the patriarch can make on his dependents' (Knights and McCabe 2001, 642).

Paternalism and Meetings of the Farmers' Union

A further manifestation of paternalism in the agricultural group studied is the informal (that is, unwritten and unstated) practice that formal industry meetings are conducted with little discussion and debate. Communication between the executive and participants in the meetings I attended was always unidirectional. In most instances, there was even little involvement from members of the executive other than the Chair. This was an issue discussed by women in the focus groups. One woman, for example, explained that because she was involved in farming two different commodities she was involved in two different agricultural organizations. She found the case study organization far less interactive and reflected that 'they are seen as a God like thing and no one will ask or question'. This reveals the way in which paternalism has become institutionalized within the case study organization. Clearly, the constituency has been taught that they do not challenge the 'authoritative, benevolent self-disciplined and wise' organizational fathers (Collinson and Hearn 1994, 13). I was given insight into the nature of this educative process at meetings I attended where responses to many questions from members were characterized by hostility, denigration and belittlement. There is also a hint of how constituents may be schooled not to question the patriarchs in the following quotation in which an elected member responds to a question about how conflict is handled at meetings.

> Nobody really speaks at my meetings anyway [laughter]. You very seldom get much comment from the floor. It's not as if it's closed. It's an open debate but people are just more laid back. They don't jump up and down too much or make good comments or bad comments. People are quite happy to take the decisions that are given to them. There's not too many radicals round here. (Elected member, Interview 2)

This male manager normalizes the lack of dialogue at meetings and presents this as simply reflective of the nonchalant attitude of the constituents, maintaining that there is opportunity for involvement but it is simply not taken up. At the same time, he conflates the asking of questions with radicalism. This is revealing as it is indicative of the strategies that have been utilized by the male leaders of the Farmers' Union to silence debate. Further insight into this issue was provided by a female focus group participant:

> Kellie: People are frightened to ask questions because of the general way they're answered. They're more or less made to feel ridiculous. At the last meeting someone asked about expansion and about why we're expanding and (a male manager) turned around and said to him, 'Well if we don't somebody else will'. I felt that was a perfectly inadequate answer to the question. But his reply really cut it off. It was as if it was below his standing that he should even be asked a question by this person. (District B, Focus Group 3)

Paternalistic managerial managers can be defined by the discourses they engage to exercise power. In the first instance, this is by 'emphasising the moral basis of cooperation' (Collinson and Hearn 1994, 13) and focusing on the need for 'group solidarity' as a means of achieving the greater good for all (McDowell 2001, 184). Within the Farmers' Union, this is achieved through the discursive script that I have labelled 'one voice'. The discourse of 'one voice' urges farmers to support the management of the Farmers' Union for the benefit of the industry as a whole. It depends on positioning a number of groups as wanting to undermine and or even threaten the industry. For example, in describing the task ahead for newly elected members at the beginning of 1998 the then Farmers' Union Chairman stated in a newsletter to constituents:

> A divided voice will take us nowhere and will give our rivals the opportunities that they are looking for to destroy our marketing system and our cane payment formula...There are forces at work seeking to demolish our present structures and they may succeed if we do not stay as a united organisation. (Chairman 1998)

The discourse of 'one voice' effectively silences dissent or even debate because these are positioned as opening the organization and the industry up to destruction. As will be discussed in detail in Chapter 6, the discourse of 'one voice' was commonly invoked to disparage the formation of networks for women in the industry. While this did not result in the dissolution of the women's groups, it seriously undermined them. They were positioned as 'diluting the voice' of the Farmer's Union and accused of being 'splinter groups'. Elected members suggested that their concern was that the collective voice – what was good for the majority – would be undermined by the existence of women's groups and it was therefore better for such groups not to exist. In this way, as Kerfoot and Knights (1993, 670) explain, paternalistic managerial masculinity operates on 'pretence of equality for the purpose of securing instrumental gain'. This is why paternalism is actually a mode of managerial masculinity that is far more complex than is often thought.

In the Farmers' Union hierarchy was important as were patriarchal relations based on seniority, but so too were fraternal relations between men. As McDowell (2001, 184) argues, the existence and fostering of 'brotherly' relations is indicative of paternalism. Men's relations with men were valued and highly prized so much that it was common for elected members to worry that women's presence at meetings would mean they could no longer swear or discuss what was important to them. Women echoed this perspective with one stating, 'the men feel more comfortable when the women aren't there'. As a rejoinder, another commented that she felt that men would be annoyed by women's attendance because men are likely to think, 'Oh, not a bloody woman. We go to meetings to get away from women'. Within the Farmers' Union men spending time with men was normal and legitimate and men spending time with women was not. As one commented,

> Elected member: I mean we're down here at a Board meeting some of us go for a walk in the morning. The guys are here and the girls are there. Why? Because they're more comfortable talking about this and that. Why do you go to a party and the guys are over here and the women there? Because they're more comfortable that way. They're talking about their interests more. (Interview 12)

Thus, elected members saw nothing problematic about holding Farmers' Union meetings at venues that were typically male dominated such as country pubs. Some also suggested that it would be awkward having women present at meetings, particularly if meetings involved staying overnight in city hotels.

In attempting to understand the elected men's continued preference for spending time with men I gained considerably from Roper's (1996) discerning discussion on the subject. He rightly says that the prevalence of these relations in male dominated organizations and the implications of these relations for women and some organizational men mean that it is critical that we name what we see. However, this is not easy when what we are witnessing typically falls 'between the categories of the social and the sexual' (Roper 1996, 223). He sees value in the term 'homosocial reproduction' (Kanter 1977) for it accentuates the way in which men's preference for other men creates male monopolies in organizations, but worries that it fails to convey the eroticism involved. Similarly, he rejects 'homosexual reproduction' for what is going on between men does not actually involve explicit sexual intimacy. Indeed, the institutionalized nature of homosexuality in many organizations would render the naming of any male to male desire impossible. Roper (1996, 223) thus engages the concept of 'homosocial desire' from Sedgwick (1985), arguing that it incorporates the 'radical discontinuities between heterosexuality and homosexuality.'

Roper's (1996) naming of 'homosocial desire' and illustration of it in operation between men in a management college in Australia allowed me to see and identify what seemed to be such a dominant undercurrent in the Farmers' Union, and central to the practice of paternalistic managerial masculinity. It was masked for me in many ways. There was, for example, the men's continued signalling of their heterosexuality in interviews as described in Chapter 3, as well as other overt displays of heterosexual identities such as through prominently displayed photographs of wives and children and/or references in informal speech to wives and children. The dominance of this 'heteronormative discourse' (Little 2003) amongst the elected leaders of the Farmers' Union was starkly represented in the numerous comments fearing women's involvement in the organization would lead to rumours of sexual impropriety/affairs. As stated above, this was seen to be a particular problem because so much of the work of the elected members involved national and international travel with overnight stays and associated nights 'on the town'. Interestingly, there was never any concern from the men that being seen dining alone with a man or going on an interstate trip with a man would be interpreted as signalling possible sexual impropriety (see also Hearn 1993). Homosexuality was never canvassed in this environment. It is this silencing of homosexuality – of the prevalence of the compulsory discourses of hetrosexuality – alongside the elected male members' constant assertions of their preferences for being with men rather than women – which highlighted the centrality of 'homosocial desire' in the managerial discourses at the Farmers' Union.

Paternalism and the Electoral System of the Farmers' Union

As well as being embedded in the conduct of meetings, paternalistic managerial masculinity is also integral to the electoral process of the Farmers' Union. This is a process that is said to be dependent upon a gender neutral benign notion of 'merit'. As one elected member asserted, 'Anyone worth their salt would want to do it on their own merit, whether it's a woman or a man. I don't care what their sex is. As long as they do it on their own merit'. Despite this assertion, feminist and pro-feminist writers have demonstrated that definitions and constructions of 'merit' in organizations are deeply value laden and gendered (Burton 1997; Blackmore 1999; Taylor 1995; Martin 1996; Scutt 1997; McKay 1997; Hovden 2000); hence, contrary to the elected member's point of view, it does matter whether 'it's a woman or a man'. Indeed, in the Farmers' Union, claims to 'merit' are undermined by a range of extraneous factors that impede the electoral process. These extraneous factors are intricately connected with assumptions embedded in paternalism. In the first instance, for example, emphasis in the electoral system is given to family background in agriculture, as one elected member explained:

> The whole industry's got a fair bit of history and background, too. And if you are somebody's daughter, you'd be a lot more noticed than if you were married into someone's family and tried to put your personal views across. But, I think the same would happen for a bloke. I mean, it takes a long time for anybody to be accepted within this industry. If he's down the same bloodline they are accepted, but a lot of times if they're a son-in-law or daughter-in-law it takes a long time for people to say, 'Well, you know, now he's a farmer. He's not someone who came in and is trying to be one'. (Elected member, Interview 11)

While this elected member attempts to present the privileging of family background in farming as ungendered and therefore not a factor that would unfairly advantage women over men, he fails to acknowledge the fact that women typically come to farming through marriage (Wallace et al. 1996; Shortall 1999) and a clear patrilineal line of inheritance is consistent across studies of family farming (Shortall 1999; Gasson 1994; Pini 2007). Thus, it would be very unlikely to find a 'son-in-law' standing for election in the Farmers' Union who has not come from a farming background, and further, inherited farming land from his parents.

The familial ideology and values that are inherent in paternalistic management are reproduced in 'father-son' relationships of mentoring between older established leaders and younger male leadership aspirants. This is not necessarily only at a symbolic level; it is very common for elected members to have fathers and/or grandfathers who were themselves leaders in the Farmers' Union. These are some of those Reed (1996, 112) calls the 'deserving' young men who benefit from paternalistic managerial masculinity as they are selected and groomed for leadership by senior organizational patriarchs. Again, elected members saw nothing problematic in the grooming of particular men for leadership or drawing such men from all male networks of service or sporting clubs.

This paternalistic managerial masculinity was an issue discussed in one of the focus groups with women farmers. In this instance, women were explaining that they may one day be interested in a leadership position but were presently concerned with what they perceived to be deficiencies in their knowledge and expertise. One participant, whose husband had been an elected leader for over a quarter of a decade, challenged the women's perceptions of their inadequacy, saying:

> Ruth: My husband's been on the committee for 26 years or something. Anyway, he was in his late twenties when he went on. And he wouldn't have known anything more than any other person, but I just think that now he's been on it all these years he has. And when they had the last election there are two new fellows on the committee. I can just see the amount of work that they've done educating them, these new members who have gone on to the committee now because there is such a lot to learn. (District A, Focus Group 3)

The 'grooming' of potential male candidates has concrete and known outcomes, almost half of the 15 elected members I interviewed explained. There are two occasions when the traditional three-yearly election is not required. The first is if there are insufficient nominations for a committee. In this case, the chairperson of the committee has the discretion to appoint someone to the committee. The second instance where an election is not required occurs if sitting elected members retire from their position or die in office six months before an election. Six of the 15 men I interviewed had first come to their position through this means. One district member explained how the process worked saying that, 'Just before the last election one gentleman resigned six months before the end of his term so that the new bloke could settle in'. I asked him what he meant by 'settle in' and he replied:

> Well, when he went for election he would have been on here for six months already. That's why the other bloke resigned six months early. Because if you resign within two years of the election, I think in the last twelve months before, there's no election and they appoint someone. And this fellow had been trying to get on before. (Elected member, Interview 8)

Importantly, the process of, as the other elected member stated, 'anointing your successor', is normalized as appropriate and not seen to be inconsistent with merit selection. Paternalism dictates that existing members, and particularly retiring and long serving senior members, are well qualified, and indeed have a right to say who should follow in their footsteps as the following quotation demonstrates:

> I think you know that there's never been any opposition for women to be fully involved in agricultural industry matters, but they need to be the same as the bloke over there…It's not a gender thing. It's an ability thing. It's a knowledge thing. They have to be able to do the job. I would hate to have someone on the job as a committee member just because she's a woman. That wouldn't be any good. That takes up one of my spots for someone who can help us run the organization. (Elected member, Interview 12)

Another unwritten cultural norm in the agricultural organization's elections is that there is no campaigning. One elected member commented that in 30 years in the industry he had only seen one person conduct a formal campaign for leadership:

> That's the funny thing about this industry, it seems to me. I find it a little strange, not that I'm one to go out campaigning, but no, it's something that by tradition you don't do…You'd talk to various people like that. But you would never put an ad in the paper or whatever. Some people might write a letter to the paper, but essentially campaigns are extremely low key, even today. (Elected member, Interview 14)

This apparent anomaly can again be explained by reference to paternalism. Paternalism often confers managerial positions on men almost as a matter of birthright. Thus, as Kerfoot and Knights (1993, 671) rightly observe, such men 'need not engage themselves in the rough and tumble of everyday struggles for power'. So, the managerial men of the Farmers' Union have no need for campaigning and even if they did would view it as demeaning and undignified. There is, however, informal campaigning, which is much more in keeping with the 'gentleman's club' culture of paternalism (Maddock and Parkin 1994). The type of 'informal' campaigning that dominates centres around discussions in male dominated contexts such as the pubs and male service clubs (Pini 2002c). This allows a range of opportunities for practising masculinity as men congregate in masculinized spaces to discuss their voting intentions and debate the virtues of different candidates. Fraternal relations between men are subsequently established and strengthened. The importance of these relations will be discussed further in the following chapter.

The final feature of the electoral system of the Farmers' Union that acts as both an expression of and reinforcement for paternalism is the system of voting. This system is one which allows only one vote per farm for elections to leadership positions. It is a system that is typical of most farmers' unions (Haslam McKenzie 1999; Dimopoulos and Sheridan 2000; Grace 1997; Elix and Lambert 1998; Alston 2000; Pini 2006b). Allocating only one vote per farm for elections serves a two-fold purpose in terms of paternalism. Firstly, it reinforces the patriarchal position of the father, investing in him all decision-making power as the singular 'head' and achieving what Collinson and Hearn (1994, 13) call 'the rule of the father'. Secondly, the voting system positions women and younger family farming members as lacking in appropriate knowledge and expertise and consequently incapable of voting. Again, we see that power is afforded to senior men in a manner that suggests it is actually in the best interests of those who are being disempowered.

Changing this franchise system was viewed as improper by the majority of Farmers' Union managers involved in the research. They agreed that women are typically excluded from voting in elections but suggested this is a 'private' matter between a husband and a wife. In this way they frame a public, formal and incredibly problematic organizational practice as a private conjugal matter requiring no debate. There is not just the issue here of the slippage between paternalistic masculinity as a practice of the home/organization, but the issue of how paternalism in one site is used to justify its practice in another and vice versa.

Paternalism and Gendered Images and Symbols in the Farmers' Union

In her analysis of the position of women in farming organizations in Canada and Ireland, Shortall (2001) affords attention to the way in which different symbols and images perpetuate the view that men are the rightful protagonists in agri-political arenas. She notes, for example, the way in which a female President of a farming organization in Ireland is continuously represented in the agricultural media as an aberration. Focus is always afforded to her gender. In contrast, when the leader of a farming organization is a man, his gender remains unstated. This is not a minor point, Shortall (2001, 179) claims, as 'symbols, the media and images create and reinforce the gendering of organizations'.

Shortall's (2001) observations are salient when examining the symbols and images constructed and promoted by the Farmers' Union. For example, leading into the boardroom of the main city office is a bronze bust of each of the past chairmen. These are clearly men to be remembered and reified. There is also a series of photographs of past managers. These present a particular staged version of managerial masculinity – one of seriousness, gravity and substance, as the managers appear always in suits, taciturn and unsmiling. Managers are remembered in terms of their length of service in text accompanying each photograph. In each of the group photographs, the Chairman and Deputy Chairman are afforded pictorial prominence reinforcing the importance of hierarchy in the Farmers' Union. These images embody a message of paternalism – that men of the past continue to be important to the organization and that heritage and tradition are to be remembered and reified. This message was also conveyed in the awarding of mementos to long serving leaders at specially convened celebratory events. These events were publicized widely in the fortnightly magazine the organization distributed to farmers, thereby circulating and legitimating the norms and values of paternalism. That is, our organizational elders are prized as are longevity, service and dedication.

Shifting Managerial Masculinities in Agricultural Organizations

The previous sections of this chapter have established the pervasiveness of paternalism in the Farmers' Union. This is not to suggest, however, that it was solely this configuration of masculinity that was evident in the case study organization. Many studies have demonstrated that it is typical for different managerial masculinities to overlap and coalesce. Reed (1996), for example, identified both entrepreneurialism and paternalism in the gendered managerial discourses of her case studies of 'self-made men'. Similarly, Kerfoot and Knights (1993) found paternalism and what they refer to as strategic managerial masculinity co-existing at banks they studied even if, at different periods, one shifted to become predominant.

These issues are explored further in the following two sections of this chapter. To begin, I examine a particular incident that occurred during the course of the research. I argue that this incident is representative of an authoritarian discourse of managerial masculinity. This is not particularly unusual for, as McDowell (2001, 184) has found, authoritarianism is often a 'subcategory' of paternalism. In the next section, I detail the establishment of the Young Farmers' Group attached to the mainstream case study Farmers' Union and explore the discourses of masculine management dominant in the narratives of executive male members of the group. In these discourses we hear a new hybrid form of managerial masculinity emerging which accentuates both professionalism and entrepreneurialism.

From Paternalism to Authoritarianism

The incident that I will use to illustrate the co-existence of authoritarianism with paternalism in the Farmers' Union concerned the women's network in one of the two districts studied. At the beginning of 2000, some of the women involved in this group expressed concern at Farmers' Union meetings about farming legislation which was to be introduced. One participant, Kim, explained:

> Kim: I felt that the new Farming Act represented a major change for farmers, yet when I talked to people, 95 to 98 per cent of them didn't even know that the bill was going before parliament. The only information I could get from the Farmers' Union was that it was a good bill and good for the industry. On two occasions I asked about it and was told, 'Don't you worry about it'. (District B, Focus Group 8)

Following this, Kim then, on her own undertaking, placed three advertisements in her local paper alerting people to the new bill, circulated letters to local business people and farmers about the legislation and organized a forum to discuss its implications. These actions were viewed incredulously by some farming leaders who reported in interviews that women in the network had 'questioned some of our decisions', 'wanted to tell us what to do' and 'wanted us to change our rules'. These men's reactions are indicative of the fact that paternalistic management within the farming group is pervasive and normalized as right. This was demonstrated even when Kim approached her district Farmers' Union office and asked for a copy of the legislation:

> Kim: And they said, 'Oh we can't give you that till it's passed'. Well this is public information. And I said, 'I beg your pardon?' I said, 'Don't you think that's why I want it. I want to have a look at it and see if I agree with it. I want to be able to put my ten cents worth in'. By the time I got home they'd left a message on the answering machine saying you can have a copy. (District B, Focus Group 8)

Collinson and Hearn (1994, 14) have argued that women who conform to the normative definitions of femininity prescribed for them typically 'experience little hostility' from paternal managers. When they do not conform, however, they will find themselves sanctioned in a range of ways. This was the case with Kim and some of the other more prominent women involved in the women's network. For example, focus group participants reported on the negative gossip that had been circulated about the women's network members, which positioned them as having 'reputations' and being troublesome, difficult and unfeminine.

Some agricultural leaders gave considerable emphasis to the fact that Kim's partner was an elected representative of an alternative agri-political group, which had been an adversary of the case study organization. She was described in one interview as 'sleeping with the enemy' and accused of raising problems with the legislation as a means of discrediting the Farmers' Union. It is a criticism that Kim was aware of, and responded to in a focus group:

> Kim: I am not a member of any alternative farming group. I live with someone who is involved with the group, but…Anyone who knows me and knows anything about me would know that it is extremely unlikely that I would be a puppet. (District B, Focus Group 8)

The representation of Kim as not capable of speaking or thinking for and by herself, again reflects the blurring of private and public paternalism within the case study site. Paternalistic assumptions about what a 'wife' would do and would think inform how women are perceived and constructed in the organizational context.

Research participants – both women and men – have reported that when Kim and others continued to raise questions about the legislation, farming leaders in the district became increasingly authoritarian in their leadership. This is the authoritarian masculinity described by Collinson and Hearn (1994, 13) as being characterized by 'an intolerance of dissent and difference, a rejection of dialogue and debate and a preference for coercive power'. As a result, when the actual forum to discuss the legislation took place, it was described by a participant as being 'more or less out of control'. One focus group participant who attended the forum was so distressed at the treatment of particular women that she telephoned me to say that she no longer wished to be involved in the research. She felt there was no possibility of changing gender relations in the industry and that her talents would be better used elsewhere. I recorded her comments in a research journal immediately after our conversation. I wrote:

> Talked to Lois about focus groups coming up in the district and she said she didn't want to participate. Seemed really frustrated and felt involvement was futile. Said, 'there is a definite gender problem'. Kept asserting that she had seen this herself and was reporting it directly. Said that at an industry meeting the men had 'got stuck right into' one of the women. Said she was 'really browned off'. Talked about how disappointed she felt and her view that the men are frightened. She believes that there might be change 'in years to come' but maintains 'it is a real boys' club'. I asked her what she meant and she said that she felt this after seeing the way this woman was treated. She said the tone was 'You upstart of a woman' and that this woman was castigated for causing problems. (Research Journal, June 1999)

The district manager of the Farmers' Union dealt with the issue by contacting the General Manager of the agricultural research and extension organization that provided financial support for the women's network. This General Manager then met with the network, and stated that the women were to focus only on education and training and not involve themselves in industry politics. In this respect, the district manager of the Farmers' Union sought institutional authority from more 'senior' men within the industry to reassert paternal rule.

From Paternalism and Authoritarianism to Entrepreneurialism and Professionalism

At the same time as the new farming legislation was being introduced and Kim was engaging in her campaign to open this up to discussion, a new Young Farmers' Group was established in District B. The group was open to young (under 30) men and women but the five member executive was, at the time of formation, all male. Despite this, the two young male executive members I interviewed were keen to stress their commitment to gender equality and their interest in involving women in the group. Both were married and said they envisaged their wives attending meetings and activities of the Group with them.

While this group did not elicit any of the degree of hostility that was directed at the women's group in the district (discussed in Chapter 6), there was some negativity from a few male leaders in the Farmers' Union. These leaders argued that the young farmers' energies would be better spent attending meetings of the mainstream organization. Another male elected member interviewed stated that while he had no cause for concern with the group, he knew others had expressed serious reservations about its formation. When I asked the nature of these reservations he replied, 'The reaction from upstairs is we don't want another group telling us what to do'. Other elected leaders as well as the CEO of the district Farmers' Union expressed cautious optimism about the group, while emphasizing the need to 'monitor it' over time. This male manager had, along with the district Chairman, organized a meeting with the President and Vice-president of the Young Farmers' Group, ostensibly to introduce themselves. However, interviews with the young farming men revealed that they had been given warnings about 'working in line' with the Farmers' Union and about people who may 'join to manipulate the system and stir trouble'. Unsurprisingly, we again see the paternal wheels in motion disciplining any potential threat to patriarchal authority.

I asked the Chairperson of the Young Farmers' Group why they had formed their own group rather than simply attend their own branch meetings. He responded:

> With us together everyone has the same ideas. No-one is going to say, 'We tried that twenty years ago' or 'We did the same thing before'. It's the same age group and the same attitudes. We need innovation. The paradigm that our parents are living in is changed. We'd like to stay at home and have things be predictable and the same, but we have to change. The meetings haven't worked to get young people involved. In the season it might be, 'Dad's going to a meeting tonight. Don't you worry about it'. (Chairperson, Young Farmers' Group, District B)

There are a number of critical points to be highlighted in this extract. First is the evidence of some resistance against the discourse of paternalism. The deference paternalism demands towards patriarchs is absent. The Young Farmers' Group is not willing to be discounted or patronized. They do not want to sit on the sidelines. They want to be involved and to make a contribution. Moreover, they are openly critical of the Farmers' Union, challenging the lack of efficacy of meetings in generating interest amongst youth. As the speaker says, 'the paradigm' is no longer the same. While to paternalists a lack of change may have been seen as indicative of dependability and steadfastness, it is seen by this new generation as antiquated and a risk to sustainability. The third key issue is that the divide the young farmer makes between the 'old' and the 'new' is age related. It is this social location that marks agricultural men as having different values and beliefs.

Like the Chairperson of the Young Farmers' Group, the Deputy Chairperson's discourse was markedly different from that of the older patriarchs of the Farmers' Union, as well as critical of paternalistic modes of management. He explained his motivation for establishing the Group:

> We want to look at the whole picture. We want to educate ourselves so we have to understand the whole picture and take a professional approach. A lot of young people get told to shut up and I feel like the young farmers are a bit intimidated. They haven't had a chance to be involved or make decisions. We want to change that but we're going to have to do things differently. (Deputy Chairperson, Young Farmers' Group, District B)

Speaking to a farming conference, another member of the Young Farmers' Group executive echoed this perspective. He spoke of the need for young farmers today to be 'professionals'. He advised his counterparts that as future farmers they needed to 'forge contacts, become comfortable with new technology, develop their skills, attend conferences and read newspapers and industry publications.'

The 'farm as business' discourse – and the associated discourses of entrepreneurship and professionalism in agriculture – have been widely circulated by Australian governments over the past decades so it is not completely unexpected to hear them articulated by this new generation of farmers (Gray and Lawrence 2001). Indeed, as the review of the literature in Chapter 2 revealed, this discourse has been found to be increasingly prevalent amongst farming people. Discourses of entrepreneurship and professionalism have also been championed in a broad range of ways and across multiple fields in the late twentieth and early twenty-first centuries. Today, write Dent and Whitehead (2002, 1), 'we are all expected to be professional, to perform professionally', while Brewis (2003, 150) reminds us of the current supremacy of the language of 'economy and efficiency'. What is notable about the young farmers is that they are not only drawing on the discourses of entrepreneurship and professionalism in terms of farming, but also in terms of agricultural management.

Conclusion

McDowell (2001, 84) emphasizes that paternalism is both evident in, and replicated by, a number of formal and informal organizational practices. In this chapter I have documented a range of these practices in the case study Farmers' Union, from the conduct of meetings to electoral practices. Despite the hegemony of paternalism in the organization it is clear that when it is under threat, a more authoritarian management discourse is engaged. Of interest is the fact that these modes of management have been superseded by other forms of management masculinities in many contemporary organizations. Within the financial services industry, for example, paternalism once enjoyed a privileged position but today it has been displaced by more adversarial and aggressive forms of managerial masculinity (Kerfoot and Knights 1996). A similar shift from paternalism to entrepreneurial masculinity has been identified in managerial masculinity practised in higher education (Whitehead 1999a).

This raises the question of why the so-called 'old order' of paternalism (Kerfoot and Knights 1996, 93) continues to manifest itself in the agricultural group under investigation. One possible explanation can be gleaned by returning to the findings of Charles and Davies (2000) and Bird (2006) reported in Chapter 2. That is, place matters in terms of the practice of management and therefore particular discursive and material conditions exist which continue to support the prevalence of paternalism in the Farmers' Union. For example, traditional family farming has typically relied upon paternalistic employment relations, decision-making processes and ownership arrangements (Wallace, Dunkerley, Cheal and Warren 1994; Bennett 2004; Price and Evans 2006). The agricultural leaders' familiarity with this type of on-farm management and their limited exposure to other forms of management[2] may

---

2 At the time of this study, only one of the 26 Board members of the Farmers' Union had undertaken formal training in management. Along with a second member, he had also worked outside the industry in another organization. In general this type of experience and management education and training are most uncommon amongst the elected leadership of the organization.

mean that paternalistic management is more common in the context of agri-politics than it is elsewhere. If one examines more context specific information about the particular organization under investigation it becomes evident that there are further material and discursive factors which may work to support the continued hegemony of paternalism as a management discourse. In particular, the Farmers' Union studied represents the interests of a group of farmers whose industry has traditionally had a high level of regulation as well as provided a secure and reasonable income for growers. These structural factors may have provided a fertile environment in which a paternalistic managerial masculinity could flourish. At the same time the Young Famers' Group provides evidence that a shift may be imminent in the types of managerial discourses hegemonic in the mainstream Farmers' Union. The young men involved in the Group espoused quite different managerial discourses from the incumbent patriarchs. Whether or not this may provide some potential for gender justice in the Farmers' Union will be discussed in the final chapter.

Chapter 5

Making Managerial Men in Agricultural Politics

Studies of gender and organizations increasingly attend to the multiplicity of masculinities within a particular site or occupational grouping (for example, Barrett 2002; Chalmers 2001; Cross and Bagilhole 2002; Lupton 2000). At the same time, this work continues to highlight Connell's (1995) claim that there is a common denominator in the process by which masculine subjects constitute themselves. That is, they all rely upon mobilizing gender discourses to establish unities and differences. In the first instance, establishing oneself as masculine involves distinguishing oneself from the feminine. Securing this masculine identity may also require positioning oneself as analogous to particular masculine subjects or alternatively, necessitate evaluating oneself against masculine subjectivities. By engaging these gender discourses in such a comparative way a boundary marker is established between one's gendered self and the identities of those deemed 'other'.

In this chapter I explore this relational and referential process as it is operationalized within the Farmers' Union. My particular concern is with identifying the process by which elected men in the organization constitute their identities. I argue that this is a two-fold process. In the first instance elected leaders situate themselves as 'masculine' by highlighting their difference/s from 'women.' In this process it is women who are 'other' either because they are not involved in on-farm physical work or because they are unsuitable for agricultural leadership. There is, however, a second dimension to the formulation of masculine subjectivities in agri-politics. Elected leaders go on to position themselves as 'different' from some 'other' farming men, emphasizing qualities such as their specialist expertise, knowledge and training. In this process of 'othering' farming men are feminized as passive, inexperienced and naïve. We thus begin to see that the work of gender identity formation is not a singular process, but a complex web of alliances and divergences.

Farmers' Union Managerial Men and the 'Othering' of Women

In the Farmers' Union elected male leaders position themselves as 'masculine' by situating women as 'other'. In large part, women are 'other' as they are not involved in on-farm physical work. However, those women who are involved in on-farm physical work are also 'othered' as agricultural leadership is defined in masculine terms. As the following will argue, the elected male leaders solidify this process of 'othering' by drawing parallels between their own displays of hegemonic masculinity with the hegemonic masculinity valourized in on-farm physical work.

Women as 'Other: Conflating the Discourses of 'Farmer'
and 'Agricultural Manager'

Gherardi and Poggio (2001, 247) write that the work of gender identity is a 'comparison activity' so that being either male or female 'entails a discourse which highlights not belonging to the other'. For the elected members I interviewed the process of constructing women as 'other' and that of creating the subject position 'masculine agricultural leader' begins with definitions of the occupational identity of farmer. As Chapter 2 revealed, examining the connections between the subject position of farmer and masculinity has been a key focus of scholarly work. This work has repeatedly reported that conventional definitions of farming emphasize its physicality, technical competence with machinery, and strength (for example, Brandth 1995; Coldwell 2007a; 2007b; Ni Laoire 1999; 2001; Saugeres 2002a). It is this traditional discourse of farming which dominated the narratives of male elected leaders of the Farmers' Union.

Like so many other farming women described in the literature, the 80 women involved in the 16 focus groups undertook a wide range of on-farm roles including all domestic and family work and the majority of financial work. However, only 11 were involved in working with tractors and machinery (see Pini 2005d). Thus the majority of the women were, by definition, not farmers nor interested in farming according to the elected members of the Farmers' Union. This was clearly enunciated by a senior Board member in responding to a question about women's lack of representation in decision-making in the organization. He stated:

> When you get right down to it, the actual level of involvement of women in the industry is extremely low, so you've got to take that across to why they don't nominate for positions… It's extremely low. Extremely low. Their basic knowledge and basic interest, most of the women, farming women, are not interested. So I have a problem when some people suggest that we're not using 48 per cent of the potential out there by not having women involved in representative positions. That's just not true. (Elected member, Interview 13)

It is not a new or surprising finding to note the propensity men had to define farming in traditional terms that exclude women and absent femininities.[1] This seems to be a remarkably intractable construction of farming. What is new and surprising is the way in which managerial men in the Farmers' Unions invoked these discourses as a means of justifying and legitimating women's exclusion from management. Men are farmers while women are not, and consequently men are the managers of the Farmers' Union and women are not.

The conflation of the discourses of farming and agricultural management was not (always) as crude as this. Rather, there was a process of what Brandth and Haugen (2000) and Liepins (1998; 2000) refer to as slippage between the two discursive fields. It was argued that farming and management are different roles but require the same type of skills and traits. Both managers and farmers are constantly involved in battle

---

1 The way in which men construct occupations as requiring particular physical traits and characteristics has been well reported in the literature on gender and organizations; see, for example, Cockburn's (1983) classic study of gender relations in the printing industry.

and as a consequence, need to demonstrate masculine strength, determination and aggression. In this way, the elected men could use the legitimacy of the 'real farming men' discourse to afford legitimacy to their own role as agricultural leaders.

The dominance of an organizational battlefield discourse predates the constitution of the case study organization. In the first edition of a journal published in 1918 by the group which paved the way for the establishment of the organization, the editor outlined the need for an agri-political group which could 'fight and fight with all its power.' At this time, at the end of World War I, the fight for farmers was with government, unions and urban based people who were positioned as not understanding the life and work of farmers. Since this time there have been some shifts in who and what the editor of the magazine called farmers, 'pitiless enemies', but the discursive construction of farmers being engaged in battle and of the agri-political leader similarly engaged have not. Farmers, for example, according to a newsletter of the Farmers' Union published in 2000, are 'always battling the elements' of 'cyclones, strong winds, excessive rainfall and flooding, drought and accidental fires' but when 'disaster does strike', the Farmers' Union is there 'striving to ensure that growers are able to recover as quickly as possible'. In undertaking this battle against the weather and other forces, male agricultural managers invoke a range of military metaphors. The Chairman, for example, introduced newly elected members in the Farmers' Union magazine by editorializing:

> There are forces at work seeking to demolish our present structures and they may succeed if we do not stay as a united organization...The brinkmanship that comes with the changing of political parties or other organizations with the task of 'bringing us to our senses' will be cold comfort if our organization is weakened because of these ill-considered attacks. Our elected members are our front line troops. Keep them fully supplied with ammunition and give them total support which will give them the encouragement and confidence to hold the line against those who would demolish our present position.

The extent of the battlefield imagery invoked in this short paragraph may be unusual, but the existence of such figurative language in the organization to describe the roles of managers is not. In a further commentary on the same theme of unity amongst farmers, the General Manager echoed his Chairman's concerns in a column headlined, 'The range war we didn't want.' Similarly, in interviews elected members referred to farmers being 'thrown to the wolves' and at risk from 'those who are out to take everything they can off us'. They emphasized that 'everything we've got we've had to fight to get' and now 'have to fight to hang on to'. The engagement of this type of military metaphor by managers is, of course, very common (Alvesson and Due Billing 1997, 112–14),[2] for it situates the manager as a champion aggressively combating the evils that lurk outside the organizational door. In a paternalistic/authoritarian culture, military analogies also reinforce the patriarch's claims to control and discipline.

---

2 There is a recursive relationship here between the masculine discourses of management engaged by managers and management theorists/writers. Look, for example, at the the nomenclature of 'strategic management' as it has been developed by populist and academic writers. Its terminology is strongly connected to masculinist military language (Bracker, 1980; Pini, 2005b).

That the strength required to fight on-farm battles and board room battles is similar was conveyed by the elected leaders who emphasized that it is their participation in on-farm physical work which gives them something to offer as agricultural leaders. They had, as one said, 'been there in the paddock' and 'gotten their hands dirty'. Others referred to themselves as having strengths as managers because they had been 'a grass roots grower' or because they 'had hands-on involvement in the industry'. What was interesting was that the capacity to make connections between an on-farm role and a managerial role was not necessarily present in all of the managerial staff of the Farmers' Union. Clearly, the elected leaders had backgrounds in farming. This was, however, not the case for staff members who were managers, such as the CEO of the organization. These managerial men thus found other means of connecting their managerial identities with the identities of the farming men. Some chose symbolic means of achieving this connection. Toy sized replica tractors and harvesters, for example, were strategically situated in two of the offices of city based male managerial staff. In another office, a framed harvesting tool evoked an empathy with the past as well as with the toil and labour associated with agricultural work. Photographs of farming men, machinery and tractors littered other walls. This constellation of symbols secured an overlap between the field and the office and between the farming men and the male managers employed by the organization.

I witnessed this overlap myself during a visit to a district to attend a conference for farmers sponsored by the Farmers' Union. Many of the senior managers from the city office were in attendance, as were elected leaders who resided in the district but with whom I had interacted during Board meetings in the city. The audience of around 200 included approximately 160 men and 40 women. By morning tea on the first day, I had recorded a note in my journal about the amount of swearing and sexual innuendos made by the managerial men chairing sessions. At morning tea I discussed my reaction with two female industry personnel   an agricultural extension officer and a trusted female staff member of the Farmers' Union. At this stage I was nearly 18 months into the study. I had been a participant observer at numerous meetings of the Farmers' Union, seen and talked to many of the elected members as well as men on staff who were managers during days working at the city office. What was interesting to me was that I had not previously encountered this type of behaviour.

This was not the other women's experiences. One said she 'barely noticed' the sexual jokes and swearing anymore, while the other told me what she considered were other worse jokes she had heard at former Farmers' Union gathering the year before. In further discussions, the female employee of the Farmers' Union added that she thought the behaviour was acceptable in this district location as it was 'more relaxed'. She suggested that it would not have been appropriate if it was 'in the city'. This was, I believe, a very insightful comment. These men were not 'doing management' as I had seen it done in the urban environment. This was a distinctly different performance. Even the costume had changed. Suit jackets were gone, sleeves were rolled up and some wore no tie. What the managerial men sought to construct was a shared sense of masculine identity with the male farmers in the audience, and simultaneously, to mark themselves as different from the women present. Men's use of sexual banter, humour and swearing to generate collective identification as masculine men and to exclude women has been well reported in the literature (Cockburn 1983; Collinson 1988; Collinson and Collinson 1989; 1992; 1996; Eveline and Booth 2002; Sinclair 1995). Cumulatively, this literature has pointed to the dominance of men's (hetero)sexuality in organizations and the interlinkages between this sexuality and power as men use sexuality to establish a hierarchy in which they share allegiances with particular men but subordinate other men and women. Such was my experience at the Farmers' Union conference.

Women in focus groups expressed a clear awareness of the way in which discourses of management and farming are conflated by elected male members, as well as their exclusion from these discourses. They consequently saw themselves as disqualified from leadership in the Farmers' Union. This was even the case with those women who did indicate that they had some leadership aspirations and potential. Two commented:

> Jacinta: As far as the Farmers' Union goes I feel as though for a woman to be in it they have to be actively involved in the field and everything in the field work...I do all the bookwork. Really, probably nothing goes on in the farm I don't know about, but I would never feel that I was a candidate for leadership because I think you have to actually be out and experience it.

> Jenny: I feel the same, because I have been approached to put my name forward to be an elected member and I was a bit hesitant...I said to the person who asked me, I said, 'I wouldn't go along to a farmers' meeting and try and put something forward'. Really, I have been living on a farm all my life. I know lots about it, but I have never actually worked the farm so I don't know. (District B, Focus Group 7)

In other focus groups women made similar statements:

> Beth: I'd say if they worked enough out in the paddock and they've had hands-on experience, I'd say they'd certainly be accepted. (District B, Focus Group 8)

> Norma: I feel they'd look at me and think, 'Well, how would she know? Haven't seen her getting her hands dirty or driving a tractor'. (District B, Focus Group 1)

Both Beth and Norma allude to the hegemonic definition of farming as one that is embodied in physical activity (Saugeres 2002b). While agricultural leaders may now have clean and even manicured hands as they sit in boardroom meetings typing away on laptops, they can lay claim to once having used their hands in more practical and manual labour. This gives credibility to their leadership which most women cannot claim. There is, of course, no reason why an aptitude with tractors or soiled hands would serve you well in taking up a leadership role. Clearly it is simply not true that you need to be able to drive a harvester to be a competent manager. However, whether this is 'true' or not is not necessarily what is important. What is important is that it is believed to be true; it is known to be true. The conflation of manager with farmer is thus powerful in regulating who can be a leader/manager in the Farmers' Union and who cannot (Weedon 1987).

I imagined that one factor that could dent the security with which essentialized gender discourses were engaged was that a small number of women in the study did meet the definition of 'farmer' as invoked by the managerial men. Of these eleven women, five had stood for leadership but been unsuccessful. In discussing these women and, in particular, why they had been unsuccessful in electoral campaigns, the men interviewed revealed another dimension to the way they construct the identity of agricultural leader. This is discussed in further detail below.

Women as Other: Farmers but Not Agricultural Leaders

In explaining why the five women who were physically active on farms and involved in tractor work on farms were unable to secure decision-making positions in agriculture, elected leaders pointed to what they perceived to be other pre-determined differences between men and women. In so doing they added further dimensions, not just to their construction of 'woman,' but also to their own gendered subjectivities as 'agricultural managers'.

Women could not be agricultural managers, it was argued, because agricultural management is a particularly tough, demanding job, requiring objective and critical thinking and the capacity to work long hours. Women, I was told, 'wouldn't be able to take the pressure'. One man commented:

> We've had a few ladies who've had some interest but when you indicate the time commitments that might be involved they aren't so willing to give up the time. You know, it might be a meeting a week or half a day a week and all of a sudden she can't arrange it. (Elected member, Interview 9)

It was not uncommon for managers to refer to women as 'ladies' in this way, which, as Ozbilgin and Woodward (2004, 678) note, has 'connotations of chivalry and protection'. The speaker is therefore not just conveying his view that women do not have the singularity of focus and level of commitment that is required of agricultural leaders, he is telling us that this is perhaps acceptable and understandable. Why would we want to subject women to the gruelling task that is agricultural management? Women, as defined by paternalism, are emotional, irrational, fragile and weak (Collinson and Hearn 1994). They should not be exposed to agricultural politics, as a Farmers' Union manager explained when I asked him why he thought there was so much opposition to establishing a women's network:

> One view that was expressed by one of the guys was that, we actually pride ourselves with not having our women heavily involved you know, that's something we can take care of. You know, we don't have to have our women sort of burdened with trying to administer the organization. (Farmers' Union staff member, Interview 1)

There are a number of salient factors that need to be elucidated from this exchange. The first point concerns the way industry administration is portrayed as a difficult and tough burden, unlike other responsibilities women are encouraged to undertake (such as all familial and domestic work). The second is the way women's exclusion from leadership is justified. It is turned around and legitimized as an act of lightening women's load and of ensuring that women are not placed under strain or stress. As the previous chapter argued, this obscuring of power is a key feature of paternalism (Collinson and Hearn 1994). The dominant group claims power in a subversive manner, suggesting it is in the best interests of the powerless and the collective good that power is held by the patriarch/s. The third crucial point is the way men's pride is associated with the capacity to keep women out of industry politics. Thus, it is not just men's involvement which renders agri-politics 'masculine', but women's exclusion from this environment. 'Real men' would not allow their wives to be involved in agri-politics as the following quotation from a woman in a focus group reveals:

> Georgie: There have been times when things have come up and I've wanted to go to a meeting, even a Landcare meeting and my husband has said he wouldn't like me to go. I think he wouldn't like the men swearing or being rough. (District B, Focus Group 1)

This quotation highlights the potential tension that may exist when women seek to enter the agri-political environment as they may destabilize masculine identities. This will be explored further in the following chapter.

Even if husbands permitted wives to attend Farmers' Union meetings, agricultural leaders suggested that there was a further aspect of femininity which rendered women unsuitable for agricultural management. This is encapsulated in the following quotation:

> Without being awful, too many women working in the one place is hard to handle. I think you need a smaller proportion, and that probably contradicts everything I just said! Women are naturally jealous and naturally bitchy. Too many women can be atrocious and probably it can be a very dangerous situation because everybody wants to be the boss, if you get very aggressive or very outspoken or very assertive women. (Farmers' Union staff member, Interview 4)

The above quotation from a Farmers' Union staff member draws on a discourse about women which emerged in multiple sites across the fieldwork. It is a discourse which positions women as irrational, over-emotional, unmanageable and unforgiving. Inversely, men are rational, non-emotional, business-like and forgive easily. Men's presence is therefore necessary to contain the natural proclivity women have towards being out of control. This is, of course, a very powerful discourse about women because it is one that has legitimacy in broader discursive fields beyond farming. Further, in the farming sector it has been a discourse that has always enjoyed currency as a means of excluding women from decision-making and even ownership of land (Pini 2007).

Given the way in which managerial men presented industry leadership as an environment that was far too challenging for women to enter, it is ironic to have had interviewees discuss the work some wives did for their elected member husbands. This work, which included monitoring press releases and reading mail and reports to highlight points of interest, was constructed by managerial men as 'helping' (see Chalmers 2001).

Farmers' Union Managerial Men and the 'Othering' of Men

The process by which managerial men in the Farmers' Union came to secure their masculine identities did not only involve 'othering' women. It also involved 'othering' some men. In the following sections I explore three ways in which this process of 'othering' occurred.

Managerial Men's Construction of Themselves as Different from Farmers

Women are not the only group constructed as different by managerial men in agricultural organizations. Another group positioned as different is 'farmers'. Positioning this group as 'different' is particularly interesting because, as explained above, the managers are also insistent that there are commonalities between themselves and what they ubiquitously referred to as the 'hands-on-farmer'. This connection is, however, qualified. What is apparent in agricultural organizations is that managerial men may once have been farmers, but not all farmers may be managerial men.

Differences between elected members and farmers were not class based in that all elected members had been farmers, and moreover, farmed the same crop. Clearly, farm size would lead to differences in wealth but there did not appear to be a relationship between farm size/wealth and access to a leadership position in the Farmers' Union. A few of the 26 member Board, the highest level of leadership in the organization, had very large farms with paid employees, but the majority had what would be described as average or small holdings. It was the case, however, that moving from the position of 'farmer' to that of 'elected leader' opened up access to new forms of capital for male managers. This was not necessarily economic, as payment for representation was nominal. Being an elected leader did, however, provide access to new forms of social and cultural capital as these men had access to international and national travel, stayed in quality accommodation and met with senior government, business and industry leaders.

The male agricultural leaders emphasized the differences between what one called the 'fairly basic' knowledge of farming and the variously described, 'intense', 'highly complex', 'onerous' and 'complicated' work of agricultural leadership. The Chairman of the Farmers' Union, for example, was dismissive of the 'simplistic unachievable solutions' he believed were offered by some constituents to the problems facing the industry. Agricultural leaders further differentiated themselves in discussions of their skills, knowledge and expertise by engaging dualistic 'us/them', 'we/they' divisions in their speech.

The agricultural leaders referred to themselves when they were 'a farmer' and compared their lack of knowledge and expertise then with what they now had as 'managers'. One stated, for example, that 'when you're a farmer you're out there farming and you don't know what goes on within the organizations'. Another elected leader echoed this construction of his constituency as knowledge poor and politically innocent. He stated:

> You'd be surprised, but 85 per cent of the farmers here would have very limited knowledge on how the organizations work, how things are negotiated, contracts are awarded. All of

the nitty gritty they would not have a clue. They don't have any reason to because it's done for them. We negotiate a deal for them. They get paid. They grow their crop, cut their crop and they're happy. (Elected member, Interview 15)

The expert knowledge of the elected leadership is not necessarily gained through formal qualifications because none of those interviewed had such qualifications. Rather, they stressed it was knowledge gained through on-site institutional and organizational learning as a result of being an industry representative. You moved along 'a big learning curve when you became an elected leader', one commented while another stated:

I have been sitting in this bloody room for twenty-three years and so have a hell of a lot of other people. One has been here for fifteen years and another for seventeen years. We didn't immediately know all the things we do. There has been a lot of training and a lot of hard work. We know how everything works and how to deal with things. You can't suddenly bring in someone and get them to be part of what's going on. (Elected member, Interview 9)

For a 'farmer' to become an 'agricultural manager' it was necessary, elected leaders said, for them to do 'an apprenticeship'. This was the process by which those interviewed had come to leadership. That is, they had all been approached by an older male in the district who encouraged them to become involved and mentored them into their role. For many this had been a father or grandfather. This apprenticeship does not necessarily end once one is elected. It goes on throughout one's membership. For example, one elected leader of the Board told me that he had nominated himself to be chair of a committee which was focused on an area in which he had particular expertise. However, he did not receive the support of his colleagues and was told later by another senior elected member that he would not be entitled to be a committee chair until at least late in his second term of office. He needed to first 'learn the ropes'.

The traits associated with the identity of 'farmer' in this rendering are those associated with normative discourses of the feminine – passivity, naivety, inexperience, simplicity and innocence. In other words, the construction of 'farmers' by 'elected leaders' is a process of feminization. The literature on masculinities reports that it is common for those men who position themselves within discourses of hegemonic masculinity to label 'other' men at the bottom of the hierarchy as symbolically associated with femininity (Gilbert and Gilbert 1998; Skelton 2001; 2003). The farmers are not masculine enough to be elected leaders. They are not quite women, of course, but there are deficiencies in their masculinity which make them lesser men, and subsequently not suitable for managerial positions in the Farmers' Union.

Managerial Men's Construction of Themselves as Different from Each Other

The 'othering' by managerial men in agricultural politics also occurred in the way they constructed managers at different levels of the organizational hierarchy. That is, those at Board level differentiated themselves from their local and district counterparts, arguing that a more particular form of managerial masculinity was necessary when you are 'the fellow at the top' or 'working at this level'. In explaining what they meant, they referred to their Chairman as embodying a specific type of management. As an agricultural representative for 27 years and the Chairman for over a decade, he was seen as, and described at different farewell speeches on his retirement as, the 'Father', the 'Godfather' and even 'the God' of the industry. Elected leaders highlighted that the Chairman was a man who was feared and gave examples of his authoritarianism and oppressive style, some of which involved themselves as the protagonists who had been 'hauled over the coals' or 'given a major blast'. At the same time, they were keen to point out that he had 'been good for the industry' and 'had respect'. The most senior agricultural manager must chastise and discipline, but ultimately this is for the good of all. Asked to describe this man's management his counterparts stated:

> He's tough. I think you have to be in that position. Probably makes you as tough as nails, hardens you up over time. But I think he always probably was [laughs]. Tough in terms of thick-skinned because you're getting it from all sides. The farmers you're helping, other members and then people outside like governments and other industry groups. Tough, also, not being walked over. I've seen him go head to head with people from the Prime Minister down and walk away the winner. He doesn't take any prisoners, but they know after all this time so he's got that reputation. (Elected member, Interview 12)

> A lot of this politics is a game. And he is a player. You have to have respect for him because he's got no real formal education and but he's street smart. A bit of a Paul Keating.[3] Not that he'd like that comparison [laughs]. He doesn't care if he's liked or disliked. He just does the job for the industry. (Elected member, Interview 10)

> You see him in Board meetings and someone's going on or saying something he thinks is stupid and he just gives them this look and they shut-up. I've seen it happen time and time again. He doesn't need to yell and scream or carry-on, just a look and that's it. (Elected member Interview 14)

Brandth (2006) has noted the lack of work on embodiment in agricultural studies and suggested that farming is an occupational role to which the body is integral. It seems from the above quotations that managerial masculinity in agricultural leadership also requires an embodied performance. This is a performance of a controlled body – one of objectivity, rationality, composure and decisiveness. Such a body is necessary in the environment of agricultural politics, which is again referred to in terms of masculine military and sporting metaphors. The Chairman is particularly admired for his singularity of purpose and his lack of bodily concern with being liked. Colouring the elected members' representations of the Chairman is the strongly ingrained conceptualization of the mind and body as dualistic, where the mind is associated with the masculine and the body with the feminine (Grosz 1987). As Kerfoot and Knights (1996) have noted, throughout history this is a dualism that has been re-inscribed on managerial discourses so that the 'good' manager is a disembodied manager. While the literature reports that new management discourses are requiring more embodied performances from managers today (for example, Hatcher 2003), the hegemony of more traditional management styles within the Farmers' Union continue to demand a Chairman with a 'closed body' (Lennie 2000, 138).

---

3 Paul Keating was Prime Minister of Australia from 1991 to 1996.

At its highest level in the Farmers' Union, management does not just require regulation of one's own body. It also requires a capacity to regulate the bodies of others – constituents, other members, organizational staff as well as external stakeholders such as government representatives and business leaders. This containment of the bodies of others does not necessarily require an exaggerated bodily performance of the Chairman. A mere raising of the eyebrows is enough to discipline the corporeal excesses of his elected members. Similarly, in dealing with government his bodily reputation for controlling the bodies of others precedes him. His capacity for aggression and his lack of willingness to compromise make him a formidable opponent. His managerial body is represented as being 'thick-skinned' and 'as tough as nails'. He has gone 'head to head' with powerful men and not been 'walked over'. This is a man who is intelligent, but not in a bookish or intellectual way. Rather, his intelligence has been written on his body, informed by nearly 30 years of confrontations and conquests.

During the period of the fieldwork I was told so many stories about the Chairman and what was constructed as his legendary leadership that these alone could fill a book. These came from people inside and outside the organization, informants and non-informants, as well as existing and retired elected members and staff. As Sinclair (2005) has reported, such storytelling plays a key role in producing and replicating the bodily authority of managerial men. Collectively the narratives, whether true or not, cloaked the Chairman with a mythology which ensured that his claim to the title of patriarch became self-sustaining. Of course, as Longhurst (1997) argues, both men and women have bodies and women also could take up the bodily performance of the Chairman. While this will be discussed in further detail in Chapter 7, it is important to state that women would face particular difficulties in 'doing masculinity' in the hegemonic fashion of the Chairman. Acker (1990, 153) has emphasized the virtual impossibility of 'women's bodies' conforming to traditional discourses of hegemonic managerial masculinity, saying this would require 'that women render irrelevant everything that makes them women'. Further, even if a woman could successfully 'do masculinity' in an equivalent manner to the Chairman, it is unlikely that she would be judged so positively, as 'doing masculinity' is interpreted very differently when it is done by a female body (see, for example, Cockburn 1991; Pierce 1995).

Managerial Men's Construction of Themselves as Different from Other Agricultural Managers

One of the difficulties of fieldwork is that you do not necessarily know what is important until after the event. We are rarely given any glimpse into how researchers deal with this because of the typically positivist style of reporting research which may have the required section on 'limitations', but rarely gives any indication of a researcher's sense of regret. In contrast, I have many regrets about this research. Of the numerous questions I wished I had asked, and trajectories I wished I had followed up, one concerns the way in which elected male members in the Farmers' Union saw themselves in relation to male agricultural leaders in other agricultural groups.

At the time of the study, I was so absorbed in understanding how managerial men in the Farmers' Union defined themselves as masculine against women and 'other' men who farmed the same crop, that I did not give sufficient consideration to outside forces. That is, the fact that managerial masculinity in the Farmers' Union would also have been constituted in relation to the masculinities practised by other managerial agricultural men.

One of the frustrations of my lack of attention to this issue is that there are many hints in the data that this was a key issue. There was a particular agricultural group, for example, which was often indirectly criticized by Farmers' Union members. It has a high media profile as it involves itself in a wide range of social issues as well as mainstream agricultural issues. It also has two women in high level management positions. At one public seminar, the CEO of the Farmers' Union made the following comparison between his organization and 'other' farming groups:

> Organizations like ours must increasingly focus on the important issues. Too many rural representative groups attempt to represent members in every aspect of their lives, tilting at every windmill – from fighting school closure to protecting the interests of local traders. If the ultimate aim is not to enhance the business success and profitability of its members, then the allocation of resources, time and effort must be questioned and priorities reassessed. (CEO Farmers' Union, Industry meeting, May 2000)

There is a very specific version of masculine management being privileged in the above quotation and another being rendered secondary/other/feminine by virtue of its softness; it lacks focus as well as attention to business outcomes. This is in comparison with the Farmers' Union and its single-minded attention to hard-core financial matters. I suspect that the managerial men of the Farmers' Union came to know and see themselves as 'real managerial men' by virtue of comparison with the activities, priorities and agendas of 'other' agricultural organizations such as those described by the CEO. This is particularly the case as a few women had been successful in achieving leadership positions in these 'other' organizations and consequently broadened the agenda of these farming organizations from focusing solely on commodity issues to focusing on social issues such as medical, transport and education services to rural areas (Liepins 1998).

Conclusion

Typically 'othered' in discourses of hegemonic masculinity is femininity and the women with whom femininity is conflated (Connell 1995; 2000). Within agricultural organizations this is also the rule. Women are positioned by the leadership as being naturally and biologically different from men. Central to women's natural and biological corporeal self is a domestic and child-care role. In contrast to the high status and visibility enjoyed by on-farm physical work, the work that is typically done by women on farms is afforded little recognition. Being a farmer is thus male. When those women who do engage in on-farm physical work have attempted to become involved in leadership, male elected leaders continue to suggest their lack of suitability. Here they draw on discourses of masculine leadership. To be an agricultural leader one needs to be independent, objective and strong. Women are identified as dependent, subjective and weak and thus not appropriate for decision-making positions within agri-politics.

The process of 'othering' women engaged in by the agricultural leaders is given potency as the men engage discourses which parallel their displays of hegemonic masculinity with the hegemonic masculinity valourized in another key agricultural discursive arena – that of the farm. Both the occupational roles of leader and farmer require a similar set of traits – strength, tenacity and aggression. It was argued that this association is furthered by a range of symbolic means such as via the types of pictures hung on the office walls of the male managers.

There is, however, another dimension to the formulation of masculine subject position 'agricultural manager'. What is interesting is that also 'othered' in the discourse of managerial masculinity in agri-politics is the identity of the 'farmer'. Despite inhabiting a male body and demonstrating in part a gendered identity which is analogous to the male leader, he is also constructed as being different. In contrast to the industry leader who is shrewd, astute, informed, knowledgeable and decisive, the 'grower' is uninformed, politically inexperienced and naïve. It is incumbent upon this leader therefore to protect the grower. Amongst this group is the younger male grower, who may in time be able to assume the characteristics which are held by the elected male leadership. This will, however, be at the discretion and behest of existing leaders, and until this occurs he too needs protection. For women, there is no such opportunity for an identity shift to leader. Their gendered feminine identity makes them, by definition, unsuitable for leadership and unable to perform leadership.

While managerial masculine identities may shift and change over time (Fondas 1997), the benefits enjoyed by male farm decision-makers as a result of existing hegemonic configurations of masculinity and leadership in the organization mean that challenging the dominant discursive constructions of gender and agricultural management in the organization will be difficult for women seeking to become involved in agri-politics. These women are unsettling taken-for-granted and normalized gender constructions and thus likely to meet resistance. This issue is taken up in the following chapters.

Chapter 6

Masculinities and Men's Response to Women's Agricultural Networks

The previous two chapters have established the dominance and privileging of hegemonic masculinities in the Farmers' Union. We have heard little of women or from women's voices. This chapter will address this silence, and particularly the question of farm women's agency, by focusing on one of the key strategies agricultural women world-wide have used to counter men's hold on organizational power.[1] That is, the establishment of women's farming groups (Carbert 1995; Liepins 1998; Shortall 2001).

In Australia, two women's networks have been established in rural areas as a means of facilitating women's increased participation in the Farmers' Union under investigation. Like other women's agricultural organizations, these networks have been central in facilitating the production and circulation of new and alternate discourses about farm women and their capacity for leadership. This was shown in the earliest work on the subject by Mackenzie (1992; 1994) who focused on the Canadian group, Women for the Survival of Agriculture, and subsequently on the Ontario Farm Women's Network. Through an analysis of data such as network newsletters, constitutions and goals, and interviews with network members, she discovered the ways farming women were developing new subjectivities which challenged the dominant agricultural discourse. These networks were using humour, women's stories and formal research projects to create a 'reverse discourse' in which the identity of 'farm wife' was being reconstituted as an important and equal 'partner' in the farm enterprise (see also Liepins 1998).

Documenting the rise of farm women's groups, geographer Elizabeth Teather (1995, 10) hypothesized that 'a backlash is to be expected from male dominated organizations as women in the agricultural industries pursue their goals of raising their profile'. However, since Teather (1995) made this claim, and despite an ongoing academic interest in rural women's networks and the increasing degree of influence these networks have achieved (Fincher and Panelli 2001), the question of resistance to farm women's networks has not been widely examined. This is a considerable limitation in the literature, given what we know about the inter-relationships between masculine subjectivities in agriculture and men's claims to power in agricultural organizations. Thus, this chapter seeks to understand the reactions of male agricultural leaders as farming women have begun to enunciate

---

1 This is, of course, a strategy women have used in many other occupational areas where men dominate, such as in trade unions (Kirton 1999; 2006; Colgan and Ledwith 2000) and local government (Pini, Brown and Ryan 2004).

new agricultural identities which are different from those which have traditionally defined the sector, and which have typically afforded men status and power and justified the systematic exclusion of women.

To address this issue, the chapter begins with some background information on the two farm women's groups established as adjuncts to the Farmers' Union. This section establishes the fact that these networks, like other agricultural women's groups, have been important sites for resistance to masculine hegemony in farming organizations. In light of this I then ask: What has been men's response to these women's networks? The discussion that follows, which is situated within the literature on men's resistance to gender equity in organizations, highlights the way in which men in the Farmers' Union trivialized, masculinized, pathologized and sexualized the women's networks.

Background to the Farm Women's Networks: Sites of Resistance

The farm women's networks that are discussed in this chapter are part of a broader 'rural women's movement' that occurred in the late twentieth century in nations such as Australia, Canada, the United States, Norway and Ireland. The emergence of such a movement has been attributed to a range of coalescing factors, including the impact of the world-wide women's movement, the downturn in agriculture and women's frustration with the continued male dominance of agri-political spaces (Wells and Tanner 1994). The work of Elizabeth Teather (1992; 1994; 1996a; 1996b; 1996c; 1997; 1998) has been critical in reporting on the emergence of this movement and the factors that distinguished these 'new' groups from past rural and farm women's groups. Her research on the subject began with an examination of the Country Women's Association of New South Wales (1992; 1994; 1996a; 1996b), and the way in which this organization (and the many Country Women's Associations around Australia) centred their mission on the nuclear family, patriarchal gender relations and rurality. Further work (1996c; 1997; 1998) drew on a survey questionnaire, in-depth interviews, document analysis and participant observation to examine the differences between newer farm women's networks such as Australian Women in Agriculture (AWiA) and the Ontario Farm Women's Network (OFWN) and more established rural women's groups such as the Women's Division Federated Farmers (WDFF) and the Federated Women's Institutes of Ontario (FWIO). Collectively, Teather's publications highlight the way in which these newer farm women's networks represent an identifiable shift away from the more traditional rural women's groups which have focused strongly on women's domestic role. She asserted that 'these newer organizations are committed to transforming the mental and cognitive attitudes of rural people' (Teather 1996c, 44). Essentially, finding that no space was available for them in the commodity groups, these farm women began creating their own space to express opinions and views and to demonstrate their capacity for leadership.

The two farm women's networks discussed in this chapter were established in 1993 and 1998, respectively, with the central aim of increasing women's participation in agricultural leadership. The first, established in District A, had its genesis in a period of hardship in the industry resulting from drought and low commodity prices.

Women attended a forum with a then leading female politician and expressed their concerns for the future of their farms and families. These events coincided with the establishment of a broad State-wide rural women's group, the Queensland Rural Women's Network. (QRWN). Three women from District A attended the QRWN's first conference in 1993 and returned home with the idea of establishing something for women in their area which would be industry focused. Meetings between the women and the CEO of the Farmers' Union district office led to the formal establishment of a network and the election of an Executive. The (male) CEO was a key supporter and champion of the Network, attending all meetings and publicly emphasizing its benefits.

The second network, established in District B, had different origins. It was established when a young female extension officer working for a government organization said she 'wondered where all the women were' when she first started attending industry meetings, and raised the issue with one woman who was a regular attendee. The extension officer then decided to organize a preliminary forum for women in the district to attempt to understand the issues women involved in farming experienced. At the forum, women expressed a reluctance to attend male dominated industry meetings, but a desire to find out more about their business.

Both networks have elected Executive committees which meet every second month. In the intervening months, open meetings are held which typically feature a guest speaker and a question period. Between 40 and 60 women attend most meetings. The very presence of these women challenges one of the commonly held 'truths' about farming women used to rationalize their lack of representation in organizational decision-making. That is the 'truth' that women are not interested in agricultural matters. Another 'truth' challenged by the networks concerns the construction of farming. Since being established, the networks have offered a wide range of education and training programmes on topics relating to personal development, future planning, change management, chemical use, workplace health and safety, stress management, industry leadership and business management. Collectively, this has challenged mainstream and limited discourses about farming as well as provided a space for growth, learning and empowerment. Asked to comment on the benefits of the Network in her district one female Farmers' Union staff member reflected:

> I think the main benefit that I can see is that we've had a group of women that have developed a lot of skills that they didn't have, a confidence they didn't have, an ability to present themselves and put their point of view forward, and as well as generally, had people acquiring knowledge because of different workshops that they've run. Personally, though, I think a lot of them have developed from being shy women who'd sit in the back row to being prepared to get up and speak to strangers, being on the microphone and have a point of view and be prepared to put that point of view across. (Farmers' Union staff member, District A, Interview 4)

The networks have also been sites of resistance in that they have created opportunities for examining and critiquing gender relations in agriculture. Their existence challenges the view that there is nothing problematic about agricultural groups and that both men and women are equally able to participate in industry forums. More directly, speakers at Network forums have questioned women's absence from leadership, the lack of representation of women in industry publications and the negative experiences of women who have attempted to become involved in industry leadership. In this they have provided, like other groups, a forum for 'articulating and stimulating debate on gender issues' (Liepins 1998, 143). Such debates have been rare in many agricultural industries.

This section has been necessarily brief as considerable detailed quality work has already documented the way in which farm women's groups have generated 'counter discourses' (Ramazanoglu 1993) about women, farming and agricultural leadership (for example, Panelli 2002; 2007; Fincher and Panelli 2001). As stated, what has not been examined in the literature is how male farmers and farming managers have responded to these challenges and disruptions. Have they embraced them or have they offered their own discursive counters to farm women's attempts at transformation?

Men's Resistance to the Farm Women's Networks

The discussion of methodology in Chapter 3 highlighted the problem of studying organizational masculinities when they are seldom seen or acknowledged. The fact that this did not seem to be an issue in examining men's responses to the farm women's networks demonstrates that organizational masculinities may become more pronounced or visible in instances where women trespass on previously male domains. This was one of the key findings of an early but still critically important examination of men's resistance to gender equity in organizations, Cynthia Cockburn's (1991) *In the Way of Women: Men's Resistance to Sex Equality in Organizations*. Cockburn's (1991) in-depth case studies of a private sector firm, a government department, a local council and a trade union in the United Kingdom demonstrate how strategies to equalize women's position with men's in the workplace are both covertly and overtly resisted by some men within organizations. She summarizes the case studies saying that men 'sexualize, threaten, marginalize, control and divide women as strategies of active resistance to equity' (Cockburn 1991, 215).

Since Cockburn's (1991) groundbreaking work, a series of other studies has added veracity and further depth to her conclusions. Particularly relevant to this book are those studies of organizational contexts such as the police/military as these, like agri-politics, are strongly infused materially, symbolically and culturally with hegemonic masculinity (see also, Herbert 2001; Woodward and Winter 2006). Women's entry to such contexts may lead to more exaggerated and aggressive forms of resistance. For example, Prokos and Padavic's (2002) analysis of women's entry to the police academy reveals that, in the absence of any legislative barriers to exclude women, some police force men have enacted informal barriers to restrict female entry. The enactment of masculinities which objectify and denigrate women is central to these barriers. Women and feminine subjectivities are positioned by the male trainees and supervisors as 'other', as a 'gendered boundary marker' against their own masculine subjectivities. In much the same way, Agostino (1997, 15) describes how Australian navy men have reacted to women's entry and policies of equal employment opportunity by adopting practices which establish and reinforce 'binaries' between discourses of masculinity and femininity. These collective male practices – which include watching pornographic videos and boasting about sexual exploits – de-centre and marginalize any alternative gender discourses beyond one focused on heterosexuality, power and strength.

In her powerful study about women in educational leadership entitled *Troubling Women*, Jill Blackmore (1999, 136) also focuses on organizational resistance to gender equity, and particularly men's struggles and contestations to retain masculine hegemony in educational workplaces. She labels the discursive practices men use in this process 'discourses of denigration'. In the following sections I take up Blackmore's (1999) terminology as a means of identifying the ways in which men in the Farmers' Union resisted the women's networks. As this discussion will demonstrate, these discourses operated as potent devices to regulate and control the behaviour and actions of farming women.

Discourses of Denigration: Trivializing Women and their Networks

When the networks were first established they had to deal with what one focus group member called 'a lot of teething problems'. One such 'teething problem' she described was being denied resources by the mainstream organization to conduct business. This was magnified by the fact that there was (and still is) no formally established policy on the relationship between the women's networks and the Farmers' Union. For example, one of the network women in District B explained the difficulty they had in attempting to advertise an education and training forum:

> Kay: It sounds petty, but they were supposed to put flyers in the newsletter to advertise the women's forum, but they didn't. They said they got lost or they forgot. They put an ad in the newsletter but it was really small. (District B, Focus Group 2)

Women reported that being denied resources by men was not such a difficulty for them once, as one said, 'we learned to work around it'. For example, Kay explained that following her difficulties in advertising the women's forum using the resources of the Farmers' Union, she subsequently advertised the meetings using local extension staff employed by the government.

Another early difficulty experienced by the networks was being ridiculed by male leaders. The District A group, for example, was called the 'knitwork' rather than referred to as a network by a number of male elected members. In addition, elected members used diminutive terms to describe/talk about the network such as asking women, 'What's your little group up to?' One long term woman member reported running into some Farmers' Union elected leaders as she left an Executive meeting of the Network. One of the leaders asked, much to the amusement of his colleagues, 'Have you women solved all the big industry problems? Can we go home now?' Clearly, the very idea of women attacking issues of magnitude, let alone solving them so that men are organizationally redundant, was comical in the extreme.

Similarly, the network in District B was an object of amusement for many leaders of the Farmers' Union when it was established. The acronym which made up its name (DEFOS) was variously called 'Don't Educate them For Our Sake' and 'Different

Education For Old Sheilas' by these men. The networks were further undermined by men who dismissed them as irrelevant, based on the view that women had nothing to contribute to industry leadership. One woman explained:

> Angela: They figured that, what would a woman know to start with? What good is it going to do? Well, why the bloody hell have it? What good is it going to do? They're not going to do anything for the industry anyway. Basically they thought that it was a waste of time. That was what they said when we first started. (District A, Focus Group 6)

Women reported that male managers had predicted the networks would enjoy only an ephemeral existence due to women's innate inability to focus long term. In similar comments, male managers suggested that women's biologically determined capacity for bitchiness and in-fighting would also see the networks implode sooner rather than later. As one woman explained:

> Josephine: I think there was an attitude of 'do what you want' because it won't last. (District A Focus Group 2)

Data from the focus groups and interviews revealed that this early resistance against the networks – positioning them as inconsequential jokes – has largely been surpassed by different forms of resistance. As one participant from District A commented, 'Things got worse rather than better for us after the first few years'. In both districts, the change in the positioning of the networks was, the women said, tied to money. In 1999, the network in District A held a national conference which attracted more than 300 participants. Their entrepreneurial drive in attracting major sponsors, as well as their thriftiness in using resources gained, meant that they made a substantial profit from the enterprise. While the network did not require significant costs for its operations, there were numerous strategies the Executive wanted to implement to increase women's participation in the industry and these required funding. The women had, they said, always been given a 'good hearing' by the Farmers' Union CEO incumbent at the time, but their windfall meant that they were now relieved of even asking.

District B women pointed to the allocation of funding from an outside research organization as the point of change in their relationship with men from the Farmers' Union. The women involved wanted the network's key role to be offering training and education for women in farming. They were concerned, however, about how they could fund these activities. The ever resourceful female extension officer saw an opportunity when a national rural and agricultural research organization, funded by levies on farmers, advertised a grants programme. Initial attempts to involve the local Farmers' Union in applying for grants were not positive, according to the organizers, who claimed that 'They tried to put us off' and 'Said no, you won't have a ghost of a chance. Don't even bother trying'. Despite this negativity, the network in District B was successful in attaining funding for three years[2] which allowed them to offer sponsorship to local women to attend outside conferences, provide a wide range of training and education programmes and organize annual conferences. Importantly, the

---

2 The research body has allocated two more grants to the District B network since this time.

three year funding provided the network in District B with resources independent of the Farmers' Union. The relationship of dependency between the impoverished women's network and the well resourced district Farmers' Union office was therefore severed. However, the women noted that this loss of paternal power was met with a level of hostility that they had previously not encountered. In one focus group, Executive members of the District B network remembered a senior Farmers' Union staff member commenting that 'You're getting a bit big for your boots aren't you?' after being told of their grant. 'We knew then that they thought we were a threat', one commented.

In the early days of the women's networks the types of 'discourses of denigration' (Blackmore 1999) engaged by managerial men in the Farmers' Union focused on trivializing the networks, their activities and the women involved. This was, of course, overlaid by the managerial masculine discourse of paternalism. The women's groups were infantilized by the fatherly managers of the agricultural organization. This belittling found expression in joke telling and name calling about the women's groups and their agendas. The factor that marked a noticeable change in the relationship between the women's networks and the Farmers' Union was financial independence. The fact that the farm women's groups had needed to ask for money from the managerial men of the Farmers' Union had kept them in their designated place. Having the monopoly on resources meant the male managers could enact what Cockburn (1991, 215) called 'institutional impediments' to equity, such as failing to distribute advertising about women's group meetings. However, once the women's networks had possession of their own resources they could bypass such impediments. It is not surprising to find, then, that after the women's networks had financial independence some male leaders of the Farmers' Union sought to attack them with new and more hostile 'discourses of denigration' (Blackmore 1999) which were much more akin to an authoritarian mode of masculine management.

Discourses of Denigration: Masculinizing Women and their Networks

Blackmore (1999, 136) argues that the 'discourses of denigration' dominant in the educational settings she studied were those directed at 'femininity in general and feminism in particular'. These types of masculinizing discourses were also directed at the network women in Districts A and B. The most prevalent discourse of this type was to attack the femininity of the women involved in the networks, particularly the members of the Executive. This is perhaps logical given that, as discussed in the previous chapters, considerable masculine energy has been dedicated to conflating masculinity and agricultural leadership.

Network women's lack of femininity was conveyed through derisive name calling. These names positioned the network women as the very embodiment of masculinity. That is, as 'having balls', being 'ball busters', 'those women in pants' or simply 'men'. What Bartky (1990, 74) calls the 'disciplinary power' of such a discourse – which 'inscribes femininity on the female body' – was not just felt by women in the network Executive, but by all women associated with the industry in the district, as the following demonstrates:

> Jessica: What worries me about women getting into these roles is you don't want to lose your femininity. You don't want to be known as someone with balls. I hate that saying. You've got to keep your feminine side, but you've also got to show that you can be smart and clever.
>
> Interviewer: How would you lose your femininity?
>
> Jessica: Being cast as one of the blokes.
>
> Leanne: She should have been a bloke, the men say.
>
> Libby: What Leanne said has already gone around town about the DEFOS women. That some of the ladies should have balls. (District B, Focus Group 4)

This discussion highlights three important factors about resistance, gender and subjectivities. The first relates to Jessica's comment on the importance of industry knowledge for elected leadership which she views as being somewhat incongruent with femininity. There is a tension between being both smart and feminine. Clearly, it is not appropriate to be *too* clever or *too* knowledgeable as you are labelled as masculine, but then it is important to be clever and knowledgeable to be taken seriously. I heard this type of ambivalence many times as women appeared to struggle with the 'tension, fragmentation and discord' of constructing new gendered subject positions (Knights and Vurdubakis 1994, 185). The second factor is that in this discussion it is men who define what is masculine and feminine. It is the men who say that involving oneself in the Farmers' Union is a masculine activity, as is participating in industry based networks or speaking out about industry issues. The third crucial point to be drawn from this discussion is the way in which women fear being named as masculine. This stigmatizing of women network members as 'unfeminine' is therefore a powerful tool men can use against women to limit their involvement in industry politics or participation in other forums. This was clearly demonstrated as the women continued the discussion. One woman, Libby, who had attended network meetings in District B, was saying how distressed she was to hear such vitriolic comments about the Executive women when they were such 'nice ladies'. I consequently asked if the women if they thought such comments would influence other women's attendance. They replied:

> Interviewer: Do you think the comments would stop other women from being involved?
>
> Jessica: I think they would because my husband has heard it. If the husbands have heard it they will say to the wife, 'Don't go. That's not a good reputation' or something like that.
>
> Leanne: My husband actually heard it and he's on his tractor all the time. He said that all those women are classed as men.
>
> Jessica: That's what my husband said. He heard that all these women that go are men. He said, 'Why do you want to go to something like that?' and I said to him, 'If you think like that you've got a narrow mind.' I can say that to my husband, but if you're an older woman and you said that to your husband you would be downtrodden. (District B, Focus Group 4)

The above extract provides an important understanding of how hegemonic gender identities are discursively reproduced within the rural community of District B. So strong is the alignment between men/masculinities and the Farmers' Union that women's mere presence at meetings of the organization means that they are named 'men'. Women who deviate from the dominant definition and role prescription of femininity – by trespassing on the domain of men – are censured and labelled as having 'a reputation'. It is irrelevant that they may be, according to Libby, 'nice ladies'. The women are aware that reputations are so powerfully conveyed that Leanne's husband did not even have to leave his tractor to hear what was being said. Husbands preserve their wives' 'reputations' by dissuading them from becoming involved in the group.

In attempting to undermine the feminine subjectivities of network women and to masculinize them, Farmers' Union leaders referred to them as 'feminists'. For many this may not be a pejorative label. Indeed, rural studies scholars have posited that the women's networks could be classified 'feminist' given that the agenda of many of these new farm women's groups is to raise women's visibility and increase women's participation in decision-making (Brandth and Haugen 1997; Shortall 1994; 1999). However, these groups have not been easily classifiable, particularly given the difficult path farm women walk as they negotiate a desire for what can been seen as explicitly feminist goals within the context of conservative agrarian culture. None of the women involved in the networks ever described themselves to me as feminists. Further, on different occasions in focus groups when the terms feminists or feminism were raised a general sense of negativity was expressed (see Pini 2002a; 2003a; 2004d).

The discourse of 'feminists/feminism' engaged by the Farmers' Union leaders mobilized around notions of authoritarianism, oppression, extremism and separatism. Elected leaders referred to the women network Executives as 'bra-burners', 'man-haters' and 'rough and angry'. This is a discourse that is implicated in wider public and popular discourses which condemn feminism and is therefore one that is readily available as well as powerful (Gough and Peace 2000; Riley 2001). One woman explained why the men she knew were critical of the network in her area:

> Greer: The perception is out there that they are a bunch of radicals trying to blow men up, thinking they can live without men…that they want to do everything separately and not work as a team. (District B, Focus Group 3)

As a means of containing the women's networks, the Farmers' Union leaders drew on the discourses of paternalism as women involved were accused of not working for the collective good – as 'a team'. As Collinson and Hearn (1994) note, the claim to power as a means of achieving the best for all is the proverbial clarion call of paternalism. The elected members' notion of 'team' is likely to be tied to discourses of paternalism so that it connotes a docile constituency following instructions from a few leading figures.

Also embedded in Greer's statement is a further dimension of the farming leaders' 'discourses of denigration' (Blackmore 1999) about the network women. That is, that they are dangerous and power-hungry. This discourse of pathologizing women is discussed in more detail below.

**Table 6.1	Farmers' Union leaders' discourses of denigration**

Discourse of denigration directed at the women's networks	Representations of women/the women's networks contained within this discourse
Trivializing	Unimportant/inconsequential Short-lived/transitory Comical
Masculinizing	Confrontational/aggressive Man hating/separatist Radical Angry/rough
Pathologizing	Dangerous/threatening Abnormal/unnatural Power-hungry/self-serving/untrustworthy Taking over
Sexualizing	Unattractive/unwanted by heterosexual men Sexually frustrated/unsatisfied

Discourses of Denigration: Pathologizing Women and their Networks

Another of the defensive responses the male agricultural leaders enlisted as a means of marginalizing the women's networks and reinscribing their patriarchal privilege within the Farmers' Union was to pathologize the women involved. At its most fundamental, this discourse asserted that because it was 'normal' for women *not* to be interested in agricultural politics, those that were must be 'abnormal'. Women involved in the networks were seen to be different and deviant. This point was made on numerous occasions as elected members of the Farmers' Union pointed out to me that, compared with the total number of women in Districts A and B, only a relatively small proportion were involved in the networks. Their point was that because 'most' women (including in all instances their wives) were 'not interested', those who were represented an aberrant category.

Another trajectory of the pathologizing discourse was one which suggested that women wanted to usurp men's roles on the farms and ultimately their positions in the Farmers' Union. This theme was similarly evident as another woman explained the reaction she had from a male relative who questioned her involvement in the network:

Emily: One said to me, 'What do you want to do, get on the tractors and take over our jobs?'. That was said to me, and I said, 'No. We just want to learn about the industry and help you with your job.' I think in this area a lot of men just want to protect their women.

Interviewer: How do they see that as protecting their women?

Emily: Not to rough them, look after them in general. That the physical type of work is a man's job and the women shouldn't have to get their hands dirty. (District B, Focus Group 7)

The gendered connection between the identities of 'farmer' and 'agri-political' leader are clearly demonstrated in this extract in the way Emily's relative conflates her involvement in the network with an on-farm physical role. She may have been working to recreate a new gendered identity around her involvement in agri-politics, but she is told that no such identity exists as the masculine territory is marked out by the possessive pronoun 'ours'. The jobs on tractors are 'ours' according to the men. Emily is acutely aware of this, saying that the goals of the women's network would be to help but the jobs remain those of men. In Emily's discursive construction, men have proprietorial rights not just over particular machine based jobs but also over 'their' women. The paternalistic discourse of 'protection' is positioned as being in the best interests of women. Thus, women are being 'looked after' when they are discouraged from, or disallowed to, participate in on-farm physical work or industry politics. The dirty and rough roles undertaken in these spheres are deemed inappropriate for women.

In reality, few of the women to whom I spoke expressed a desire to be involved in formal positions of leadership in their networks, or in the parlance of the Farmers' Union men, to 'take-over'. In general, their aspirations were limited to wanting to understand and learn about the industry. One commented that, 'I don't think I've ever wanted to be a leader. I just wanted to know that if something happened to my husband that I could cope', while another said, 'I don't want to be King Pin or President or anything like that. I just want to be able to be involved'. This was in contrast to Farmers' Union men who constantly referred to women having usurpatory motives. Indeed, this was sometimes presented as women having already 'taken-over' as the following quotation indicates:

> The network women have stepped on a few toes and upset people. Given the impression that they're trying to muscle in. There is still the perception that they're getting carried away and trying to muscle in through the back door. Some of them have been pretty prominent in general meetings and in the press lately. They had a lot to say about the new industry legislation. They've used the media and public meetings to question some of our decisions and it makes people worried that women are taking over. (Elected member, Interview 13)

The claim that there is anxiety that women are 'taking over' is extraordinary given that, at the time of the interview, there was still not a single woman leader amongst the 181 elected members of the Farmers' Union. It is however, an illustration of what Nirmal Puwar (2004) identifies as 'amplification' which is, she claims, a common response to the entry of women and minorities to spaces where they have previously been unknown. While Puwar's (2004, 49) focus is Westminster, her critique of how white men respond to 'bodies out of place' through exaggerating the numbers of women/minorities present is illuminating. She begins her discussion by establishing the way in which certain public spaces have been traditionally reserved for specific bodies, but that this claim to space has been largely masked and unstated. She then explains that, in very recent years, new bodies – those of women and minorities – have begun to enter spaces previously designated for only elite groups of white males. The new bodies are, as the title of her book suggests, *Space Invaders* (2004), and when they are encountered by those bodies that have been the traditional incumbents of powerful spaces they face considerable resistance. Amplification – a process of exaggerating the presence of women/minorities so that they are constructed as an organizational threat – is one way in which dissonant bodies have been constructed by those that have been normalized as the rightful inhabitants of certain occupational spaces.

Puwar's (2004) evocative reading of the bodies of women/minorities as dissonant in public spaces resonates strongly with the reaction of the Farmers' Union men to the women's networks. It is interesting to note the prevalence of bodily metaphors in the above quotation from the leader of the Farmers' Union. Women's bodies are everywhere and they are relentless. They are muscling in, stepping on toes, saying too much, questioning, coming in back doors and upsetting people. Moreover, women's bodies are not just pervasive within the Farmers' Union but also prominent in the media. One can hear the 'shock and surprise' and the 'disorientation and terror' in this elected member's response, that are, as Puwar (2004, 55) notes, common reactions to the 'arrival of women and racialized minorities in privileged occupational spaces'. Men's proprietorial rights over the agenda, processes and activities of the organization are clearly marked by the elected member as 'ours'. However, women's presence – however small – threatens this claim and the numbers of women are suddenly amplified so that the elected leader is talking about 'take overs'.

A final way in which the network women were pathologized was by presenting them as devious and dangerous. Those women involved were considered to be pushing their own interests for individual gain to the detriment of the industry as a whole. One woman (whose husband was a Farmers' Union leader) articulated this position in explaining her negative reaction to the women's network in her local area:

> Fiona: I question the motives for the network as having a hidden agenda for their own political life. I am interested in working collectively not in pushing your own barrow. (District B, Focus Group 5)

Farmers' Union leaders used a vocabulary of terms such as 'ratty', 'radical', 'manipulative', 'negative', 'there for the glory' and 'damaging' as a means of pathologizing the women's networks and their membership. This discourse, of course, was strongly connected to discourses condemning the women's alleged lack of femininity.

Discourses of Denigration: Sexualizing Women and their Networks

In the previous chapter, I emphasized the way in which discourses of sexuality were utilized by the Farmers' Union elected members as a means of constructing and consolidating a collective identity and also as a means of excluding women. Deploying discourses of sexuality was also a strategy to control and contain the women's networks. It is difficult to separate these discourses from other discursive strategies such as those which pathologized and masculinized women, as a (hetero)sexist undercurrent ran through most derogatory statements made about the women's networks. That is, the women involved are sexually unattractive to men. Men would not want to be seen with or be with network women who were depicted as far removed from normative definitions of heterosexual femininity.

Thus, asked about one of the network women who had stood for election, a Farmers' Union leader replied laughing, 'I don't have a problem with Doris... Wouldn't want to be married to her though.' Women in the networks claimed such comments were common. A young female Farmers' Union secretary confirmed that, much to her discomfort, it was customary for similar remarks to be made at the all-male meetings of the Farmers' Union district Executive when the women's network was discussed. In writing the minutes of meetings she was specifically instructed by the Chairman not to record any disparaging remarks made about the women's group members.

Women network members were also sexualized by elected members who suggested that their political activism was a response to sexual frustration. One network woman, for example, described the reaction she had received about her involvement from a male relative who was also a Farmers' Union leader. This interaction occurred at a large family gathering:

> Rosa: He said, 'What have you been deprived of at home?' I said, 'My husband hasn't deprived me of anything.' And he said, 'Well, why get involved with it?' (District B, Focus Group 5)

This discourse which suggests women's channelling of their energies into the public sphere/politics/leadership/work is inappropriate/unnatural and therefore representative of sexual frustration is one that has often been directed at powerful women (DiTomaso 1989). Here, the male elected member exerts power by making Rosa's sexuality not just a problematic matter, but also a public matter.

Farm Women's Networks: Responding to the Discourses of Denigration

The impact of the Farmers' Union men's trivializing, masculinizing, pathologizing and sexualizing of the network women was well summed up by what one elected member called the 'campaign to slow down the women's group'. I asked him to explain what he meant and he responded:

> Oh, slow down well...you just don't recognize them, you discredit them to a large extent. Farmers talk around the place and you just don't help and pass on information. You can do all sorts of things if you want to discredit a group and when you're in a position like this, there's probably lots of things you could do that could make them a bit weak. (Elected member, Interview 10)

What is clear from this extract is that those male farmers and agricultural leaders who actively mobilized discourses against the women's networks did so with an understanding of their discursive power and the impact of this power on women's participation in the groups. Women networks members were equally aware of the regulatory power of the 'discourses of denigration' (Blackmore 1999) mobilized against them. They consequently sought numerous means of countering the men's discursive framing of them as trivial, masculine, pathological and sexual.

The key strategy the network women utilized to counter the men's disparaging construction of them was to highlight their commitment to the sustainability of family farming. This repertoire focused on threats to family farming and positioned the women's networks as integral to the battle for an agricultural future. In this battle very traditional (and paternalistic) notions of woman as helper/supporter to men were deployed. Women network members distanced themselves from feminist labels, expressing the view that they would not be involved in anything that was branded as such. They expressed similar sentiments about discourses which attempted to position them as 'taking over', again emphasizing their desire to work alongside men rather than in opposition to men. One stated:

> Cynthia: I'm all for the women's network, not from any bra burning aspect...I would be the first one to pull out if it was them and us. As far as I am concerned we're just another branch. We're the women's side. With the men working together. It should be a united thing for all the community. We should be all working together because we're all the same thing, aren't we? (District B, Focus Group 5)

Another, in a later focus group expressed a similar sentiment:

> Nicole: We've got to get that message through that we aren't against the men. We only want to learn and support them. And helping them, helping ourselves, helping our family, helping our community. (District B, Focus Group 7)

Both Cynthia and Nicole's comments are illustrative of how the network women attempted to position themselves and their groups. They de-emphasized women's lack of decision-making power in the Farmers' Union and the associated intent of the networks to foster women's involvement in mainstream farming leadership. In contrast, they accentuated their desire to work for the benefit of the industry as a whole and to assist husbands, family and the broader community. In this respect they spoke to what are very widely held beliefs and assumptions in rural locales which suggest that farm women should forego their own interests for the betterment and harmony of their families, farms and communities (Little 1987; Poiner 1990). By positioning their networks within well-established and accepted discourses about 'farm women' and 'family farming', the women involved in the networks sought to foster legitimacy for their groups. This is an approach Brandth and Haugen (1998, 342) note has been adopted by the Norwegian Society for Rural Women. They explain that the group has chosen a line of co-operation rather than confrontation with men, emphasizing the need to recognize farm women in order to meet common goals such as 'protection of the family unit, tradition, culture and a living rural community' (see also Carbert 1995, 29).

In seeking to exploit discourses about 'family farming' to promote the women's networks, prominence was given to the education and training aims of the groups. It was through knowledge that women were going to be best placed to assist and help in the struggle to survive on family farms. The language of partnerships, collaboration, and co-operation was constantly highlighted. The fact that these were networks first established for 'women' because men dominated leadership in the Farmers' Union was repeatedly played down. Indeed, the word 'women' does not even appear in the network names, while promotional material for meetings was directed at 'men and women in the industry' rather than women alone. On many occasions, network women attempted to present themselves as gender neutral and/or minimize the importance of the gendered nature of the networks as the following quotation from a network Executive member demonstrates:

Kim: We want to improve women's knowledge, understanding, skills and self-confidence through organized education programs at a local level. In doing this we have been accused of being radical feminists, who want to take over, but there is nothing further from the truth. We are just farmers who happen to be women. (District B, Focus Group 8)

Attempts to de-gender the networks appear nonsensical and contradictory given that we are talking about 'women's networks', but demonstrate the women's continued strategic attempts to rework the derogatory discourses that had been used against the groups.

Conclusion

The question of agency has been a problematic one in much feminist post-structural writing (for example, Davies 1997; Jones 1997; The London Feminist Salon Collective 2004). Butler (1990), like other proponents of feminist poststructuralism, has been simultaneously accused of conceptualizing agency/subjectivity in an overly voluntaristic manner and an overly deterministic manner (Barvosa-Carter 2005). However, in this chapter we have seen both the repressive and the liberating possibilities of discourse (Barrett 1991; Bordo 1988). Women within the Farmers' Union have utilized the spaces provided by the formation of networks to articulate discourses of farming, agriculture and leadership which have opened up a range of new subject positions. They have, as a consequence, unsettled the assumption that the identity of 'farmer' is unquestionably male by asserting that there is nothing dissonant in being both a 'woman' and 'farmer'. They have, as well, created room for feminine subjectivities within agri-politics, through practices such as engaging women in education and training programmes and encouraging women to attend industry meetings

This is not to suggest, however, that the farm women have been free to choose any identity off the shelf unencumbered by the norms, assumptions and practices which 'work, animate and constrain the gendered subject' (Butler 1993, 22). Further, the 'new' identities being articulated by farming women are fragile and contingent in light of men's discursive resistance against them, and in terms of the asymmetrical power relations through which they are deployed and circulated. In terms of discursive resistance, men have utilized four key 'discourses of denigration' against the women's networks (Blackmore 1999). These are summarized in Table 6.1 as trivializing women, masculinizing women, pathologizing women and sexualizing women. Men's access to extensive resources within the Farmers' Union as well as their 75 year claim to power in the organization have provided them with considerable means of circulating these derogatory discourses.

Men's engagement of such negative discourses about the networks has not simply been directed at censuring women. Their discursive task has been much broader than this as they have also been attempting to re-gender the terrain on which farming women have trespassed. What we see is reminiscent of Burton's (1991) phrase 'masculinity protection strategies'. As Agostino (1997) and Prokos and Padavic (2002) have demonstrated, these strategies work to recuperate masculinities when they are threatened by women's presence. In a more recent theorization of how men 'do masculinity' in organizations, Martin (2001, 588) coins the term 'mobilizing masculinities' to describe 'practices, wherein two or more men concertedly bring to bear, or bring into play, masculinity/ies'. While Martin's (2001) interest is in men's collective behaviour at work which does not intend harm to women, what we have seen in the Farmers' Union is quite different. In this context, male agricultural leaders knowingly and deliberately 'mobilized masculinities' to re-masculinize the identity of the agricultural manager as well as the space of agricultural politics.

In turn, women involved in the networks, have, as agentic subjects, resisted the men's mobilization of masculinities and the derogatory discourses directed at them. In doing so they have drawn on very conservative gender discourses which emphasize their identities as 'wives', 'mothers' and 'members of farming families'. They have positioned themselves as wanting to help and work co-operatively and in partnership to assist their husbands and communities. The 'new' agricultural identity they are attempting to construct is thus closely grounded in some of the paternalistic discourses of the Farmers' Union leaders. While this seems at odds with what could be described as the more 'feminist' goals of the networks, it is a framing that has been commonly used by rural and farm women's groups attempting to traverse a very difficult discursive path. However, even when network women have located themselves within submissive and subordinate positions as 'helpers' or 'learners', Farmers' Union managers have not desisted from denigrating them. Indeed, even discourses where women say they simply want to 'support' men are viewed with a high level of suspicion and animosity. It therefore seems highly likely that there will be much further discursive contestation between the Farmers' Union and the women's networks.

Given the level of resistance that has been directed at the women's networks, one wonders what life is like for those few women who have actually achieved positions of leadership in agricultural organizations. This question is addressed in the following chapter.

Chapter 7

The Third Sex: Women and Masculinities in Agricultural Management

This book has established that hegemonic masculinities are central to how the identity of agri-political manager is defined and how agricultural management is deployed, as well as demonstrated the concurrent marginal position of feminine subjectivities in these processes. What then of women who are agricultural leaders – those who make up the 13 per cent (or less)[1] of elected leaders within Australian farming unions (DoTARS 2005)? What are their organizational experiences in an environment where managerial constructions and processes are so strongly masculinized?

In endeavouring to address these questions, I am, as I have been throughout this book, particularly guided by the work of Liepins (1998; 2000) and Brandth and Haugen (2000). In seeking to extend those earlier studies of gendered agricultural subjectivities, I ask: How do women in mainstream agricultural organizations construct and negotiate their identities? Liepins (1998; 2000) provides a useful launching pad for addressing this question in her analysis of gendered farming media and organizational discourses in New Zealand and Australia. For example, she identifies the emergence of a new feminine subject position in agri-politics, that of the 'alternative agricultural activist' (Liepins 1998, 376). This new subjectivity is said to repudiate a leadership style of aggression and control in favour of one that is communicative and nurturing. This was a subject position Liepins (1998) found being made available in the types of farm women's groups discussed in the previous chapter. Is it possible that now we are seeing this identity emerge within mainstream farming groups? That despite the dominance of hegemonic masculinities within farming unions, women are engaging new and different ways of managing that are focused on inclusiveness and communication rather than exclusivity and confrontation? In contrast, perhaps things are as they were a decade ago when Liepins (1998, 384) noted that the only discourses of femininity in farming organizations were those of 'industry-based femininity' and 'woman as masculine'. Are the women still being restricted to decision-making tasks and roles associated with normative definitions

---

1 Even this low figure may overstate the actual situation. There are three reasons for this. Firstly, it is common for women to be members of several boards. Secondly, in some areas of decision-making women's participation is actually decreasing. This is the case for the number of women chairs on Commonwealth boards and as board participants in Landcare panels. Finally, in some sectors and states women's representation is extremely low. In the Northern Territory, for example, women hold just 8.5 per cent of leadership positions in agriculture while in the Australian sugar industry only two of the 181 positions of leadership are held by women (1.1 per cent).

of femininity, while male leaders are afforded the right to take on a much broader agenda? Alternatively, is there evidence that women farming leaders are doing 'woman as masculine', performing the hegemonic masculinity of the managerial farming men? If so, are these pioneer woman leaders comfortable with this discourse or are they struggling with an identity that situates them as akin to men?

In order to address these many questions, this chapter draws on data from interviews with 20 women agricultural leaders. As stated previously, at the time of my study there were no women elected leaders and just one woman manager on staff at the Farmers' Union. Thus, to understand what it may mean to be a woman leader in agriculture I sought participants from other agricultural organizations. Before the exploration of the women's stories begins, the following section provides some brief background information on these 20 women.

Interviewing Women Agricultural Managers

Data for this chapter are drawn from 20 one-hour interviews with Australian women on the boards of agriculture and producer groups. The method was particularly appropriate to the task of the study – that is, to gain insight into and knowledge about women leaders' own experiences of agricultural leadership and interpretations of these experiences (Kvale 1996).

The interviews were semi-structured in line with what Mason (2002, 67) calls a 'conversation with a purpose'. A list of general themes and questions to be covered was prepared, allowing sufficient flexibility in the approach for participants to elaborate on particular points. To elicit descriptive detail, a range of questions about being a board member was asked, such as the types and usefulness of training women had received, whether they had a leadership mentor and what previous leadership roles they had undertaken. Women were also asked what advice they would give to aspiring women leaders in agriculture and why they believed women were an under-represented group in farming leadership.

Interview participants were selected across a range of industries and types of agricultural boards. To assist with selection, I used three key informants. All were personally known to the participants and gave me permission to use their names in approaching possible interviewees.

The 20 women interviewed were all on state, national and in one case, international, agricultural boards. The boards differed in terms of type of industry (for example, poultry, dairy, organics, sugar, seafood and horticulture) as well as function (for example, marketing, research, agri-political). Just four of the 20 women were on only one board with the remainder serving on two to three boards. The exception was a participant who sat on five boards. The length of time served on a board varied from six months to 12 years. All participants were, or had at some time been, on an agricultural board where they were the only woman. Further, 60 per cent reported being the only woman ever elected or appointed to positions in board histories which dated back for periods of over a century.

Of the 20 women interviewed, only one had bought into agriculture with her husband after marriage, one was single and employed by a state government department of agriculture, and the other 18 lived and worked on the farms their partners had operated before their marriage. These agricultural enterprises were located across rural and regional Australia, some in very remote areas. As a consequence, it was not uncommon for women to have to travel enormous distances to attend board meetings.

Agricultural boards in Australia are not just dominated by men but by a particular group of men, namely white Anglo-Saxon property-owning older men. While similar in the first two respects to these men, the 20 women agricultural leaders interviewed were relatively young. Four of the women interviewed were younger than 40, the youngest was 32. A further group of 12 was aged between 40 and 50 while the remaining four were over 50. Only two of the women had no children.

Like the broader population of farming women from which this group of participants was drawn, the women interviewed were well educated (Gooday 1995). Sixteen of the women had tertiary qualifications in areas such as agricultural science, engineering, teaching, law, accountancy and marketing. Some had completed post-graduate studies and one a doctorate. In addition to this education, all but two had undertaken courses in leadership and/or in corporate governance.

The majority of women interviewed had become board members by appointment rather than by election. This is not surprising given that, as Chapter 4 explained, Farmers' Unions typically allow only one vote per farm. This patriarchal practice severely disadvantages women because it is typically the senior male who votes in elections.

Woman and Agricultural Manager: Competing Discourses

Martin (2003) writes that gender is, in a number of respects, like riding a bicycle, not least because it is something that we often do automatically and with a limited degree of reflexivity. What is of particular interest in terms of respondents to this study is that for them, becoming an agricultural leader meant that they were suddenly aware of riding this gender bicycle, which entailed (re)learning a masculine practice. There was no sense of the ordinary or the familiar. Instead, they felt awkward and concerned as to their ability to negotiate all the moves competently. Respondents referred to the fact that in the past they had 'not been into gender', 'had little time for gender' or 'weren't into things about men and women'. For the majority, their board appointment had changed this. The heightened gender consciousness appeared to result from constant reminders and/or references to their feminine status. As this book has demonstrated (see also Liepins 1998; 2000; Brandth and Haugen 2000), there is compatibility and coherence between constructions of masculinity and leadership in agricultural organizations, but no such corresponding congruence between constructions of femininity and leadership. Gender is consequently of great salience for women in leadership in farming unions.

For women with young children, their differential gendered position was most significantly emphasized in terms of responsibilities for domestic work and childcare. While a leader is assumed to be free of domestic and childcare responsibilities, women board members with families were responsible for organizing what would occur in terms of childcare in their absence, as well as for undertaking the majority of household and domestic work when they were present on their farms. There was a range of illustrations by which women had learned that their male counterparts were advantageously positioned in terms of this work (Eveline 1994). These included having meetings called at short notice, meetings being held over a week-long period rather than for shorter times and meetings being held late into the evenings. This point of difference between men and women was made explicitly in one interaction described by a participant:

> Sacha: I was at a board meeting in June and I said it was a bit of a scramble getting away this time. It was the end of the week and we were drought feeding and the kids had sports most days. I just stuck all my clothes in a bag un-ironed and one of the guys on the board said, 'Look, my wife does all that. She puts all my things out on the bed and I just pick what I'm taking away'. (Interview 4)

Even when women organized their domestic responsibilities so that they did not intrude on their position as leader, thus emulating the masculine notion of manager as someone unencumbered by family duties, other aspects of their difference from the male board members was given emphasis. One participant, for example, described how the simple task of greeting became something which marked her as the exception:

> Lucy: They didn't know what to do with me, how to greet me. They'd walk in, shake hands with each other and then just stop at me. I said one day, 'If you guys don't start shaking my hand I'm going to give you all a big kiss'. (Interview 5)

Lucy's claims echo Puwar's (2004) work on bodies out of place introduced in the previous chapter. Here we see the confusion, chaos and discord that are generated by the entry of women's bodies into male dominated spaces. Men's bodies are unmarked, normal, known and understood because they belong in the spaces of agricultural organizations. Women's do not. The very ordinary and everyday task of simply greeting another board member is thus turned into something complex and fraught because of Lucy's bodily difference from the men. Like so many of the other women I interviewed, she took responsibility for alleviating the men's discomfort but in a manner which demonstrated considerable humour and resistance. In her joking threat to kiss the men, she names and exposes the men's fear of the dangers of her femininity/sexuality and asserts her right for her body to be treated as any other body.

There were a number of other ways in which men gave prominence to women's difference from them. One was by asking women members to speak for and about all women. It was common, one respondent said, for her to be brought into a discussion with comments such as 'Would the girls go for that?'. The shift from 'token' status and the sharp relief this brought was noted by one participant:

> Imogen: There's a distinct difference when you go from one to three (women). The culture changes. The focus on women, as representing more of womankind changes. A woman is allowed to be there on her own individual expertise. Not, 'She has a bad day, it reflects all of womankind', but 'She has a good day, it is a reflection on her abilities'. (Interview 14)

This problem of being the 'token women' as a woman manager, always seen to be representative of all women as well as able to speak for all women is not a new one for managerial women (Kanter 1977). However, for the women managers in farming groups it constantly highlighted their identity as 'woman' while men were simply allowed to be 'managers'. No-one, of course, ever questioned men as men. They were always simply managers.

Another way of accentuating women's difference was for men to apologize for swearing or for any lewd remark made in a woman's presence. Alternatively, men would comment – in the presence of the woman board member – that behaviour and speech would have to change with female entry into agri-politics. Collectively, in these situations men highlighted not just women's difference from them as men, but women's difference from them as leaders. It was a difference one woman described as being a member of the 'third sex':

> Ruby: You are not male because you're not one of the blokes and you are not a woman because you're not doing kitchen things and you're talking about industry stuff not painting the house. You're identified as another group. The third sex. (Interview 6)

The metaphor of being androgynous was a recurring theme in the interviews. Women suggested that they were not just different from their male counterparts, but also from other women. The following sections describe the strategies used by agricultural women leaders to perform as a member of 'the third sex'.

Gender Management Strategies

In the literature on gender and organizations, writers have struggled to render tangible the tensions of being both 'manager' and 'woman'. They have subsequently turned to metaphors such as 'travellers' (Marshall 1984; 1995), 'pioneers' (Gherardi 1995), 'intruders' (Gherardi 1996), the 'homeless' (Kvande 1999) and 'the other' (Gherardi and Poggio 2001) as a means of explanation. The choice of figurative language engaged by writers is indicative of the uneasy fit between socially constructed notions of what it means to be a 'woman' and a 'manager'.

As metaphorical outsiders and itinerants, women in management engage in strategies to circumvent the masculine embodiment of leadership and secure and legitimate their position. Sheppard (1989, 144) labels these 'strategies of managing gender', in that they require women to redefine and rework masculinity and femininity. Sheppard (1989) makes two critical points about gender management strategies. The first is that it is women, not men, who have to manage their gender. The male body and masculinity are unproblematic, but the female body and femininity must be accommodated and adapted. As Kvande (1999, 306) revealed in examining women's entry into the engineering profession, it is women who have to modify or relinquish their 'gender status'. Second, gender management is highly risky. Sheppard (1989) explains that women are highly vulnerable because their under-representation leads to higher visibility and because at any time men may give prominence to a woman's femininity or her sexuality. Barrett (2002, 171) concurs in summing up his work on women's experiences as members of the US navy. He has written that managing gender is fraught for women given that they do not have 'the same freedom to manoeuvre, the same access to informal socialization, the same opportunity to make mistakes and until recently, the same access to prestigious jobs'. Despite this precariousness, Sheppard (1989, 144) reported that what unified the accounts of the 34 woman managers in her study was their 'reference to strategies of gender management'. Two key strategies are highlighted as existing on a continuum. At one end, she says, are blending in strategies whereby women managers seek to minimize their sexuality/femininity and conform to the prevailing workplace orthodoxies. At the other end are strategies which Sheppard (1989, 146) labels 'claiming a rightful place'. Women who utilize 'claiming a rightful place' strategies do not seek to make accommodations for their sexuality/gender. Instead, these women challenge and critique male organizational dominance and masculine modes of managing.

Sheppard (1989) qualifies her categorization, emphasizing that she did not aim to provide an exhaustive list of 'gender management strategies', and suggests that researchers are likely to find diversity in stories of managing gender as they talk to different participants from various organizational settings. However, as scholars have continued to study the complex identity work involved in being a 'woman' and 'manager', they have found Sheppard's (1989) typology to be robust and relevant (for example, Blackmore 1999; Sinclair 1998; Wajcman 1999).

In light of the continued weight of Sheppard's (1989) observations, I want to apply her discussion of 'gender management strategies' to the experiences of women managers in agriculture. I first examine those strategies that could be grouped around the far end of the continuum – that is, blending in strategies. However, I break this up into two different categories as it seemed to me that blending in had two quite different components. The first group of blending in strategies comprise those that aim to neutralize one's femininity/sexuality, while the second aim to highlight one's masculine credentials. Thus, I suggest that 'blending in' (Sheppard 1989) for women managers is a two-fold process which requires simultaneous assertion and subjugation of gender. The view of women managers who adopted the blending in strategies was that the agri-political environment is a male environment and women simply had to learn to fit in. If women could not, they should not be there (see also, Eveline and Booth 2002, 570).

From blending in strategies, I move to examine the women agricultural managers' experiences of 'claiming a rightful place' (Sheppard 1989). While these latter strategies were less common, the particular stories of two women who have challenged the status quo illuminate and reinforce the key themes of this book. That is, agricultural organizations are 'men's organizations' (Shortall 1999, 96) because they are infused with hegemonic masculinities which facilitate men's participation in leadership and render problematic the participation of women.

Blending In: Women in Agricultural Management Minimizing Femininity

Like Sheppard (1989), I found the most common of the 'gender management strategies' used by women leaders were those that aimed to neutralize their femininity and sexuality. A key site for achieving this aim was through self-surveillance of the body (Bartky 1990). This is problematic, of course, given that women are seen to have a particularly embodied status – messy bodies, leaking bodies, irrational bodies and bodies of desire. As Bordo (1993, 6) writes, 'Frequently even when women are silent their bodies are seen as "speaking" a language of provocation'. As a means of quietening this forever noisy body, women agricultural managers gave particular attention to dress. One woman described her wardrobe as being in compartments which were representative of different identities she inhabited – as farmer, member of an aristocratic wool growing family, mothers' club participant and board member. The dark blue and black suits that were the uniform of her latter role were important in concealing her femininity. Typically women expressed this in terms of being 'professional', as Lydia does in the quotation below:

> Lydia: When I'm in any kind of professional role I always try to be as professional as I can…I know I probably consciously wear a professional kind of uniform – a traditional suit and stuff like that because I just think it stops people – they focus on what you're saying and not what you're wearing. (Interview 17)

Dressing like 'a professional' for Lydia and many other women meant masking the female body, for the female body does not signify a managerial body, nor one of command, authority and power (Brewis and Sinclair 2000). Again, like Lydia, women were adamant that dress was critical if you wanted to be 'taken seriously' and 'treated equally'. Thus, when they described the efforts to dress in the particular way outlined by Lydia in the quotation above, they did so by locating themselves within discourses of professionalism. This was therefore not, in their representation, about disguising/ obfuscating their femininity, but about 'being professional' (Barrett 2002).

Like other women leaders described (for example, Sinclair 1998), the farm women leaders had to decouple their leadership and sexual identities, and thus present themselves, while visible in their leadership role, as devoid of sexuality. Again, this is not a straight-forward task given that, as Halford and Leonard (2001, 157) remark, 'Sexuality is something that women have to bring into the public realm, it is not something they can choose to leave at home'. Further, as the authors note, this is not just any old sexuality but a specific form: 'A jolly, cheerful sort of heterosexuality which hints at constant availability' (Halford and Leonard 2001, 157). Farmers' Union male leaders often called upon this very narrow construction of female sexuality in their interactions with board counterparts. As we saw in earlier chapters, this was not just a regulatory technique directed at women leaders, but also a means of enacting and consolidating the male managers' collective heterosexual identities. Typically, these efforts would be shrouded in terms of 'humour' or 'jokes'. One participant with an obviously keen sense of humour and vivacious personality explained what this meant for her:

> Sally-Anne: I am always careful when one of the boys tells a joke and it's a bit rough. You know, maybe they get a bit bawdy. I never laugh. Even if I go home and tell my husband and have a good laugh, I wouldn't at the time because you set the tone and if you want their respect you have to do that. (Interview 2)

The question of monitoring and repudiating one's sexuality was particularly acute for the women leaders when they discussed interacting with male colleagues outside the boardroom. Most board meetings are held in capital cities over a period of days. It is common practice for members, accommodated at the same hotel, to meet at the end of the day for drinks and/or a meal. In the main, women leaders joined their male colleagues at the bar, saying they enjoyed the opportunity to talk about what had occurred during the day in an informal environment. Yet their stories revealed that they did so with a degree of caution:

> Anna: If you're a woman you've got to be very careful...you've got to watch your step in that you don't sort of look as though you're there to chase the guys... You've got to be very sensible and don't start cracking a lot of jokes and all this sort of thing because that can be taken in the wrong context. [Laughs] You've got to be fairly serene but not be a sour old bitch. (Interview 20)

In her detailed study of professional women's embodied identities at work, Trethewey (1999, 425) writes of her participants constantly navigating 'complex, ambiguous and precarious "in-between"'s (for example, masculinity/femininity, revealing/hiding one's body, conservative/fashionable dress, social conformity/individual creativity and sexuality/asexuality)'. This is precisely what Anna is describing. She emphasizes the need for care and caution in managing gender, acknowledges the surveillance of women in management and laments the near impossibility of attempting to occupy that position 'in-between' what is viewed as 'serene' and what is viewed as a 'sour old bitch'.

Blending In: Women in Agricultural Management Doing Masculinity

The women I interviewed gained a great deal of pleasure and satisfaction from their managerial roles. Like the male managers at the Farmers' Union, they found the power and privilege their board positions garnered highly seductive. They spoke of their enjoyment at meeting important people, having access to insider information, travelling internationally, making decisions that had a large impact and dealing with significant financial resources. The majority were very complimentary about the male chairs of the boards they were on as well as in awe of the prestige and entitlements these men commanded. One commented:

> Clara: Our president has such an incredible mind. His whole persona is speedy. The circles he moves in. It's just beyond me. And his knowledge. He's just so astute. And he has the major ear of people in the UN and EU. (Interview 17)

Like other participants, this female farming leader had invested in some aspects of the hegemonic masculine discourses informing agricultural politics and leadership. She presented being an agricultural manager as requiring high levels of specialist expertise, a capacity for logic and reason, a wealth of important connections and a commitment to work long hours. Further, she suggested that these were not the traits and characteristics found in many women who said they aspired to a leadership position in agriculture. In this sense, she positioned herself as 'different' from these 'other' women who she saw as flighty, impracticable, naïve and lacking in knowledge. She stated:

Clara: There's a lot of women out there that want to be active in their industry which is all very nice, but they're going to make us look like idiots if, when they get there, they don't have something really concrete to contribute other than a passion. Passion's just the icing on the cake. You've got to have theory and knowledge behind you. (Interview 17)

Clara's quotation is reminiscent of the masculine discourses of agricultural management centred on 'pinnacle leadership' and 'power' identified as prevalent by Liepins (1998; 2000) and Brandth and Haugen (2000). Her representation of the identity of agricultural leader also reverberates with the masculine discourses engaged by the Farmers Union men as they described their role in Chapters 4 and 5. This was not the only way in which the women farming managers I interviewed demonstrated complicity with masculinist definitions of leadership. It was also the case that some participants embedded their identities as 'women agricultural leaders' within discourses linking farming leadership and on-farm tractor work. These discourses, described in detail in Chapter 5, have played a crucial part in marking most women as unsuitable for leadership in agri-politics. They were, however, a resource to some of the women agricultural leaders as they dealt with difficulties in their position. One explained:

Anna: Before I went to the meetings I always braced myself and said, 'Well look, some of the guys have never driven a harvester and they don't know as much as I do'. So I thought, 'Well, I'm just as good as them and if they ask a few questions, I should be able to give them just as good an answer as the men'. (Interview 20)

This quotation demonstrates that identity construction for women leaders in agriculture, in part, imitates that of men in the sector. Anna refers, not just to her involvement in dirty on-farm physical labour, but also her competence with a particularly large piece of machinery. In this way she positions herself within the hegemonic masculine discourses of on-farm technical expertise, mechanical competence and strength that have been so important to traditional definitions of farming (see Chapter 2, and Brandth 1995), and consequently affirms her right to a place in the boardroom.

A final way in which the farming women invested in the dominant discourses of masculinity prevalent in agri-politics was in relation to their preferred leadership styles. Three women described their leadership as distinctly different from normative definitions of femininity. One remarked:

Tammy: I've learnt to be blunt in a man's world. Put it this way. When you're in business with men you have to act, not act like men, but you have to be in business too. You've got to get to the point quickly. Be tough. Say it like it is across a board table. (Interview 1)

Tammy's quotation suggests that her style of leadership has changed and that this has been a deliberate strategy – something she has learnt to do – in order to operate in the masculine world of agri-politics. The leadership mode that is most common and has most currency in the farming boardrooms where Tammy has a seat values tough talking and directness to the point of bluntness. The ambivalence that Tammy experiences in positioning herself within this discourse of hegemonic masculinity is conveyed at her equivocation, naming her behaviour as acting 'like men'. She substitutes 'men' for 'business', attempting to neutralize the gender dimensions of the leadership discourse she has adopted. This is not a way of 'doing masculinity', rather a way of 'doing business'.

Tammy and the two other women managers who described their leadership style in more masculine terms asserted that this was only problematic when working with women. One suggested, for example, that being a 'Napoleon' type leader who was focused on 'process not people' meant she had difficulty working on female dominated community boards and consequently did not participate in leadership at this level. Another said that her style of not 'having strong leanings in terms of "touchy feely"' meant she typically enjoyed better working relationships with men than with women. The third claimed she thought men appreciated her way of operating.

The women's claim that their style of leadership was acceptable when performed by them as women was contradicted by other participants. These participants were openly critical of women they perceived as acting in stereotypical masculine ways. Moreover, they suggested that this criticism was shared by male colleagues. This demonstrates Sheppard's (1989) argument that managing gender is a 'tight-rope' walk for women in leadership positions. The danger is not only in being too feminine, but equally in being too masculine. Across her case studies Cockburn (1991) provides a range of illustrations of this bind for the woman manager. What she demonstrates is that when women engage in activities that emulate the men they work with or operate in a manner equivalent to men, they are castigated and criticized. Her observation (Cockburn 1991, 156) that 'A woman cannot operate by men's rules and get away with it' is well illustrated by the following quotation:

> Rosa: When you've got men who don't think that women should be there some women feel as though they need to puff up, roll up their sleeves and act like men. All it does is make people turn off, or talk in the corridors. (Interview 16)

In this extract Rosa continues to signal the importance of the masculine body as a key marker of manager/ment and to cite the deficiencies of the female body as a signifier of manager/ment. The male managerial body is large (puffed up) as well as focused and industrious (sleeves rolled up).Women managers who want to emulate men must then enact a masculine bodily performance. This manoeuvre, however, may have negative consequences. As Rutherford (2001, 330) has reminded us, 'It is not masculinity *per se* that is valourized in organizations, it is masculinity in men'. Men can 'do femininity' in organizations such as in relation to the 'new' feminine styles of leadership and be rewarded and commended for it. Women who want to 'do masculinity' in organizations are not likely to be applauded in the same way, as Rosa acknowledges. These women will find themselves censured.

Women in Agricultural Management: Doing Leadership Differently?

The 12 Australian women managers interviewed by Sinclair (1998), like the 20 women agricultural managers I interviewed, describe themselves engaged in a number of gender management strategies as a means of negotiating a space in boardrooms where femininity is considered a pejorative term. While documenting the range of strategies used by the women to neutralize or obscure their femininity, Sinclair (1998) asks whether it is possible to do leadership differently, that is, to theorize, practice, celebrate and legitimate a mode of leadership that is not embedded in notions of hegemonic masculinities?

If asked Sinclair's (1998) question, many of the women agricultural managers would answer positively as they disassociated themselves and their preferred leadership style from conventional masculine discourses of leadership. Of the 20 women interviewed, 17 described their leadership style as being distinctly different from men. They typified themselves as feminine, by noting their nurturing, communicative, consultative, holistic, empathic and inclusive qualities. Furthermore, they indicated that such attributes could be proudly claimed as attractive commodities for leadership. Praise for their 'different' style of leadership had come from male board chairs as well as from other male board members. Two commented:

> Samantha: My chairman said to me, you know the Board changed immeasurably when you came on. Because women do things differently. They think differently. (Interview 7)

> Sarah: That's where I've seen that the dynamics change when women come onto boards. Because the men will actually say, 'Well we're over here and you're over there'...Quite often the role I've had to take around a board table is when there is conflict with two opposing sides and I say 'It appears there is some middle ground here'. (Interview 18)

These women pointed to changing societal expectations as well as challenges in the agricultural sector to argue that traditional authoritarian and hierarchical leadership styles associated with men no longer hold currency. They expressed a frustration with adversarial styles of leadership which were favoured by some males on their boards and which they saw as being highly inefficient and antiquated. There was consequently a high degree of pride in what they saw as women's innate differences from men.

The apparent acceptance of women displaying this 'new' style of leadership is not surprising. Australian government and industry policy directed at increasing women's representation in agricultural leadership has been predicated on the argument that women have naturally occurring skills and interests that would be of benefit to the agricultural sector (Pini 1998; 2003b; Pini and Brown 2004). Beyond my own shores, the discourse of 'new' feminine styles of management has had wide currency in international popular and academic management texts (Hatcher 2003). Further, the discourse being adopted by so many of the women agricultural managers is also likely to be met with little resistance from the men as it is entirely consistent with orthodox assumptions about essentialized and biologically determined differences between men and women. The adoption of this discourse was also useful for men. As Sarah explained in the above quotation, it has meant her role is that of negotiator and intermediary. Other women talked of using their more inclusive leadership styles in similar ways to open up channels of communication, intercede on behalf of board members or smooth the waters in a conflict. Thus, women's 'different' style of leadership is a valuable asset and resource for the male agricultural leaders. At the same time, because this 'difference' is seen to be innate, women are given no individual credit for the considerable skills, traits and knowledge they are demonstrating in their 'new' style of leadership.

While the majority of women asserted that they did indeed 'do leadership differently' in terms of style of communication (Sinclair 1998), there was little else that was 'different' from the masculine norm in terms of their construction of leadership. For example, while a number found managing family and their leadership role problematic, they were not critical of the fact that few agricultural groups provided child-care for board members, claiming child-care was a responsibility of individuals. There was also no critique of the culture of long work hours, extensive travel and incursions of board work into leisure and family time. These were seen to be requirements of the position and again to be negotiated at an individual level. There were also ongoing assertions that leadership revolved around objectivity, rationality, instrumentality and detachment. Sentiment and emotion were seen to have little place in a boardroom.

Of the 20 women interviewed, two did offer a sharp critique of the values and norms of boardroom Australia and suggested they had attempted to 'do leadership differently' (Sinclair 1998). The first of these women, Catherine, was a board member of a national organic farming organization. The literature review in Chapter 2 demonstrated that 'new' farming masculinities are emerging in the organic farming sector which are notable for articulating a more egalitarian view of gender relations than is evident in traditional discourses of farming masculinity (Peter et al. 2000; Barlett and Conger 2004; Barlett 2006). It seems quite likely that these on-farming discourses are spilling over into the agri-political arena as Catherine's experience of farming leadership as a woman is quite distinct compared with other women. She described herself as passionate and expressive and said she brought these qualities to her leadership. Unlike the other women agricultural managers interviewed, Catherine deliberately attempted to 'stand out' in how she dressed. She saw her bright suits and colourful scarves as sources of subversion against the dreary greyness of the uniform of the suit. She claimed she was proud of her body and worried women tried to hide their 'gorgeous curves' in a world of 'square suits'. Taking up this argument further she contended:

> Catherine: There are some fairly hard-nosed women that are very tough. Faceless kind of. I don't know where you need to be. I have those dilemmas myself of how I should approach the boardroom. And there's plenty of people on my board who are so hard-nosed, so critical, so exact and so pointy – that it just makes everyone prickle and it's not conducive to team work. And team responses. I have seen women who have done that as well, who have tried to emulate that...Sometimes I see women who have been placed on boards and they become – they lose themselves. They take on the role of being tough blokes. And I would, my advice would be to be yourself. To allow your beauty and your femininity – and I don't mean that in a long nails and lipstick mode, but those caring and nurturing aspects of women – to remain there around the board table as well. (Interview 3)

Catherine's quotation reveals that she has not been immune to the challenge of reconciling the competing definitions of 'woman' and 'manager', particularly with a lack of role models. She clearly does not want to emulate the 'hard-nosed' and 'pointy' men of the board. This is a strategy she has witnessed some women adopting but is opposed to it. The strategy she has adopted for herself was not to deny her femininity/sexuality, but to allow them to inform and embody her leadership.

Catherine differentiates between first, a definition of femininity which mobilizes around lipstick and long nails and second, a femininity which focuses on caring and nurturing. The former is positioned as trivial and superficial while the latter is positioned as central to the practice of leadership. After making this statement, Catherine went on to give different examples of how she achieved this in practice. She talked of using 'touch' as a means of connecting with board members, as well as explained how she sought to value, nurture and care for her fellow board members. Overall, Catherine espoused an extremely radical discourse of leadership which was imbued with femininity. She was not inhibited from taking up this discourse despite the presence of some 'pointy' men on the board. She is likely to have been assisted in this by the fact that she appeared to have a particularly good relationship with the board chair who is himself widely respected. Catherine may also have had some immunity to any attempts to circumscribe her behaviour/actions/beliefs as she appeared to have a very strong sense of self and a disregard for any negativity.

The second of the farming women leaders who had attempted to 'do leadership differently' (Sinclair, 1998) was a woman called Clare. One of the important themes evident in Clare's story is how fraught and difficult the process of gender management is for women leaders (Sheppard 1989). Earlier narratives have suggested that success as a woman leader is about managing one's drinking, socializing, joke-telling and sexuality, but in this process of self-management (Knights and Willmott 1999), a strategy of non-participation or avoidance does not appear to be acceptable. Clare reflected these efforts as she explained that she was not re-appointed to her very senior and prominent board position after one term:

> Clare: You know, I was never invited to any of those [dinners] because I don't drink and I really like to get up early and meditate and go for a run. I was sort of out of sync with the rest of them who would drink and go to the bar. So I missed out on that because they're all boys and they do all that stuff, I really had to be taken on my own terms which was difficult for people. (Interview 10)

Clare's insistence to be 'taken on my own terms' may have contributed to her removal from office. In another anecdote, she related a similar experience of failing to attend to the norms and conventions of masculine definitions of leadership; that is, to take on the masculine imperative to be unemotional. The event in question occurred, she said, at a particularly difficult time for her in that the family farm was in its fifth year of drought, her husband was depressed and resentful of her involvement in leadership, her five school age children were anxious and unsettled, and farm labour was an unaffordable luxury. She was exhausted from farm, domestic and board work and when she addressed the audience to talk about the drought she began to cry:

> Clare: One of the other board members, who was a good mentor, used to have a chat to me fairly often about the embarrassing catch in my voice – but it was more than that this time. He pulled me aside after, 'You don't want to do that too often, people will think you've got problems'. And I just looked at him and I said, 'But I have'. But...you're not allowed to actually admit it. (Interview 10)

In what she said and how she said it, Clare contravened what Foucault (1972, 216) termed the 'rules of exclusion'. He wrote:

> In a society such as our own, we all know the rules of exclusion. The most obvious and familiar of these concerns what is prohibited. We know perfectly well that we are not free to say just anything, that we cannot simply speak of anything, when we like or where we like; not just anyone, finally, may speak of just anything.

Talking about hardship and not coping is clearly an aberration in this culture. As is crying a violation of what it means to be a leader. As stated, in describing their own experiences of leading, women generally accepted this convention, asserting that a failure to do so would mean compromising one's standing on the board. Clare, however, saw things differently – and attempted to lead differently. Ultimately this is very likely to have contributed to her removal from the board.

Conclusion

As I talked to the women agricultural managers and read over their transcripts, I had many 'me too' experiences. I knew what they were talking about. I have lived variants of these stories in teaching at all-boys' schools, working in senior management positions in the public sector and being employed in a business school. Other female researchers studying women in male dominated organizations have reported a similar sense of familiarity with the narratives of their participants (see, for example, Kronsell 2005; Katila and Merilainen 2002a; 2002b). I wonder now how many women reading this chapter will also find themselves nodding and perhaps feeling a sense of discomfort, frustration or maybe humour as they are taken back to their own organizational contexts and witness themselves having to manage their 'femaleness'. It was thirty years ago that the conundrum was noted by Kanter (1977, 123) who wrote that 'women are measured by two yardsticks – how as women they carried out the management role, and how as managers they lived up to the images of womanhood'. Despite this considerable lapse in time and other significant social changes, women managers remain Kanter's (1977) Os in organizations, and men the Xs.[2] In farming unions this gender disparity in managerial positions is dramatically marked. It thus requires a particular performance in terms of gender management.

It is notable that the women pioneers in leadership positions in mainstream farming groups are actively and creatively attempting to develop new subjectivities as political participants in agriculture. In this chapter, particular time was spent describing the stories of Catherine and Clare. There appears to be considerable latitude for Catherine 'doing leadership differently' in her agricultural board work (Sinclair 1998).

---

2 Kanter (1977) famously attempted to analogize what it is like to be a minority position as a woman manager in an organization by referring to the 'case' of Xs and Os. If one looks at an O in a group of Xs, she said the difference of the O calls it into attention. It is seen to represent all other Os and other Os to represent it. It is examined, studied and scrutinized in a way the Xs are not as they are everywhere. The O is isolated but cannot fit in.

Clare's experience is sobering. She found her leadership experiences painful to recount. I did not find them easy to listen to or even to read now – quite some time after the initial interview. It is clear that hegemonic masculinity in farmers' unions is vociferous in its intolerance of challenge because Clare had so over-stepped the boundaries that she had to be physically removed from office. When in a leadership position, she had constantly transgressed explicit and implicit norms, codes and values of hegemonic masculinity. She did not perform the bodily enactments prescribed by the masculine discourses of agricultural management – she was emotive rather than taciturn, went running instead of drinking and enjoyed time alone rather than socializing with board members. Clare's story is not a hopeful one on which to finish, for it suggests that the forces of male resistance to women's entry to farming leadership are strong and powerful. I take this issue up in greater detail in the next chapter as I seek to draw the threads of the book together and assess what all of this may mean for a more equitable agricultural sector emerging in the future.

Chapter 8

Conclusion

In a 1981 article published in the American journal, *The Rural Sociologist*, Frances Hill outlined a research agenda for the future study of farm women. Six areas requiring investigation were identified. These included studies which dissected gendered assumptions and ideologies surrounding family farming, documented farm women's work, explored women's on-farm decision roles, examined farm women's off-farm work, described the implications of divorce and widowhood for farm women and queried women's invisibility in mainstream organizations. As the introductory chapter explained, a rich literature has been assembled on gender relations in farming since this time, much of which has contributed significantly to addressing Hill's (1981, 371) 'guideposts' for research (for example, Argent 1999; Bokemeier and Garkovich 1987; Dempsey 1992; Deseran and Simpkins 1991; Duggan 1987; Fink 1992; Garcia-Ramon and Canoves 1988; Haugen 1998; Little 1986; 1987; 1997; Perry and Ahearn 1994; Pini 2003d; 2007; Poiner 1990; Voyce 1993; Wallace, Abbott and Lankshear 1996).

In terms of the last of Hill's (1981) suggestions for future research, that of studies on women and farm organizations, we have also made some progress. We have a plethora of evidence that has substantiated Shortall's (1999, 96) claim that farming unions internationally are indeed 'men's organizations' because of the sheer preponderance of men in managerial and leadership positions within them. However, we have learnt little about why this is the case. The aim of this book was to redress this gap in scholarship through the lens of critical studies of masculinities. Such a lens has been little used in rural sociology where traditionally men and masculinities have been unmarked and unexamined. In contrast, this book placed masculinities at the centre of its inquiry. In shifting the focus of investigating the under-representation of women in agri-politics away from 'women' to 'masculinities', the book has revealed a great deal about why farming unions have historically been and remain today organizations of and for men. The following section of the chapter summarizes these findings before turning to the question of generalizability.

Summary

The book began by examining the interview interactions I had with 15 male elected leaders. Three different displays of masculinity by elected members were identified and discussed. These focused on heterosexuality, knowledge and importance. In attempting to understand these performances of masculinity I drew on Schwalbe and Wolkomir's (2001) advice that the gender dynamics of interviewing need to be seen in the context of 'who is asking whom about what.' This was a useful framing device for clearly my position as a woman, relatively youthful and a student talking to older men in positions of seniority coloured the interviews as did the gender focus of the research. My contention was, however, that this did not explain the gendered interview interactions in their entirety for the question of 'where' was also important. As this book has demonstrated, the Farmers' Union investigated is an organization where men's presence and power are rarely questioned or challenged. Women's exclusion is seen as natural, logical and inevitable. In this environment the problem of what Sinclair (2000, 90) says is the 'undiscussability of masculinities' is magnified.

Chapter 3 raised a number of methodological and epistemological difficulties I experienced as a woman researcher undertaking qualitative interviews with men investigating masculinities in an environment hostile to equity for women. My aim was not to suggest that we should confine our study of gender to accommodating environments or that this type of work would be more properly carried out by men. I did suggest that when such gender work is undertaken we need to be critical and reflexive about the research process. The gendered dynamics of our data gathering need to be recognized and analyzed, rather than ignored as subjective and/or marginalized as not central to the findings. Certainly in this study, the hostility of the male interviewers to the topic under investigation was a crucial finding. So too was the finding that the male elected members of the Farmers' Union assert and confirm their right to lead and differentiate themselves from 'others' such as women, by enacting a masculinity in which heterosexuality, power and knowledge are emphasized. As the following chapters demonstrated, the displays of masculinity provided excellent preliminary data for the study. Yet traditional interview textbooks did little to encourage me to see this at the time of the research. As Alvesson (2002, 126) writes in his critique of modernist approaches to interviewing, we have been taught to view 'the interview as a technique or tool', and as researchers to work 'hard in interview encounters in order to get interviewees to be honest, clear and consistent'. His message that we need to consider the 'shakiness of interviews' suggests that the types of silences, evasions and criticisms that I encountered in the interactions described in Chapter 3 were key findings of the research.

Chapter 4 introduced a framework of managerial masculinities developed by Collinson and Hearn (1994). It was argued that the dominant form of managerial masculinity in the Farmers' Union is that of paternalism. However, when there is a challenge to paternal rule a more authoritarian form of masculinity is deployed. There is no single organizational practice which produces and reproduces paternalism in the Farmers' Union. Rather, it is a constellation of both formal and informal practices that coalesce to inscribe paternalistic managerial masculinity. These include the way meetings are conducted, the way male and female staff and male elected members interact and the way labour is divided in the organization. One of the most salient of organizational practices through which paternalism is enacted and replicated in the Farmers' Union is the electoral system. Importantly, this is heavily concealed and suppressed behind a dominant discourse of 'merit' which suggests that the processes for gaining a leadership position in the organization are gender-neutral. On closer inspection, however, one sees that being elected is dependent upon paternalistic assumptions about one's family background, seniority and grooming. This involves the sponsorship, typically of a junior male by a senior male. Incumbent senior patriarchs have considerable professional resources to support these junior men inviting them into what are largely male or male-only networks, coaching them on industry knowledge, and instructing them on the informal norms of the organization. Campaigning is not just uncommon; it is shunned. There is no necessity for such vulgarity in the gentlemanly arena of the Farmers' Union as the senior patriarchs, rather than the constituents, indirectly determine who will become leaders. Ultimately, paternalism is manifest in the electoral system by virtue of the continued process of allowing only a single vote per farm.

One of the critical questions for this book is why paternalism retains such eminence in the Farmers' Union when, in contemporary management discourse, it is typically depicted as antiquated. It may be that the omnipresence of paternalism in the Farmers' Union is related to its connection to discursive gender regimes outside of the organization. That is, on the farm and in the rural community. Bennett's (2006) detailed reading of interactions occurring in a Dorset farmhouse kitchen focuses attention on the way in which discourses of paternalism inform the daily lives of farming families. It may be that the hegemony of paternalism on-farm has spilled over into organizational life in the Farmers' Union. Farming constituents' familiarity with paternalism may lead it to be seen as the most logical and rightful of managerial approaches even if it has been replaced in other organizations. This finding challenges much gender and management research which has largely ignored the question of place, and the particular ways in which discourses of rurality may intersect with discourses of gender to privilege particular forms of managerial masculinity.

Chapter 4 emphasized the emergence of new discourses of managerial masculinity in the Farmers' Union as enunciated by male members of a Young Farmers' Group. This is a discourse which focuses on the twin themes of entrepreneurship and professionalism. In their narratives the young men derided discourses which legitimated the overt exclusion of women from involvement in agri-politics and suggested that they were seeking to welcome women into the group. This may appear to offer some hope for change in the future. However, the extent to which this is the case will require further examination. Evidence from the broader literature on masculinities and management offers little in the way of optimism as it reports that the 'new' dominant discourses of management such as 'feminine management' (Maile 1995), 'managerialism' (Whitehead 1999), Total Quality Management (Kerfoot and Knights 1996) and Business Process Re-engineering (Knights and McCabe 2001) are as constraining for women as was paternalism. This is clear in Hopton's (1999, 77) critical reading of more contemporary post-modern management theories which reveals that while they espouse a rhetoric of teams, flattened hierarchies and co-operation, these new managerial discourses are actually embedded in traditional discourses of the past. He subsequently wonders if these apparently new management styles may be the 'Trojan horse for the reassertion of patriarchal and authoritarian values and attitudes in the workplace'. They may look and sound very different from the managerial masculinities of the past, but have the same detrimental effects for aspiring women leaders.

The dominance of paternalistic managerial masculinity in the Farmers' Union was further illuminated in Chapter 5. However, the specific focus of this chapter was on how paternal managers and leaders construct their identities, taking up Alvesson's (1998, 995) claim that 'the constituting and reconstituting of a particular identity requires that one defines oneself in relation to some other person or social category...You are a man if somebody else is a woman'. What Chapter 5 revealed is that the process of 'doing masculinity' as an elected member in the Farmers' Union is not straight-forward. It is a complex performance involving the 'othering' of women as well as some men. In the first instance, elected men draw a putative link between their own work and the work of farming men. They argue that both are engaged in battle and require the same traits of aggression, toughness, tenacity and strength. The conflation of the discourses of farming and agricultural management in the Farmers' Union positions farming women as 'other'. Indeed, the conflation of the discourses of farming and agricultural leadership in the Farmers' Union leads many women to exclude themselves from nominating for election.This is particularly so because participation in on-farm physical work involving tractors and heavy machinery is presented as a necessary precursor to agricultural leadership. Many women absent themselves believing that they would not be seen as credible electoral candidates because they have not been involved in such work. Studies of gender and farming have highlighted the critical role the tractor plays as a boundary marker delineating on-farm differences between the categories masculinity/femininity and men/women (Brandth 1995; Saugers 2002a). It is clear from this study that the tractor also plays a role in gender boundary setting in the agricultural organization. Of course, not all women are absented or marginalized by a discourse which suggests that agricultural leadership is akin to tractor work on the farm for some women engage in this work. Such women are consequently 'othered' in different ways by men in the Farmers' Union. In this repertoire, women are presented as overly emotional, easily distracted and irrational, while agricultural leadership is constructed as requiring the polar opposites of these characteristics.

One of the key themes of Chapter 5 was that the performance of masculinity is a relational act involving not just femininities but 'other' masculinities. This was demonstrated by examining the way in which the elected members of the Farmers' Union construct their identities by demarcating a particular version of masculinity that is different from the masculinities of 'other' farmers. In this respect, elected members claim they are 'different' from 'other' farming men, highlighting their extensive and detailed expertise and knowledge. They are seasoned and tried on the prestigious stages on which they are required to perform. This is not the case with 'other' farming men who are positioned as inexperienced and unsophisticated. With appropriate grooming and training from older incumbent patriarchs some of these 'other' farming men may one day become leaders, but this will only be a select group. The majority will need the paternal fathers to provide care and protection.

Chapter 5 also argued that further differentiation between men occurs as they move up the organizational hierarchy. Those at higher tiers 'other' men at the next level and so on. More exaggerated displays of the traits and attributes of the masculine managerial man are required in the upper levels of the organizational hierarchy. The hierarchical relations between the managerial men in the Farmers'

Union are firmly embodied. Thus, while all managerial men are valourized as tough and strong, the Chairman must be tougher and stronger. Similarly, while all elected leaders are constructed as informed about the industry and well connected with influential figures, the Chairman is positioned as omnipotent.

The gender identity work undertaken by male agri-political leaders in the Farmers' Union serves them well on a number of counts. Most importantly, it increases and validates their position and status. Given that the simple farming folk who are 'the farmers' are unversed in the harsh realities of business and politics, it is not just necessary but critical that managerial positions are held by those currently in position. If not, they should at least be held by those chosen by the incumbents as appropriate successors. Further, when male leaders position agricultural leadership as being a difficult burden and women as lacking the strength and fortitude for such a task, power relations and women's subordination are obscured. Women should, in fact, be grateful that men hold all leadership positions. It is not possible to have younger members (than the incumbents in their late fifties and sixties) because they have not engaged in the years of learning or done the necessary 'apprenticeship'. One day, once appropriately groomed by the existing leadership, they may be suitable for management. For women no such options exist as they are situated within discourses which position them as weak, uninformed and overly emotional and these discourses are framed in opposition to discourses of leadership based on strength, knowledge and objectivity.

Chapter 6 introduced the subject of farm women's networks, and more specifically, the discourses by which men in the Farmers' Union have resisted networks for women. Cockburn's (1991, 100) work has demonstrated the pervasiveness of male resistance to gender equity claiming the males in her study were 'not exceptional in their resistance to change'. This is not to suggest that there was any uniformity to the nature of the resistance Cockburn (1991) identified. It came in a variety of guises – as sexist humour and sexual harassment as well as via disparaging comments and exclusionary practices. A similar diversity of resistance strategies were mobilized by the male elected members of the Farmers' Union in response to the establishment and success of two adjunct farm women's networks. In order to categorize these disparate resistance strategies I drew upon Blackmore's (1999, 136) notion of 'discourses of denigration'. Four discourses of denigration were identified. That is, those that trivialize women, masculinize women, pathologize women and sexualize women.

One of the important aspects of Chapter 6 was that it focused attention on organizational resistance as performed by power-holders and decision-makers. This group has rarely been the focus of studies of resistance in the organizational literature Agocs (1997, 47). More generally, 'resistance' has been discussed in terms of middle managers, supervisors, shop floor or unionized workers resisting a change that senior management wants to implement. This omission is significant, given that a person's position in the organizational hierarchy will influence their capacity to resist change. Those who have access to resources, and moreover, access to determine the allocation of resources, as well as the authority to establish organizational rules, priorities and practices are clearly well positioned to resist calls for change. This is not to suggest that resistance is one-sided or that power is absolute and monolithic, but that in organizations such as the Farmers' Union, the male elected leaders mobilizing resistance operate from a structurally and discursively more powerful position than groups such as women. This is important in considering why farm women involved in the networks have had such difficulty in challenging and nullifying the derogatory constructions of themselves and their networks as frivolous, unfeminine, dangerous and sexually frustrated/troublesome. As Weedon (1987) has argued, discourses are particularly powerful when they are institutionalized and when they can be linked to other dominant discourses. The Farmers' Union has considerable organizational strength. It has significant physical and financial resources as well as a legitimacy and credibility with government, other industry groups and the media. This means that it has the capacity to control the dissemination of discourses about farming or leadership that serve its own interests and the interests of the men who predominate in decision-making positions. It helps, of course, that the discourses the farming men mobilized against the women's networks are those which are widely propagated as 'truths' in broader discursive fields relating to gender and specifically, women and management. These are discourses which align organizational leadership with masculinity and any female involvement in leadership as unfeminine; classify women as generally difficult, emotional and unforgiving and therefore a problematic presence in organizational life; and identify women's rightful place as being located within the private rather than public sphere. While 'new' discourses about women and women's right to participate in management have emerged in recent years, more conservative and stereotypical discourses retain currency and legitimacy, particularly in non-metropolitan areas. Such discourses are thus easily called upon by Farmers' Union men to discredit and marginalize the women's networks.

In Chapter 7 attention moved to documenting the experiences of women who are currently elected leaders in agri-political groups. Again, emphasis was on understanding how gender is 'performed' in the terms described by Butler (1990). What was revealed was that the gendered performance of agricultural leadership is, for women, a dynamic, ambiguous and contradictory process. In the first instance it requires the amplification of a range of normative traits of femininity. This appears to be the case in relation to the style of women leaders. In describing themselves as communicative, relationship builders and people-oriented, the majority of agricultural women marked themselves as distinctly different from hegemonic definitions of masculine management articulated by men in the Farmers' Union. In part, the discourse of the feminine advantage in leadership (Rosener 1990) and the alleged relationship between this style and business success has presented agricultural women with an opportunity to breach the duality of being both 'woman' and 'leader'. At the same time, asserting a link between women as a group and a specific set of attributes and skills is problematic in that it relies on the very stereotyping that has disqualified women from leadership. Further, rather than opening up a range of ways for women to lead, it prescribes a particular way and reinforces the view that any diversion from this type of leadership by women is abnormal (Due Billing and Alvesson 2000).

Women's claim to leadership in agriculture is not just asserted through magnifying aspects of femininity. Contradictorily, leadership also requires women to suppress other aspects of femininity and to celebrate some traits of masculinity. Chapter 7 demonstrated that women can also 'do masculinity' and that we cannot always assume that masculinity is the preserve of biological men (Alvesson 1998, 973). The oppositional positioning of leader and woman is consequently re-magnified. Being an agricultural woman leader requires the reification of on-farm skill and expertise. It also requires one to be objective, desexualized and rational, unencumbered by domestic and household duties. Gender performance is thus highly complex and precarious – while displaying masculine characteristics, agricultural women are nonetheless required to present themselves as not completely devoid of softness, sexual attractiveness and conviviality. There is consequently a fragile balancing act for the woman agricultural leader as she manages her sexuality, dress, intelligence, speech, emotions and knowledge to be feminine enough but not too feminine. In order to negotiate this path women leaders in agriculture are involved in an ongoing process of self-surveillance (Foucault 1977). This does not mean, however, that they are immune from being sanctioned or stigmatized as they attempt to manage their gender. Even the most accomplished performer, however, can be vulnerable as men may give prominence to a woman's femininity or her sexuality.

Chapter 7 revealed that women pioneers in leadership positions in mainstream farming groups are actively and creatively attempting to develop new subjectivities as political participants in agriculture. Like the women involved in the networks, many female agri-political leaders engage practices and discourses that 'challenge or disrupt prevailing power relations and the norms that sustain and reproduce them' (Bordo 1993, 199). They are, however, constrained and curtailed in such a task given the central and seemingly immovable place men and dominant masculinities occupy in the definition and enactment of farming leadership. Unfortunately, this does not augur well for women's increased participation in farming leadership in the future because, as the following discussion highlights, the case study has implications beyond Australian shores.

Masculinities and Management in Agricultural Organizations Worldwide?

This book has presented a case study of the preponderance and practice of managerial masculinities in an Australian agricultural organization. There are, of course, inherent problems in the examination of a single case study in terms of generalizations and theory development. There are also difficulties in attempting to generalize when the theoretical orientation of the study was to give descriptive emphasis to the temporal specificities and particularities of the case. There is, however, an important key point to make in order to connect this case study with other Farmers' Unions worldwide. That is, the numerical patterns of gendered leadership within the Farmers' Union under investigation mirror those of other agricultural organizations both across Australia and in other western industrialized nations. In short, in farming organizations from Ireland to Iceland, Norway to New Zealand and France to Finland men significantly outnumber women in decision-making positions. Regardless of the commodity focus of the group, whether it be, for example, sugar, wheat, corn or beef, it is men not women who lead. This is particularly striking when one considers the multiple differences which would exist between these organizations in terms of, for example, their national context, their size and their history. The preponderance of male leaders is the key common denominator. This book has taken this very critical shared characteristic of agricultural organizations as its starting point to ask how this is maintained and reproduced. Given the shared starting point between the case study organization and other Farmers' Unions the findings have resonance internationally. That is, ethnographic studies of other agricultural groups world-wide are likely to reveal a similar story of gendered organizational power manifest in the deployment and reproduction of hegemonic masculinities. Drawing on Connell's (2000) theorization of hegemonic masculinities one can assume that what the case study describes is likely to be illustrative of how masculine power operates in Farmers' Unions internationally where men predominate. There will, of course, be key variations and nuances in the type of hegemonic masculinities performed and in how they are performed so a key focus for future studies will be to explore the particular shape hegemonic masculinities may take in Farmers' Unions in other national contexts. An obvious question will be the extent to which paternalism dominates, given that while it was prominent in the case study there is evidence of clear resistance to it from the Young Farmers' Group and further evidence in the literature that is rarely seen in contemporary organizations.

Future Research

The case study of the Farmers' Union has demonstrated the potential importance of place to how management is practised in organizations and why women may be under-represented in organizational leadership. There is, however, little work that has considered the intersections between gender, management and rurality. Thus, it is important that future work attends to the way in which leadership is practised in rural locales not associated with agriculture such as regional development, local government and natural resource management organizations (for example, Sheridan, Pini and Conway 2006; Pini 2006a; 2008).

As well as broader studies of gender, management and rurality, more specific work on gender, management and agricultural organizations also needs to continue. Agri-political governance is currently being reconfigured as a result of globalization so that today new trans-national organizations are increasingly important to the governance of agriculture. While mainstream rural and agricultural studies have afforded considerable attention to this shift (see for example, Higgins and Lawrence 2005), there has been no attempt to critique what is occurring from a gender perspective. This is despite the argument of Connell (1998b, 3) who has stated that while we have learnt a great deal from local studies of masculinities 'in a globalizing world we must pay attention to very large scale structures' and the masculinities inherent in them. Here, scholars have argued that while there may have been slight increases in the number of women holding positions of national leadership in recent years (such as in agriculture) this is not necessarily cause for rejoicing as this has been accompanied by a shift in organizational and management power from national to international arenas. As power has shifted women have been appointed to positions of national leadership, and men to positions of international leadership (Calas and Smircich 1993). What is clear then, is that as studies of gender and farming organizations continue, focus must move beyond the national to the international sphere and to the new forms of agricultural governance being established in the globalized world of the twenty-first century.

Accompanying the shift to internationalization in agri-political governance has been the growth in the importance of agricultural biotechnologies. Again, mainstream rural and farming studies have generated a strong body of literature on this subject, and particularly the question of the governance of genetically modified agriculture (for example, Levidow 2001; MacMillan 2003; McAfee 2003), but failed to incorporate an analysis of gender. It is this absence which has led to calls for work which examines the gendered nature of new governance bodies focused on agricultural biotechnologies, which submits the agricultural biotechnology policies of Farmers' Unions to a gender analysis and which views new agricultural activist groups through a gender lens (Bryant and Pini 2006). In short, requiring scrutiny are the 'gendered discourses about wealth creation, development, progress and the public good' in which discussions about genetically modified agricultural governance are embedded (Bryant and Pini 2006, 275). Thus, as studies of masculinities and the public sphere of agriculture continue and move outside of national boundaries they need to attend to the increasing importance of capital relations in agriculture as they are manifest in biotechnologies.

Conclusion

The question of the enactment of masculinities by male agricultural leaders has been addressed in this book by adopting an understanding of gender as 'mobilized' (Martin 2001, 600), 'achieved' (Skelton 2000, 7), 'constructed' (Collinson and Hearn 1996, 65), or 'done' (West and Zimmerman 1987, 125). These verbs convey the view that men and women are active agents, engaged in an ongoing process of creating and recreating gender identities as they take up different discourses of masculinity and/or femininity across a range of sites. As the introductory discussion argued such a view of gender runs counter to biologically grounded discourses which ascribe normative sets of fixed characteristics/behaviours as naturally belonging to the unity category 'men' and the unity category 'women'. While adopting such a theoretical perspective and documenting empirical evidence to support such a view, I was fascinated when reading the transcripts by the dominance of the vocabulary of 'normal' and 'natural'. Such terms peppered the data. There was little sense of ambivalence or uncertainty in the claims made about the polarized categories 'men' and 'women' by participants. This highlights Butler's (1990, 43) observation that repeated performances of gender congeal over time giving the appearance of rigidity and normalcy. Yet, as Butler (1990) reminds us, gender is a fabrication. It *is* possible to 'undo gender' (Butler 2004) and create new ways of being, legitimate different bodies and support other types of actions and behaviours, but this first requires an understanding of the complex inter-relationship between particular gender discourses and power. In this book I have made a small contribution to this task of 'undoing gender' in the agricultural sector. At the same time, I am aware of the enormity of what remains to be done in deconstructing and shifting those dominant gender discourses which continue to delimit leadership opportunities for so many farming women and some farming men.

Appendix

A Note on Methodology

Data for this book were obtained from a three year ethnographic study (1998–2001) of one of the largest farmers' unions in Australia as well as from interviews with 20 women agricultural leaders from a range of different farmers' groups.

The ethnography of the Farmers' Union drew on data from participant observation, document analysis, interviews and focus groups. Data from all these methods are used throughout the book.

During the period of the research I was given office space at the city based head office of the Farmers' Union. Over this period I averaged two to three days a week there conducting my work and maintaining an ongoing reflective journal recording observations, interpretations and experiences (Pini 2004d). The extended period in the field provided multiple opportunities to participate in both formal and informal facets of organizational life. This participant observation was enriched by an analysis of organizational documents, and particularly the fortnightly publication of the Farmers' Union which is sent to all constituents.

Further to the participant observation and document analysis I conducted 15 interviews with male managers within the Farmers' Union. In Chapter 3 of the book I explore these interview interactions in detail, drawing particular attention to the ways in which the interviews were used by the male managers as a means of signifying masculinity. Specific details about the processes for the selection of the interviewees, the design of the interviews and methods of data analysis are detailed at the beginning of this chapter. Interviews were also undertaken with five staff of the Farmers' Union from two district locations where farm women's networks had been established.

The final data sources for the study were 16 focus groups with women in the agricultural industry associated with the Farmers' Union. Elsewhere I have documented the rationale for these focus groups in detail as well as documented the positive aspects of the focus groups as a feminist method (see Pini 2003a). These women lived in two district locations in the central and northern areas of the state of Queensland. These districts were selected for investigation as in both locations women's networks had been established to foster greater female participation in industry politics. Women involved in the networks were invited to participate in focus groups as well as asked to suggest other women who may be able to contribute to the research. In total, 80 women participated in the focus groups. Of these women, the majority were married (n=69), ten were widowed and one was living in a de facto relationship with her partner. Prior to marriage, focus group participants had been involved in a wide range of occupations that they no longer pursued including quality control; laboratory work and cane testing at a sugar mill; running a saw mill; policing; retail work; teaching and nursing. Ten of the 80 women were involved in non-farm paid work. Three had part time and casual work in administrative positions, one ran family day care from her home, the fifth worked in public administration full time, the sixth in a retail position and the seventh ran her own computer training business. The three remaining women all worked as school teachers – one in a full time position and two casually. Over half (n=43) had grown up on farms, yet just two had inherited farms. A significant majority, 69 women (86.2 per cent), farmed in partnership with their husband's extended families. It was apparent that the majority of participants were over the age of forty, but a specific question about age was not asked.

As stated, at the time of the study there were no women in positions of elected leadership in the case study Farmers' Union. Thus, in order to gain a perspective on gender relations in farming unions from women agricultural leaders I had to go outside of the case study site and interview women from other organizations. Details of these interviews are provided in Chapter 7.

In terms of the qualitative data, Miles and Hubermann (1994, 9) identify 'a fairly classic set of analytical moves' common across different qualitative research types as: coding; reflecting; sorting to identify patterns, similarities or differences between variables; isolating these and using them to focus follow-up fieldwork; developing a small set of generalizations; and using these generalizations with the literature to develop theory. These stages reflect my own approach to data analysis. Importantly, these are not discrete phases or linear. They were engaged in a circular and ongoing process throughout the analysis. The feminist theoretical orientation of the study and specifically the conceptual focus on subjectivities, knowledges and power informed each stage of the analysis.

In the initial stages of data analysis, coding was guided by the structure provided by the interview and focus group guides, which in turn were developed from the literature and early participant observation. In the second stage of data analysis, prior to follow-up visits to case study locations, data was re-coded using NVivo (Qualitative Solutions and Research 1999) into themes and grouped into categories and sub-categories for the sorting and identification of patterns, similarities and differences between the variables. This preliminary analysis provided an opportunity to identify areas requiring further clarification in follow-up fieldwork.

After return visits to fieldwork locations and the input of the further data into NVivo (Qualitative Solutions and Research 1999), a third stage in the data analysis took place with some re-coding and re-organization of themes and categories. At this stage I found the data display techniques of Miles and Huberman (1994) as a means of data analysis particularly useful and developed matrices and diagrams to display comparative elements of the data.

Two additional strategies were used as part of the data analysis. Firstly, a research journal was maintained throughout the process to record both analytical and reflective notes as part of the data, and correspondingly, as part of the process of analysis. These provided 'links across' data and also become part of the 'analytical files' developed to begin to collate data (Glesne and Peshkin 1992, 128). In recognition of the ongoing nature of data analysis, these memos were a useful means of recording interpretations throughout the research.

Secondly, interpretations and findings were discussed and reviewed on both informal and formal occasions with participants, colleagues and associated industry personnel. Again, on these occasions I recorded what occurred in these discussions and reviews in my journal. Thus, for example, following attendance at an industry conference where swearing and sexual innuendos were commonplace from the men chairing sessions, I discussed my reaction with two female industry personnel – an extension officer and a Farmers' Union staff member.

Bibliography

Aaltio, I. and Mills, A.J. (eds) (2002), *Gender, Identity and the Culture of Organisations* (London: Routledge).

Acker, J. (1990), 'Hierarchies, Jobs, Bodies: A Theory of Gendered Organizations', *Gender and Society* 4:2, 139–58.

Agocs, C. (1997), 'Institutional Resistance to Organizational Change: Denial, Inaction and Repression', *Journal of Business Ethics* 16, 917–31.

Agostino, K. (1997), 'Masculinity, Sexuality, and Life On Board Her Majesty's Royal Australian Ships', *Journal of Interdisciplinary Gender Studies* 2:1, 15–33.

Alcoff, L.M. (1988), 'Cultural Feminism Versus Post-Structuralism: The Identity Crisis in Feminist Theory', *Signs* 13:31, 405–36.

Alloway, N. and Gilbert, P. (2004), 'Shifting Discourses about Gender in Higher Education Enrolments: Retrieving Marginalised Voices', *International Journal of Qualitative Studies in Education* 17:1, 99–112.

Alsop, R., Fitzsimmons, A. and Lennon, K. (2002), 'Natural Men and Women', *Theorizing Gender* (Cambridge: Polity Press).

Alston, M. (ed.) (1990), *Key Papers No.1: Rural Women* (Wagga Wagga: Centre for Rural Welfare Research).

—— (1995), *Women on the Land: The Hidden Heart of Rural Australia* (Kensington: UNSW Press).

—— (2000), *Breaking Through the Grass Ceiling* (Amsterdam: Harwood).

Alvesson, M. (1998), 'Gender Relations and Identity at Work: A Case Study of Masculinities and Femininities in an Advertising Agency', *Human Relations* 51:8, 969–1005.

—— (2002), *Postmodernism and Social Research* (Buckingham: Open University Press).

Alvesson, M. and Due Billing, Y. (1997), *Understanding Gender and Organizations* (London: Sage).

Anahita, S. and Mix, T.L. (2006), 'Retrofitting Frontier Masculinity for Alaska's War against Wolves', *Gender and Society* 20:3, 332–53.

Arendell, T. (1997), 'Reflections on the Researcher-Researched Relationship: A Woman Interviewing Men', *Qualitative Sociology* 20:3, 341–68.

Argent, N. (1999), 'Inside the Black Box: Dimensions of Gender, Generation and Scale in the Australian Rural Restructuring Process', *Journal of Rural Studies* 15:1, 1–15.

Aslin, H.J., Webb, T. and Fisher, M. (2000), *Fishing for Women: Understanding Women's Roles in the Fishing Industry* (Canberra: Bureau of Rural Sciences).

Bacchi, C. (2005), 'Discourse, Discourse Everywhere: Subject "Agency" in Feminist Discourse Methodology', *Nordic Journal of Women's Studies* 13:3, 198–209.

Barbic, A. (1993), 'Farm Women in Slovenia: Endeavours for Equality', *Agricultural Human Values* 10:4, 13–25.

Barlett, P.F. (2006), 'Three Visions of Masculine Success on American Farms', in H. Campbell, M. Bell and M. Finney (eds), 47–66.

Barlett, P.F. and Conger, K.J. (2004), 'Three Visions of Masculine Success on American Farms', *Men and Masculinities* 7:2, 205–27.

Barrett, F.J. (2002), 'Gender Strategies of Women Professionals: The Case of the U.S. Navy', in M. Dent and S. Whitehead (eds), 157–73.

Barrett, M. (1991), *The Politics of Truth: From Marx to Foucault* (Stanford: Stanford University Press).

Barry, J., Dent, M. and O'Neil, M. (eds) (2003), *Gender and the Public Sector: Professionals and Managerial Change* (London: Routledge).

Bartky, S.L. (1990), *Femininity and Domination: Studies in the Phenomenology of Oppression* (New York: Routledge).

Barvosa-Carter, E. (2005), 'Strange Tempest: Agency, Poststructuralism and the Shape of Feminist Politics to Come', in M. Sonser Breen and W.J. Blumenfeld (eds), 175–90.

Bell, D. (1997), 'Anti-idyll: Rural Horror', in P. Cloke, and J. Little (eds), 94–108.

—— (2000a), 'Eroticizing the Rural', in R. Phillips, D. Watt and D. Shuttleton (eds), 83–101.

—— (2000b), 'Farm Boys and Wild Men: Rurality, Masculinity and Homosexuality', *Rural Sociology* 65:4, 547–61.

—— (2006), 'Cowboy Love', in H. Campbell, M. Bell and M. Finney (eds), 163–82.

Bell, D., Caplan, P. and Jahan Karim, W. (eds) (1993), *Gendered Fields: Women, Men and Ethnography* (London: Routledge).

Bell, D. and Klein, R. (eds) (1996), *Radically Speaking: Feminism Reclaimed* (Melbourne: Spinifex).

Bell, J.H. and Pandey, U.S. (1989), 'Gender-role Stereotypes in Australian Farm Advertising', *Media Information Australia* 51, 45–9.

Benhabib, S. (1994), 'Feminism and the Question of Postmodernism', in Polity Press (ed.), 76–107.

Bennett, K. (2004), 'A Time for Change? Patriarchy, the Former Coalfields and Family Farming', *Sociologia Ruralis* 44:2, 147–66.

—— (2006), 'Kitchen Drama: Performances, Patriarchy and Power Dynamics in a Dorset Farmhouse Kitchen', *Gender, Place and Culture* 13:2, 49–56.

Beynon, J. (2002), *Masculinities and Culture* (Buckingham: Open University Press).

Bird, S. (2006), 'Masculinities in Rural Small Business Ownership: Between Community and Capitalism', in H. Campbell, M. Bell and M. Finney (eds), 67–86.

Blackmore, J. (1999), *Troubling Women, Leadership and Educational Change* (Buckingham: Open University Press).

Blair-Loy, M. (2001), 'Cultural Constructions of Family Schemas: The Case of Women Finance Executives', *Gender and Society* 15:5, 687–709.

Bock, B. (2004), 'Fitting in and Multi-Tasking: Dutch Farm Women's Strategies in Rural Entrepreneurship', *Sociologia Ruralis* 44:3, 245–60.

Bock, B. and de Haan, H. (2004), 'Rural Gender Studies in the Netherlands', in H. Goverde, H. de Haan and M. Baylina (eds), 106–26.

Bock, B. and Shortall, S. (eds) (2006), *Rural Gender Relations: Issues and Case Studies* (Oxfordshire: CABI Publishing).

Bokemeier, J. and Garkovich, L. (1987), 'Assessing the Influence of Farm Women's Self-identity on Task Allocation and Decision Making', *Rural Sociology* 52:1, 13–36.

Bonnett, A. (1996), 'The New Primitives: Identity, Landscape and Cultural Appropriation in the Mythopoetic Men's Movement', *Antipode* 28:3, 273–91.

Bordo, S. (1988), 'Anorexia Nervosa: Psychopathology as the Crystallization of Culture', in I. Diamond and L. Quinby (eds), 87–117.

—— (1993), 'Feminism, Foucault and the Politics of the Body', in C. Ramazanoglu (ed.), 179–202.

Boulding, E. (1980), 'The Labor of US Farm Women: A Knowledge Gap', *Sociology of Work and Occupations* 7:3, 261–90.

Bouquet, M. (1982), 'Production and Reproduction of Family Farms in South-West England', *Sociologia Ruralis* 22:3, 227–44.

Boyle, P. and Halfacre, K. (eds) (1999), *Migration and Gender in the Developed World* (London: Routledge).

Bracker, J. (1980), 'The Historical Development of the Strategic Management Concept', *Academy of Management Review* 5:2, 219–24.

Brandth, B. (1994), 'Changing Femininity: The Social Construction of Women Farmers in Norway', *Sociologia Ruralis* 34: 2/3, 127–49.

—— (1995), 'Rural Masculinity in Transition, Gender Images in Tractor Advertisements', *Journal of Rural Studies* 11:2, 123–33.

—— (2002a), 'Gender Identity in European Family Farming: A Literature Review', *Sociologia Ruralis* 42:3, 181–200.

—— (2002b), 'On the Relationship between Feminism and Farm Women', *Agriculture and Human Values* 19:2, 107–17.

—— (2006), 'Agricultural Body-Building: Incorporations of Gender, Body and Work', *Journal of Rural Studies* 22:1, 17–27.

Brandth, B. and Haugen, M.S. (1998), 'Breaking into a Masculinist Discourse: Women and Farm Forestry', *Sociologia Ruralis* 38:3, 427–42.

—— (2000), 'From Lumberjack to Business Manager: Masculinity in the Norwegian Forestry Press', *Journal of Rural Studies* 16:3, 343–55.

—— (2005a), 'Doing Rural Masculinity – From Logging to Outfield Tourism', *Journal of Gender Studies* 14:1, 13–22.

—— (2005b), 'Text, Body and Tools: Changing Mediations of Rural Masculinity', *Men and Masculinities* 8:2, 148–63.

—— (2005c), 'The Gendered Embodiment of Agricultural Work: Nature, Machinery and Patriarchy', in D. Morgan, B. Brandth and E. Kvande (eds), 89–100.

Breen, M.S. and Blumenfeld, W.J. (eds) (2005), *Butler Matters: Judith Butler's Impact on Feminist and Queer Studies* (Aldershot: Ashgate).

Brewis, J. (2003), 'On the Front Line: Women's Experiences of Managing the New Public Services', in J. Barry, M. Dent and M. O'Neil (eds), 136–53.

Brewis, J. and Sinclair, J. (2000), 'Exploring Embodiment: Women, Biology and Work', in J. Hassard, R. Holliday and H. Willmott (eds), 192–214.

Brooks, A. (1997), *Postfeminisms: Feminism, Cultural Theory and Cultural Forms* (London: Routledge).

Brueggemann, J. (2000), 'The Power and Collapse of Paternalism: The Ford Motor Company and Black Workers, 1937–1941', *Social Problems* 47:2, 220–40.

Bruni, A. and Gherardi, S. (2002), 'En-gendering Differences, Transgressing the Boundaries, Coping with the Dual Presence', in I. Aaltio and A.J. Mills (eds), 21–38.

Bruni, A., Gherardi, S. and Poggio, B. (2005), *Gender and Entrepreneurship: An Ethnographical Approach* (London: Routledge).

Bryant, L. (1999), 'The Detraditionalization of Occupational Identities in Farming in South Australia', *Sociologia Ruralis* 39:2, 236–61.

—— (2003), 'Gendered Bodies, Gendered Knowledges', *Social Science Computer Review* 21:4, 464–74.

—— (2006), 'Marking the Occupational Body: Young Women and Men Seeking Careers in Agriculture', *Rural Society* 16:1, 62–79.

Bryant, L. and Pini, B. (2006), 'Towards an Understanding of Gender and Capital in Constituting Biotechnologies in Agriculture', *Sociologia Ruralis* 46:4, 261–79.

Buchy, M. (2001), *Listening to Women's Voices in the Australian Forestry Industry Workforce* ANU Occasional Paper (Canberra).

Burch, D., Lawrence, G., Rickson, R.E. and Goss, J. (eds) (1998), *Australasian Food and Farming in a Globalised Economy: Recent Developments and Future Prospects* (Melbourne: Monash Publications in Geography).

Burgess, R.G. (1984), *In the Field: An Introduction to Field Research* (London: Allen and Unwin).

Burton, C. (1991), *The Promise and the Price* (Sydney: Allen and Unwin).

—— (1997), *Women's Representation on Commonwealth and Private Sector Boards* (Canberra: Department of the Prime Minister and Cabinet).

Butler, J. (1990), *Gender Trouble: Feminism and the Subversion of Identity* (New York: Routledge).

—— (1993), *Bodies that Matter: On the Discursive Limits of Sex* (New York and London: Routledge).

—— (1999), *Gender Trouble – Feminism and the Subversion of Identity* 10th edition (New York: Routledge).

—— (2004), *Undoing Gender* (Abington, Oxfordshire: Routledge).

Butz, D. and Berg, L.D. (2002),'Paradoxical Space: Geography, Men and Duppy Feminism', in P. Moss (ed.) (Oxford: Blackwell), 87–102.

Bye, L. (2003), 'Masculinity and Rurality at Play in Stories About Hunting', *Norsk Geografisk Tidsskrift* 57:3, 145–53.

Byrne, A. and Lentin, R. (eds) (2002), *Feminist Research Methods in the Social Sciences in Ireland* (Dublin: Institute of Public Administration).

Cacoullos, A. (2000), 'Feminist Ruptures in Women's Studies and American Studies', *American Studies International* 38:3, 89–99.

Calas, M.B. and Smircich, L. (1993), 'Dangerous Liaisons: The Feminine in Management Meets Globalization', *Business Horizons* 36:2, 223–8.

Campbell, E. (2003), 'Interviewing Men in Uniform: A Feminist Approach?', *International Journal of Social Research Methodology* 6:4, 285–304.

Campbell, H. (2000), 'The Glass Phallus: Public Masculinity and Drinking in Rural New Zealand', *Rural Sociology* 65:4, 562–81.

Campbell, H. and Bell, M.M. (2000), 'The Question of Rural Masculinities', *Rural Sociology* 65:4, 552–46.

Campbell, H., Bell, M. and Finney, M. (eds) (2006a), *Country Boys: Masculinity and Rural Life* (Pennsylvania, US: Pennsylvania State University Press).

—— (2006b), 'Masculinity and Rural Life: An Introduction', in H. Campbell, M. Bell and M. Finney (eds), 1–22.

Campbell, H. and Kraack, A. (1998), 'Beer and Double Vision: Linking the Consumer to the Rural through New Zealand Television Beer Advertising', in D. Burch, G. Lawrence, R.E. Rickson and J. Goss (eds), 159–76.

Campbell, H. and Phillips, E. (1995), 'Masculine Hegemony and Leisure Sites in Rural New Zealand and Australia', in P. Share (ed.), 107–26.

Caplan, P. (1993), 'Introduction', in D. Bell, P. Caplan and W. Jahan Karim (eds), 19–27.

Carbert, L. (1995), *Agrarian Feminism: The Politics of Ontario Farm Women* (Toronto: University of Toronto Press).

Carrigan, T., Connell, R.W. and Lee, J. (1987), 'Hard and Heavy: Toward a New Sociology of Masculinity', in M. Kaufman (ed.), 139–92.

Chalmers, L.V. (2001), *Marketing Masculinities: Gender and Management Politics in Marketing Work* (Westport: Greenwood).

Charles, N. and Davies, C.A. (2000), 'Cultural Stereotypes and the Gendering of Senior Management', *The Sociological Review* 48:4, 542–67.

Clatterbaugh, K. (1990), *Contemporary Perspectives on Masculinity: Men, Women and Politics in Modern Society* (Colorado and Oxford: Westview Press).

—— (1998), 'What is Problematic about Masculinities?' *Men and Masculinities* 1:1, 24–45.

Cloke, P. (2006), 'Rurality and Racilialized Others: Out of Place in the Countryside', in P. Cloke, T. Marsden and P.H. Mooney (eds), 379–87.

Cloke, P. and Little, J. (eds) (1997), *Contested Countryside Cultures: Otherness, Marginalisation and Rurality* (London: Routledge).

Cloke, P., Marsden, T. and Mooney, P.H. (eds) (2006), *Handbook of Rural Studies* (London: Sage).

Coad, D. (2002), *Gender Trouble Down Under: Australian Masculinities* (Paris: Presses Universitaires de Valenciennes).

Cockburn, C. (1983), *Brothers: Male Dominance and Technological Change* (London: Pluto).

—— (1991), *In the Way of Women: Men's Resistance to Sex Equality in Organizations* (New York: ILR Press).

Coldwell, I. (2007a), 'New Farming Masculinities: "We're More Than Just Shit-Kickers": We're "Switched On" Farmers wanting to "Balance Lifestyle, Sustainability and Coins"', *Sociology* 43:1, 87–103.

—— (2007b), 'Young Farmers, Masculinities and the Embodiment of Farming Practices in an Australian Setting', *Rural Society* 17:1, 19–33.

Collier, R. (1998), *Masculinities, Crime and Criminology* (London: Sage).

Collinson, D.L. (1988), 'Engineering Humour: Masculinity, Joking and Conflict in Shopfloor Relations', *Organization Studies* 9:2, 181–99.

Collinson, D.L. and Collinson, M. (1989), 'Sexuality in the Workplace: The Domination of Men's Sexuality', in J. Hearn, D.L. Sheppard, P. Tancred-Sheriff and G. Burrell (eds), 91–109.

Collinson, D.L. and Hearn, J. (1993), 'The Big Picture: Masculinities in Recent World History', *Theory and Society* 22:5, 597–623.

—— (1994), 'Naming Men as Men: Implications for Work, Organization and Management', *Gender, Work and Organization* 1:1, 2–22.

—— (1995), *Masculinities* (St Leonards: Allen and Unwin).

—— (1996a), 'Breaking the Silence: On Men, Masculinities and Managements' in D.L. Collinson and J. Hearn (eds), 1–24.

—— (eds) (1996b), *Men as Managers, Managers as Men* (London: Sage).

—— (1998a), 'Introduction: Studying Australian Masculinities', *Journal of Interdisciplinary Gender Studies* 3:2, 1–8.

—— (1998b), 'Masculinities and Globalization', *Men and Masculinities* 1:1, 3–23.

—— (1998c), 'Reply', *Gender and Society* 12:4, 474–7.

—— (2000), *The Men and the Boys* (St Leonards: Allen and Unwin).

—— (2001), 'Studying Men and Masculinity', *Resources for Feminist Research* 19:1/2, 43–55.

—— (2003), 'Masculinities, Change, and Conflict in Global Society: Thinking about the Future of Men's Studies', *Journal of Men's Studies* 11:3, 249–66.

—— (2005), 'Men and Masculinities in Work, Organizations and Management', in M.S. Kimmel, J. Hearn and R.W. Connell (eds), 289–310.

—— (2006), 'Country/City Men', in H. Campbell, M. Bell and M. Finney (eds), 255–66.

Connell, R.W. and Messerschmidt, J.W. (2005), 'Hegemonic Masculinity: Rethinking the Concept', *Gender and Society* 19:6, 829–59.

Cooper, B.J. (1989), 'Farm Women: Some Contemporary Themes', *Labour/Le Travail* 24:3, 167–80.

Cross, S. and Bagilhole, B. (2002), 'Girls' Jobs for the Boys? Men, Masculinity and Non-traditional Occupations', *Gender, Work and Organization* 9:2, 204–26.

Cupples, J. (2002), 'The Field as a Landscape of Desire: Sex and Sexuality in Geographical Fieldwork', *Area* 34:4, 382–90.

Dale-Hallett, L., Panelli, R., Diffey, R., May, C. and Pini, B. and the members of the Women on Farms Heritage Group (2006), 'Creating Collaborative Living History: The Case of the Victorian Women on Farms Gathering Heritage Collection', *History Australia* 3:1, 15.1–15.14.

Davidson, M.J. and Burke, R.J. (eds) (1994), *Women in Management: Current Research Issues* (London: Paul Chapman).

Davies, B. (1995), 'What about the Boys? The Parable of the Bear and the Rabbit', *Interpretations* 28:2, 1–17.

—— (1997), 'The Subject of Post-Structuralism: A Reply to Alison Jones', *Gender and Education* 9:3, 271–83.

—— (2004), 'Introduction: Poststructuralist Lines of Flight in Australia', *International Journal of Qualitative Studies in Education* 17:1, 3–9.

Davies, B., Flemmen, A.B., Gannon, S., Laws, C. and Watson, B. (2002), 'Working on the Ground. A Collective Biography of Feminine Subjectivities: Mapping the Traces of Power and Knowledge', *Social Semiotics* 12:3, 291–313.

Davies, B. and Harre, R. (1990), 'Positioning the Discursive Production of Selves', *Journal for the Theory of Social Behaviour* 20:1, 43–63.

Day, K. (2001), 'Constructing Masculinity and Women's Fear in Public Space in Irvine California', *Gender, Place and Culture* 8:2, 109–27.

Deem, R. (2003), 'Gender, Organizational Cultures and the Practices of Manager-Academics in UK Universities', *Gender, Work and Organization* 10:2, 239–59.

Demetriou, D. (2001), 'Connell's Concept of Hegemonic Masculinity: A Critique', *Theory and Society* 30:3, 337–61.

Demossier, M. (2004), 'Women in Rural France: Mediators of Change?', in K. Hoggart and H. Butler (eds), 164–84.

Dempsey, K. (1992), *A Man's Town: Inequality Between Men and Women in Rural Australia* (Melbourne: Oxford University Press).

Dent, M. and Whitehead, S. (eds) (2002a), *Managing Professional Identities: Knowledge, Performativity and the 'New' Professional* (London: Routledge).

—— (2002b), 'Introduction: Configuring the "New" Professional', in M. Dent and S. Whitehead (eds), 1–16.

Department of Transport and Regional Services (DoTARS) (2005), *Women's Representation in Rural and Regional Australia* (Canberra: DoTARS).

Deseran, F.A. and Simpkins, N.R. (1991), 'Women's Off-farm Work and Gender Stratification', *Journal of Rural Studies* 7:1–7:2, 91–8.

Diamond, I. and Quinby, L. (1988a), 'Introduction', in I. Diamond and L. Quimby (eds), xi–xix.

—— (eds) (1988b), *Feminism and Foucault: Reflections on Resistance* (Boston: North-Eastern University).

Dimopoulos, M. and Sheridan, M. (2000), *Missed Opportunities: Unlocking the Future for Women in Australian Agriculture, Stage 2 Report* (Canberra: Rural Industries Research and Development Corporation).

DiTomaso, N. (1989), 'Sexuality in the Workplace: Discrimination and Harassment', in J. Hearn, D.L. Sheppard, P. Tancred-Sheriff and G. Burrell (eds), 71–90.

Donaldson, M. (1993), 'What is Hegemonic Masculinity?' *Theory and Society* 22:5, 643–57.

Due Billing, Y. and Alvesson, M. (2000), 'Questioning the Notion of Feminine Leadership: A Critical Perspective on the Gender Labeling of Leadership', *Gender, Work and Organization* 7:3, 144–57.

Duffield, B. (1996), 'Professional Women in Agriculture – Do They Have a Future?', *Women in Management Review* 11:4, 20–27.

Dyck, I., Lynam, J. and Anderson, J. (1995), 'Women Talking: Creating Knowledge Through Difference in Cross-Cultural Research', *Women's Studies International Forum* 18:5/6, 611–26.

Easterday, L., Papademas, D., Schorr, L. and Valentine, C. (1997), 'The Making of a Female Researcher', *Urban Life* 6:3, 333–48.

Effland, A.B., Rogers, D.M. and Grim, V. (1993), 'Women as Agricultural Landowners: What Do We Know about Them?' *Agricultural History* 67:2, 235–62.

Elix, J. and Lambert, J. (1998a), *Missed Opportunities—Harnessing the Potential of Women in Australian Agriculture, Volume 1* (Canberra: Rural Industries Research and Development Corporation).

—— (1998b), *Missed Opportunities: Harnessing the Potential of Women in Australian Agriculture, Volume 2, Economic Module* (Canberra: Rural Industries Research and Development Corporation and Department of Primary Industries and Energy).

El-Tobshy, Z. (2005), 'Gender and Culture in Egypt', in P. Motzafi-Haller (ed.), 115–40.

Elwood, S.E. and Martin, D.G. (2000), 'Placing Interviews: Location and Scales of Power in Qualitative Research', *Professional Geographer* 52:4, 649–57.

England, P. (ed.) (1993), *Theory on Gender/Feminism on Theory* (New York: Aldine De Gruyter).

Eveline, J. (1994), 'The Politics of Advantage', *Australian Feminist Studies, Special Issue: Women and Citizenship* 19 (Autumn), 129–54.

Eveline, J. and Booth, M. (2002), 'Gender and Sexuality in Discourses of Managerial Control: The Case of Women Miners', *Gender, Work and Organization* 9:5, 556–77.

Fellows, Q. (1996), *Farm Boys: Lives of Gay Men from the Rural Midwest* (Madison: University of Wisconsin Press).

Fenstermaker, S. and West, C. (eds) (2002), *Doing Gender, Doing Difference: Inequality, Power and Institutional Change* (New York: Routledge).

Fincher, R. and Panelli, P. (2001), 'Making Space: Women's Urban and Rural Activism and the Australian State', *Gender, Place and Culture* 8:2, 129–48.

Fink, D. (1992), 'Farm Wives and Agrarianism in the United States', in M. Alston (ed.), 1–7.

Fink, V.S. (1991), 'What Work is Real? Changing Roles of Farm and Ranch Wives in South-Eastern Ohio', *Journal of Rural Studies* 7:1/2, 17–22.

Finney, M., Campbell, H. and Bell, M.M. (2004), 'Rural Masculinities: Toward a New Research Agenda', Paper presented to Working Group 7, *Challenging Gender Relations in a Context of Rural Change*, World congress of the International Rural Sociological Association. Trondheim, 25–30 July.

First-Dilic, R. (1978), 'The Productive Roles of Farm Women in Yugoslavia', *Sociologia Ruralis* 18:2, 124–39.

Fitzsimons, A. (2002), *Gender as a Verb: Gender Segregation at Work* (Aldershot: Ashgate).

Flax, J. (1990), 'Postmodernism and Gender Relations in Feminist Theory', in L. Nicholson (ed.), 39–62.

Fondas, N. (1997), 'Feminization Unveiled: Management Qualities in Contemporary Writings', *Academy of Management Review* 22:1, 257–82.

Fonow, M.M. and Cook, J.A. (2005), 'Feminist Methodology: New Applications in the Academy and Public Policy', *Signs: Journal of Women in Culture and Society* 30:4, 2211–36.

Foucault, M. (1972), *The Archaeology of Knowledge* (New York: Harper Colophon).

—— (1977), *Language, Counter-Memory, Practice: Selected Interviews and Essays*, D. Bouchard (ed.) (New York: Cornell University Press).

—— (1978), *The History of Sexuality Volume 1: An Introduction* (London: Penguin).

—— (1980), *Power/Knowledge: Selected Interviews and Other Writings 1972–1977*, C. Gordon (ed.) (New York: Pantheon Press).

—— (1981), *The History of Sexuality Volume 1: The Will to Knowledge* (London: Penguin).

—— (1987), 'The Ethic of Care for the Self as a Practice of Freedom', *Philosophy and Social Criticism* 12:2, 113–31.

—— (1997), *Ethics, Essential Works of Foucault 1954–1984 Volume 1*, Paul Radinow (ed.) (London: Penguin).

Francis, B. (2000), *Boys, Girls and Achievement* (London: Routledge).

Franklin, M.A., Short, L.M. and Teather, E.K. (eds) (1994), *Country Women at the Crossroads* (Armidale: University of New England Press).

Friedland, W.H. (1991), 'Women and Agriculture in the United States: A State of the Art Assessment', in W. Friedland, L. Busch, F. Buttel and A. Rudy (eds), 315–38.

Friedland, W.H., Busch, L., Buttel, F. and Rudy, A. (eds) (1991), *Towards a Political Economy of Agriculture* (Boulder, CO: Westview Press).

Fulton, A. and McGowan, C. (2005), 'Fostering Women's Participation in On-farm Programs', *Meat and Livestock Australia* (Sydney).

Garcia-Ramon, M.D. and Canoves, G. (1988), 'The Role of Women on the Family Farm: The Case of Catalonia', *Sociologia Ruralis* 28, 263–70.

Garcia-Ramon, M.D., Canoves, G. and Valdovinos, N. (1995), 'Farm Tourism, Gender and the Environment in Spain', *Annals of Tourism Research* 22:2, 267–82.

Gardiner, J.K. (2002a), 'Introduction', in J.K. Gardiner (ed.), 1–30.

—— (ed.) (2002b), *Masculine Studies and Feminist Theory: New Directions* (New York: Columbia University Press).

Garkovich, L. and Bell, A.M. (1995), 'Charting Trends in Rural Sociology: 1986–1995', *Rural Sociology* 60:4, 639–87.

Gasson, R. (1980), 'Roles of Farm Women in England', *Sociologia Ruralis* 20:3, 165–80.

—— (1994), 'Women's Management Roles in Agriculture', *Farm Management* 8:11, 513–22.

Gasson, R. and Winter, M. (1992), 'Gender Relations and Farm Household Pluriactivity', *Journal of Rural Studies* 8:4, 387–97.

Gergen, M. and Davis, S. (eds) (1997), *Toward a New Psychology of Gender* (London: Routledge).

Gherardi, S. (1995), *Gender, Symbolism and Organizational Cultures* (London: Sage).

—— (1996), 'Gendered Organizational Cultures: Narratives of Women Travelers in a Male World', *Gender, Work and Organization* 3:4, 187–201.

Gherardi, S. and Poggio, B. (2001), 'Creating and Recreating Gender Order in Organizations', *Journal of World Business* 36:3, 245–59.

Gilbert, R. and Gilbert, P. (1998), *Masculinity Goes to School* (London: Routledge).

Glesne, C. and Peshkin, A. (1992), *Becoming Qualitative Researchers: An Introduction* (London: Longman).

Gooday, J. (1995), *Women on Farms* (Canberra: Australian Bureau of Agricultural and Resource Economics).

Gough, B. and Peace, P. (2000), 'Reconstructing Gender at University: Men as Victims', *Gender and Education* 12:3, 385–98.

Gourdomichalis, A. (1991), 'Women and the Reproduction of Family Farms: Change and Continuity in the Region of Thessaly, Greece', *Journal of Rural Studies* 7:1/2, 57–62.

Goverde, H., de Haan, H. and Baylina, M. (eds) (2004), *Power and Gender in European Rural Development* (Aldershot: Ashgate).

Grace, M. (1994), *Women in Rural Queensland: An Exploration of Cultural Contexts, Educational Needs and Leadership Potential* (Brisbane: Queensland University of Technology).

—— (1997), *Networking Systems for Rural Women* (Canberra: Rural Industries Research and Development Corporation).

Gray, I. and Lawrence, G. (2001), *A Future for Regional Australia: Escaping Global Misfortune* (Cambridge: Cambridge University Press).

Grosz, E. (1987), 'Notes Towards a Corporeal Feminism', *Australian Feminist Studies* 2:1, 1–16.

Gubar, S. (1998), 'What Ails Feminist Criticism?', *Critical Inquiry* 24:4, 878–902.

Gullifer, J. and Thompson, A.P. (2006), 'Subjective Realities of Older Male Farmers', *Rural Society* 16:1, 80–97.

Gunn, H. (1997), 'Women's Bodies, 1924–1926. A Site for Rural Politics', in J. Long, J. Gothard and H. Brash (eds), 181–201.

Gurney, J.N. (1985), 'Not One of the Guys: The Female Researcher in a Male-Dominated Setting', *Qualitative Sociology* 8:1, 42–62.

Halfacree, K. (1995), 'Talking about Rurality: Social Representations of the Rural as Expressed by Residents of Six English Parishes', *Journal of Rural Studies* 11:1, 1–20.

Halford, S. and Leonard, P. (2001), *Gender, Power and Organizations: An Introduction* (Basingstoke: Houndsmills).

Hall, S. (1996), 'Introduction: Who Needs Identity?', in S. Hall and P. Du Gay (eds), 1–17.

Hall, S. and Du Gay, P. (eds) (1996), *Questions of Cultural Identity* (London: Sage).

Haney, W.G. and Knowles, J.B. (eds) (1988), *Women and Farming: Changing Roles, Changing Structures* (Boulder: Westview Press).

Harter, L.M. (2004), 'Masculinity(ies), the Agrarian Frontier Myth, and Cooperative Forms of Organizing', *Journal of Applied Communication Research* 32:1, 89–118.

Haslam McKenzie, F. (1999), 'Boys' Clubs: Discriminatory Voting Practices in Agricultural Industry Organizations', *International Review of Women and Leadership* Special Issue, 39–52.

Hassard, J., Holliday, R. and Willmott, H. (eds) (2000), *Body and Organization* (London: Sage).

Hatcher, C. (2003), 'Refashioning a Passionate Manager: Gender at Work', *Gender, Work and Organization* 10:4, 391–412.

Haugen, M.S. (1994), 'Rural Women's Status in Family and Property Law: Lessons from Norway', in S. Whatmore, T. Marsden and P. Lowe (eds), 87–101.

—— (1998), 'The Gendering of Farming: The Case of Norway', *The European Journal of Women's Studies* 5, 133–53.

Haywood, C. and Mac an Ghaill, M. (2003), *Men and Masculinities: Theory, Research and Social Practice* (Buckingham: Open University Press).

Hearn, J. (1992), *Men in the Public Eye: The Construction and Deconstruction of Public Men and Public Patriarchies* (London: Routledge).

—— (1993), *Researching Men and Researching Men's Violence*, Research Paper No. 4.BD7 (Bradford: University of Bradford).

—— (1996), 'Is Masculinity Dead? A Critique of the Concept of Masculinity/ Masculinities', in M. Mac an Ghaill (ed.), 202–17.

—— (1997), 'The Implications of Critical Studies on Men', *NORA* 3:1, 48–60.

—— (1998), 'Theorizing Men and Men's Theorizing: Varieties of Discursive Practices in Men's Theorizing of Men', *Theory and Society* 27:6, 781–816.

—— (2000), 'The Hegemony of Men: On Construction of Counterhegemony in Critical Studies on Men', in P. Folkesson, M. Norberg and G. Smirthwaite (eds).

—— (2004), 'From Hegemonic Masculinity to the Hegemony of Men', *Feminist Theory* 5:1, 49–72.

Hearn, J., Sheppard, D.L., Tancred-Sheriff, P. and Burrell, G. (eds) (1989), *The Sexuality of Organization* (London: Sage).

Heather, B., Skillen, L., Young, J. and Vladicka, T. (2005), 'Women's Gendered Identities and the Restructuring of Rural Alberta', *Sociologia Ruralis* 45:1/2, 86–97.

Hekman, S. (2000), 'Beyond Identity: Feminism, Identity and Identity Politics', *Feminist Theory* 1:3, 289–308.

Herbert, S. (2001), '"Hard Charger" or "Station Queen"? Policing and the Masculinist State', *Gender, Place and Culture* 8:1, 55–71.

Herod, A. (1993), 'Gender Issues in the Use of Interviewing as a Research Method', *Professional Geographer* 45:3, 305–17.

Higgins, V. and Lawrence, G. (eds) (2005), *Agricultural Governance: Globalization and the New Politics of Regulation* (London: Routledge).

Hill, F. (1981), 'Farm Women: Challenge to Scholarship', *The Rural Sociologist* 1:6, 370–82.

Hodgson, D. (2003), '"Taking it like a Man": Masculinity, Subjection and Resistance in the Selling of Life Assurance', *Gender, Work and Organization* 10:1, 1–21.

Hoggart, K. and Butler, H. (eds) (2004), *Women in Rural Europe* (Aldershot: Ashgate).

Holloway, L. and Kneafsey, M. (eds) (2004), *Geographies of Rural Cultures and Societies* (London: Ashgate).

Holstein, J.A. and Gubrium, J.F. (eds) (2003), *Inside Interviewing: New Lenses, New Concerns* (Thousand Oaks, CA: Sage).

Hooper, C. (2001), *Manly States: Masculinities, International Relations and Gender Politics* (New York: Columbia University Press).

Hopton, J. (1999), 'Militarism, Masculinism and Managerialisation in the British Public Sector', *Journal of Gender Studies* 8:1, 71–82.

Horn, R. (1997), 'Not One of the Boys: Women Researching the Police', *Journal of Gender Studies* 6:3, 297–308.

Hovden, J. (2000), 'Gender and Leadership Selection Processes in Norwegian Sporting Organizations', *International Review for the Sociology of Sport* 35:1, 75–82.

Imms, W.D. (2000), 'Multiple Masculinities and the Schooling of Boys', *Canadian Journal of Education* 25:2, 152–65.

Jackson, P. (2001), 'Making Sense of Qualitative Data', in M. Limb and C. Dwyer (eds), 199–214.

James, K. (1989), 'Introduction', in K. James (ed.), 1–19.

—— (ed.) (1989), *Women in Rural Australia* (St Lucia: Queensland University Press).

—— (1990), 'Women's Decision Making in Extended Family Farm Businesses', in M. Alston (ed.), 29–37.

Jefferson, T. (2002), 'Subordinating Hegemonic Masculinity', *Theoretical Criminology* 6:1, 63–88.

Jeffreys, S. (1996), 'Return to Gender, Post-Modernism and Lesbian and Gay Theory', in D. Bell and R. Klein (ed.), 359–74.

Jermier, J., Knights, D. and Nord, W. (eds) (1994), *Resistance and Power in Organizations* (London: Routledge).

Jervell, A.M. (1999), 'Changing Patterns of Family Farming and Pluriactivity', *Sociologia Ruralis* 39:1, 100–116.

Jodahl, T. (1994), 'Farm Women in the Nordic Countries', in L. Van der Plas and M. Fonte (eds), 112–18.

Jones, A. (1997), 'Teaching Post-Structuralist Feminist Theory in Education: Student Resistances', *Gender and Education* 9:3, 261–9.

Jones, L. (2002), *Mamma Learned Us to Work* (Chapel Hill: University of North Carolina Press).

Jones, O. (1995), 'Lay Discourses of the Rural; Development and Implications for Rural Studies', *Journal of Rural Studies* 11:1, 35–49.

—— (1999), 'Tomboy Tales: The Rural, Nature and the Gender of Childhood', *Gender, Place and Culture* 6:2, 117–36.

Kanter, R.M. (1977), *Men and Women of the Corporation* (New York: Basic Books).

Katila, S. and Merilainen, S. (2002a), 'Metamorphosis: From "Nice Girls" to "Nice Bitches": Resisting Patriarchal Articulations of Professional Identity', *Gender, Work and Organization* 9:3, 336–54.

Katila, S. and Merilainen, S. (2002b), 'Self in Research: Hopelessly Entangled in the Gendered Organizational Culture', in I. Aaltio and A.J. Mills (eds), 185–200.

Kaufman, M. (ed.) (1987), *Beyond Patriarchy: Essays by Men on Pleasure, Power and Change* (Toronto: Oxford).

Kenway, J., Kraack, A. and Hickey-Moody, A. (2006), *Masculinity Beyond the Metropolis* (Basingstoke, UK: Palgrave).

Kenway, J., Willis, S., Blackmore, J. and Rennie, L. (1994), 'Making "Hope Practical" Rather than "Despair Convincing": Feminist Post-Structuralism, Gender Reform and Educational Change', *British Journal of Sociology of Education* 15:2, 187–210.

Kerfoot, D. and Knights, D. (1993), 'Management, Masculinity and Manipulation: From Paternalism to Corporate Strategy in Financial Services', *Britain Journal of Management Studies* 30:4, 659–77.

—— (1996), 'The Best Is Yet to Come? The Quest for Embodiment in Managerial Work', in D.L. Collinson and J. Hearn (eds), 81–95.

Kerfoot, D. and Whitehead, S. (1998), '"Boys' Own Stuff": Masculinity and Management of Further Education', *Sociological Review* 46:3, 436–57.

Kerfoot, S. (2002), 'Managing the Professional Man', in M. Dent and S. Whitehead (eds), 81–95.

Kimmel, M. (1996), *Manhood in America* (New York: Free Press).

Kimmel, M.S., Hearn, J. and Connell, R.W. (eds) (2005), *Handbook of Studies on Men and Masculinities* (Thousand Oaks: Sage).

Kirton, G. (2006), *The Making of Women Trade Unionists* (Aldershot: Ashgate).

Knights, D. and McCabe, D. (2001), '"A Different World": Shifting Masculinities in the Transition to Call Centers', *Organization* 8:4, 619–45.

Knights, D. and Vurdubakis, T. (1994), 'Foucault, Power and All That', in J. Jermier, D. Knights and W. Nord (eds), 167–98.

Knights, D. and Willmott, H. (1999), *Management Lives: Power and Identity in Work Organizations* (London: Sage).

Knoppers, A. and Anthonissen, A. (2005), 'Male Athletic and Managerial Masculinities: Congruencies in Discursive Practices?' *Journal of Gender Studies* 14:2, 123–35.

Kohl, S.B. (1977), 'Women's Participation in the North American Family Farm', *Women's Studies International Quarterly* 1:1, 47–54.

Kronsell, A. (2005), 'Gendered Practices in Institutions of Hegemonic Masculinity', *International Feminist Journal of Politics* 7:2, 280–98.

Kulick, D. and Wilson, M. (eds) (1995), *Taboo: Sex, Identity and Erotic Subjectivity in Anthropological Fieldwork* (London: Routledge).

Kvale, S. (1996), *Interviews* (Thousand Oaks: Sage).

Kvande, E. (1999), 'In the Belly of the Beast: Constructing Femininities in Engineering Organizations', *European Journal of Women's Studies* 6:3, 305–28.

Leckie, G.J. (1996), 'Female Farmers and the Social Construction of Access to Agricultural Information', *Library and Information Science Research* 18:4, 297–321.

Lee, D. (1997), 'Interviewing Men: Vulnerabilities and Dilemmas', *Women's Studies International Forum* 20:4, 553–64.

Lennie, I. (2000), 'Embodying Management', in J. Hassard, R. Holliday and H. Willmott (eds), 130–46.

Letherby, G. (2003), *Feminist Research in Theory and Practice* (Buckingham: Open University Press).

Levinson, B.A. (1998), 'Can a Man do Feminist Ethnography of Education?', *Qualitative Inquiry* 4:3, 337–68.

Leyshon, M. (2005), 'No Place for a Girl: Rural Youth, Pubs and the Performance of Masculinity', in J. Little and C. Morris (eds), 104–122.

Liepins, R. (1998), 'The Gendering of Farming and Agricultural Politics: A Matter of Discourse and Power', *Australian Geographer* 29:3, 371–88.

—— (2000), 'Making Men: The Construction and Representation of Agriculture-based Masculinities in Australia and New Zealand', *Rural Sociology* 65:4, 605–620.

Limb, M. and Dwyer, C. (eds) (2001), *Qualitative Methodologies for Geographers: Issues and Debates* (London: Arnold).

Limerick, B., Burgess-Limerick, T. and Grace, M. (1996), 'The Politics of Interviewing: Power Relations and Accepting the Gift', *Qualitative Studies in Education* 9:4, 449–60.

Lingard, B. and Douglas, P. (1999), *Men Engaging Feminisms: Pro-Feminism, Backlashes and Schooling* (Buckingham: Open University Press).

Linstead, A. and Thomas, R. (2002), '"What Do You Want from Me?": A Poststructural Feminist Reading of Middle Managers' Identities', *Culture and Organization* 8:1, 1–20.

Little, J. (1986), 'Feminist Perspective in Rural Geography: An Introduction', *Journal of Rural Studies* 2:1, 1–8.

—— (1987), 'Gender Relations in Rural Areas: The Importance of Women's Domestic Role', *Journal of Rural Studies* 3:4, 335–42.

—— (1997), 'Constructions of Rural Women's Voluntary Work', *Gender, Place and Culture* 4:2, 197–209.

—— (2002a), 'Rural Geography: Rural Gender Identity and the Performance of Masculinity and Femininity in the Countryside', *Progress in Human Geography* 26:5, 665–70.

—— (2002b), *Gender and Rural Geography: Identity, Sexuality and Power in the Countryside* (London: Prentice Hall).

—— (2003), 'Riding the Rural Love Train: Heterosexuality and the Rural Community', *Sociologia Ruralis* 43:4, 401–17.

—— (2006), 'Gender and Sexuality in Rural Communities', in P. Cloke, T. Marsden and P.H. Mooney (eds), 365–78.

—— (2007), 'Constructing nature in the performance of rural heterosexualities', *Environment and Planning: Society and Space* 25:5, 851–66.

Little, J. and Leyshon, M. (2003), 'Embodied Rural Geographer: Developing Research Agendas', *Progress in Human Geography* 27:3, 257–72.

Little, J. and Morris, C. (eds) (2005), *Critical Studies in Rural Gender Issues* (Aldershot: Ashgate).

Little, J. and Panelli, R. (2003), 'Gender Research in Rural Geography', *Gender, Place and Culture* 10:3, 281–9.

—— (2007), 'Outback romance? A Reading of Nature and Heterosexuality in Rural Australia', *Sociologia Ruralis* 47:3, 174–88.

Lohan, M. (2000), 'Extending Feminist Methodologies: Researching Masculinities and Technologies', in A. Byrne and R. Lentin (eds), 167–87.

Long, J., Gothard, J. and Brash, H. (eds) (1997), *Forging Identities: Bodies, Gender and Feminist History* (Perth: University of Western Australia Press).

Longhurst, R. (1997), 'Disembodied Geographies', *Progress in Human Geography* 21:4, 486–501.

Lorber, J. (1998), 'Men's Gender Politics', *Gender and Society* 12:4, 469–72.

Lucas, R. (2006), 'Dragging It Out: Tales of Masculinity in Australian Cinema, from "Crocodile Dundee" to "Priscilla, Queen of the Desert"', *Journal of Australian Studies* 56, 138–9.

Lupton, B. (2000), 'Maintaining Masculinity: Men Who Do "Women's Work"', *British Journal of Management* 11:1, 33–48.

Lyson, T.A. (1990), 'A Note on the Increase of Female Farmers in the United States and New Zealand', *The Australian and New Zealand Journal of Sociology* 26:1, 59.

Mac an Ghaill, M. (ed.) (1996), *Understanding Masculinities* (Buckingham: Open University Press).

MacInnes, J. (1998), *The End of Masculinity* (Buckingham: Open University Press).

Mackenzie, F. (1992), 'The Worse it Got, the More we Laughed: A Discourse of Resistance Among Farmers of Eastern Ontario', *Environment and Planning D: Society and Space* 10:6, 691–713.

—— (1994), 'Is Where I Sit Where I Stand? The Ontario Farm Women's Network, Politics and Difference', *Journal of Rural Studies* 10:2, 101–115.

Maddock, S. and Parkin, D. (1994), 'Gender Cultures: How They Affect Men and Women at Work', in M.J. Davidson and R.J. Burke (eds), 29–40.

Maile, S. (1995), 'The Gendered Nature of Managerial Discourse: The Case of a Local Authority', *Gender Work and Organization* 2:2, 76–87.

Maloney, M. and Fenstermaker, S. (2002), 'Doing Difference', in S. Fenstermaker and C. West (eds), 55–79.

Marshall, J. (1984), *Women Managers: Travellers in a Male World* (Chichester: John Wiley and Sons).

—— (1995), 'Researching Women and Leadership: Some Comments on Challenges and Opportunities', *International Review of Women and Leadership* 1:1, 1–10.

Martin, P.Y. (1996), 'Gendering and Evaluating Dynamics: Men, Masculinities and Managements', in D.L. Collinson and J. Hearn (eds), 186–209.

—— (1998), 'Why Can't a Man Be More Like a Woman? Reflections on Connell's Masculinities', *Gender and Society* 12:4, 472–4.

—— (2001), 'Mobilizing Masculinities: Women's Experiences of Men at Work', *Organization* 8:4, 587–618.

—— (2003), '"Said and Done" Versus "Saying and Doing": Gendering Practices, Practicing Gender at Work', *Gender and Society* 17:3, 342–66.

Mason, J. (2002), *Qualitative Researching* (London: Sage).

Massey, D. (1994), *Space, Place and Gender* (Cambridge: Polity Press).

Maynard, M. (1995), 'Beyond the "Big Three": The Development of Feminist Theory in the 1990s', *Women's History Review* 4:3, 259–81.

Maynard, M. and Purvis, J. (eds) (1994), *Researching Women's Lives from a Feminist Perspective* (London: Taylor and Francis).

McDowell, L. (1992), 'Space, Place and Gender Relations, Part 1, Feminist Empiricism and the Geography of Social Relations', *Progress in Human Geography* 17:1, 157–79.

—— (1998), 'Elites in the City of London: Some Methodological Considerations', *Environment and Planning A* 30, 2133–46.

—— (1999), *Gender Identity and Place: Understanding Feminist Geographies* (Cambridge, Oxford: Polity Press).

—— (2001), 'Men, Management and Multiple Masculinities in Organizations', *Geoform* 32, 181–98.

McDowell, L. and Court, G. (1994), 'Missing Subjects: Gender, Power and Sexuality in Merchant Banking', *Economic Geography* 70:3, 229–51.

McKay, J. (1997), *Managing Gender: Affirmative Action and Organizational Power in Australian, Canadian and New Zealand Sport* (Albany: State University of New York).

McKeganey, N. and Bloor, M. (1991), 'Spotting the Invisible Man: The Influence of Male Gender on Fieldwork Relations', *British Journal of Sociology* 42:2, 195–210.

McLaren, M.A. (2004), 'Foucault and Feminism: Power, Resistance, Freedom', in D. Taylor and K. Vintges (eds), 235–57.

McMahon, A. (1993), 'Male Readings of Feminist Theory: The Psychologization of Sexual Politics in the Masculinity Literature', *Theory and Society* 22:5, 675–96.

Messerschmidt, J.W. (2005), 'Men, Masculinities and Crime', in M. Kimmel, J. Hearn and R.W. Connell (eds), 196–212.

Messner, M. (1997), *Politics of Masculinities, Men in Movements* (Thousand Oaks, Sage).

Meyer, K. and Lobao, L.M. (1994), 'Engendering the Farm Crisis: Women's Political Response in USA', in S. Whatmore, T. Marsden and P. Lowe (eds), 80–90.

Miles, M.B. and Huberman, A.M. (1994), *Qualitative Data Analysis* 2nd edition (Thousand Oaks: Sage).

Miller, G.E. (2004), 'Frontier Masculinity in the Oil Industry: The Experience of Women Engineers', *Gender, Work and Organization* 11:1, 47–73.

Miller, T. (1998), 'Commodifying the Male Body, Problematizing "Hegemonic Masculinity"?', *Journal of Sport and Social Issues* 22:4, 431–47.

Modleski, T. (1991), *Feminism Without Women: Culture and Criticism in a Post Feminist Age* (New York and London: Routledge).

Morell, I.A. and Bock, B. (eds) (2008), *Gender Regimes, Citizen Participation and Rural Restructuring* (Oxford: Elsevier).

Morgan, D., Brandth, B. and Kvande, E. (eds) (2005), *Gender Bodies and Work* (Aldershot: Ashgate).

Morris, C. and Evans, N. (2001), '"Cheese Makers Are Always Women": Gendered Representations of Farm Life in the Agricultural Press', *Gender, Place and Culture* 8:4, 375–90.

—— (2004), 'Agricultural Turns, Geographical Turns: Retrospect and Prospect', *Journal of Rural Studies* 20:1, 95–111.

Moss, P. (ed.) (2001), *Geography and Gender: A Guide to Methodology* (Oxford: Blackwell).

Motzafi-Haller, P. (ed.) (2005), *Women in Agriculture in the Middle East* (Aldershot: Ashgate).

Mulholland, K. (1996), 'Entrepreneurialism, Masculinities and the Self-Made Man', in D.L. Collinson and J. Hearn (eds), 123–49.

Murrie, L. (1998), 'The Australian Legend: Writing Australian Masculinity/Writing "Australian" Masculine', *Journal of Australian Studies* 56, 68–77.

Nash, K. (1994), 'The Feminist Production of Knowledge: Is Deconstruction a Practice for Women', *Feminist Review* 47: Summer, 65–77.

Neth, M. (1988), 'Building the Base: Farm Women, the Rural Community, and Farm Organizations in the Midwest, 1900–1940', in W.G. Haney and J.B. Knowles (eds), 339–55.

Ni Laoire, C. (1999), 'Gender Issues in Irish Rural Out Migration', in P. Boyle and K. Halfacre (eds), 223–7.

—— (2001), 'A Matter of Life and Death: Men, Masculinities and Staying "Behind" in Rural Ireland', *Sociologia Ruralis* 41:2, 220–36.

—— (2002), 'Young Farmers, Masculinities and Change in Rural Ireland', *Irish Geography* 35:1, 16–27.

—— (2004), 'Winner and Losers? Rural Restructuring, Economic Status and Masculine Identities among Young Farmers in South-West Ireland', in L. Holloway and M. Kneafsey (eds), 283–301.

Ni Laoire, C. and Fielding, S. (2006), 'Rooted and Routed Masculinities Among the Rural Youth of North Cork and Upper Swaledale', in H. Campbell, M. Bell, and M. Finney (eds), 105–120.

Nicholson, L. (ed.) (1990), *Feminism and Postmodernism* (London and New York: Routledge).

Nilan, P. (1995), 'Masculinity as Social Practice and Cultural "Becoming"', *Journal of Interdisciplinary Gender Studies* 1:1, 57–69.

Nussbaum, M.C. (1999), 'The Professor of Parody', *The New Republic* 220:8, 37–45.

O'Farrell, C. (2005), *Michel Foucault* (London: Sage).

O'Hara, P. (1998), *Partners in Production? Women, Farm and Family in Ireland* (New York: Berghahn Books).

O'Sullivan, J. and Sheridan, A. (2005), 'The King is Dead, Long Live the King: Tall Tales of New Men and New Management in "The Bill"', *Gender, Work and Organization* 12:4, 299–318.

Oakley, A. (1981), 'Interviewing Women: A Contradiction in Terms', in H. Roberts (ed.), 30–61.

—— (2000), *Experiments in Knowing: Gender and Method in the Social Sciences* (New York: New Press).

Oldrup, H. (1999), 'Women Working off the Farm: Reconstructing Gender Identity in Danish Agriculture', *Sociologia Ruralis* 39:3, 343–58.

Ozbilgin, M.F. and Woodward, D. (2004), '"Belonging" and "Otherness": Sex Equality in Banking in Turkey and Britain', *Gender, Work and Organization* 11:6, 668–88.

Panelli, R. (2002), 'Contradictory Identities and Political Choices: "Women in Agriculture" in Australia', in B.S.A. Yeoh, P. Teo and S. Huang (eds), 136–55.

—— (2006), 'Rural Society', in P. Cloke, T. Marsden and P.H. Mooney (eds), 63–90.

—— (2007), 'Time-space Geometries of Activism and the Case of Mis/placing Gender in Australian Agriculture', *Transactions* 32, 46–65.

Panelli, R. and Pini, B. (2005), '"This Beats a Cake Stall": Farm Women's Shifting Encounters with the Australian State', *Politics and Policy* 33:3, 489–503.

Pearson, J. (1979), 'Note on Female Farmers', *Rural Sociology* 44:1, 189–200.

Pease, B. (2000), *Recreating Men: Postmodern Masculinity Politics* (London: Sage).

Pedersen, K. (1998), 'Doing Feminist Ethnography in the "Wilderness" Around My Hometown: Methodological Reflections', *International Review of the Sociology of Sport* 33:4, 393–402.

Pedersen, K.B. and Kjaergard, B. (2004), 'Do We Have Room for Shining Eyes and Cows as Comrades? Gender Perspectives on Organic Farming in Denmark', *Sociologia Ruralis* 44:4, 373–94.

Perry, J.E. and Ahearn, M.C. (1994), 'Farm Women Blend Off-farm Work', *Rural Development Perspectives* 9:3, 24–31.

Peter, G., Bell, M.M., Jarnagin, S. and Bauer, D. (2000), 'Coming Back Across the Fence: Masculinity and the Transition to Sustainable Agriculture', *Rural Sociology* 65:2, 215–33.

Phillips, M., Fish, R. and Agg, J. (2001), 'Putting Together Ruralities: Towards a Symbolic Analysis of Rurality in the British Mass Media', *Journal of Rural Studies* 17:1, 1–27.

Phillips, R., Watt, D. and Shuttleton, D. (eds) (2000), *De-centering Sexualities: Politics and Representation Beyond the Metropolis* (London: Routledge).

Philo, C. (1992), 'Neglected Rural Geographies', *Journal of Rural Studies* 8:3, 193–207.

Phoenix, A. (1994), 'Practising Feminist Research: The Intersection of Gender and Race in the Research Process", in M. Maynard and J. Purvis (eds), 49–71.

Phoenix, A. and Frosh, S. (2001), 'Positioned by "Hegemonic" Masculinities: A Study of London Boys' Narratives of Identity', *Australian Psychologist* 36:1, 27–35.

Pierce, J. (1995), *Gender Trials* (Berkeley: University of California Press).

Pini, B. (1998), 'The Emerging Economic Rationalist Discourse on Women and Leadership in Australian Agriculture', *Rural Society* 8:3, 223–34.

—— (2002a), 'Constraints to Women's Involvement in Agricultural Leadership', *Women in Management Review* 17:6, 276–84.

—— (2002b), 'Focus Groups and Farm Women: Opportunities for Empowerment in Rural Social Research', *Journal of Rural Studies* 18:3, 330–51.

—— (2002c), 'The Exclusion of Women from Agri-political Leadership: A Case Study of the Australian Sugar Industry', *Sociologia Ruralis* 42:1, 65–76.

—— (2003a), 'Feminist Methodology and Rural Research: Reflections on a Study of an Australian Agricultural Organisation', *Sociologia Ruralis* 43:4, 418–33.

—— (2003b), 'Sheep, Shadows and Silly Saints: Constructions of Women in Leadership in Australian Agriculture', *Rural Society* 13:2, 193–207.

—— (2003c), 'Strategies for Increasing Women's Representation in Agricultural Leadership', *Australian and New Zealand Academy of Management* 9:1, 66–79.

—— (2003d), 'We Could Have Had the Old Girl out in the Paddock Years Ago: Widowed Women, Farming and Agricultural Leadership', *Work, Employment and Society* 17:1, 171–82.

—— (2004a), 'Counting Them In, Not Out: Surveying Farm Women about Agricultural Leadership', *Australian Geographical Studies* 42:2, 249–59.

—— (2004b), 'Farm Women and Off-farm Work: A Study of the Australian Sugar Industry', *Labour and Industry* 15:1, 53–64.

—— (2004c), 'Gender and Farming in the Information Economy', *Australian and New Zealand Journal of Communication* 31:2, 135–48.

—— (2004d), 'On Being a Nice Country Girl and an Academic Feminist: Using Reflexivity in Rural Social Research', *Journal of Rural Studies* 20:2, 169–79.

—— (2004e), 'Paternalism and Managerial Masculinities in the Australian Sugar Industry', *Rural Society* 14:1, 22–35.

—— (2005a), 'Interviewing Men: Gender and the Collection and Interpretation of Qualitative Data', *Sociology* 41:2, 1–16.

—— (2005b), 'Progress Not Pipelines: A Case Study of the Need for the Strategic Management of Equity in an Australian Agricultural Organisation', *Strategic Change* 14:3, 133–40.

—— (2005c), 'The Third Sex: Women in Leadership in Australian Agriculture', *Gender, Work and Organisation* 12:1, 73–88.

—— (2005d), 'Women, Tractors and Gender Management', *International Journal of the Sociology of Food and Agriculture* 13:1, 1–12.

—— (2006a), 'A Critique of New Regional Governance: The Case of Gender in a Rural Australian Setting', *Journal of Rural Studies* 22:4, 383–502.

—— (2006b), 'Will We Have to Wait for Another Hundred Years? Gender and Franchise in Australian Agri-Political Organizations', *Hecate* 32:1, 123–31.

—— (2007), 'Always an Outlaw: Daughters-in-law and Australian Family Farming', *Women's Studies International Forum* 30:1: 40–47.

—— (2008), 'Men, Masculinities and the (Re)gendering of Local Government in Rural Australia', in, I.A. Morell and B. Bock (eds), 299–316.

Pini, B. and Brown, K. (2004), 'Farm Women and Femocrats', *Australian Journal of Political Science* 39:1, 161–74.

Pini, B., Brown, K. and Previte, J. (2004), 'Politics and Identity in Cyberspace: A Case Study of Australian Women in Agriculture', *Information, Communication and Society* 7:2, 167–84.

Pini, B., Brown, K. and Ryan, C. (2004), 'Women Only Networks as a Strategy for Change? A Case Study from Local Government', *Women in Management Review* 19:6, 286–92.

Pini, B., Brown, K. and Simpson, L. (2003), 'Australian Women in Agriculture: 1992–2002', *Australian Journal of Public Administration* 61:1, 24–31.

Pini, B., Panelli, R., Dale-Hallett, L. and the Women on Farms Heritage Group (2007), 'The Victorian Women on Farms Gatherings: A Case Study of the Australian "Women in Agriculture" Movement', *Australian Journal of Politics and History* 53:4, 569–81.

Pini, B., Panelli, R. and Sawer, M. (2008), 'Managing the Woman Issue! The Australian State and the Case of Women in Agri-Politics', *International Journal of Feminist Politics* 10:2, 173–97.

Pini, B. and Shortall, S. (2006), 'Gender Equality in Agriculture: A Comparative Study of State Intervention in Australia and Northern Ireland', *Social Policy and Society* 5:2, 199–206.

Poiner, G. (1990), *The Good Old Rule: Gender and Power Relations in a Rural Community* (Sydney: Sydney University Press and Oxford University Press).

Polity Press (ed.) (1994), *The Polity Reader in Gender Studies* (Cambridge UK: Polity Press).

Price, L. and Evans, N. (2005), 'Work and Worry: Revealing Farm Women's Way of Life', in J. Little and C. Morris (eds), 45–59.

—— (2006), 'From "As Good as Gold" to "Gold Diggers": Farming Women and the Survival of the British Family Farming', *Sociologia Ruralis* 46:4, 280–98.

Probyn, E. (1993a), 'Introduction: Speaking the Self and Other Feminist Subjects', in E. Probyn (ed.), 1–6.

—— (ed.) (1993b), *Sexing the Self. Gendered Positions in Cultural Studies* (London: Routledge).

Prokos, A. and Padavic, I. (2002), '"There Ought to be a Law Against Bitches": Masculinity Lessons in Police Academy Training', *Gender, Work and Organization* 9:4, 439–59.

Puwar, N. (2004), *Space Invaders: Race, Gender and Bodies Out of Place* (Oxford: Berg).

Qualitative Solutions and Research (1999), *NUD*IST VIVO for Qualitative Research* (Melbourne: La Trobe).

Ramazanoglu, C. (1993), 'Introduction', in C. Ramazanoglu (ed.), 1–25.

—— (ed.) (1993), *Up Against Foucault: Explorations of Some Tensions Between Foucault and Feminism* (London: Routledge).

Ramazanoglu, C. and Holland, J. (2002), *Feminist Methodology: Challenges and Choices* (London: Sage).

Ramirez-Ferrero, E. (2005), *Troubled Fields: Men, Emotions and the Crisis in American Farming* (New York: Columbia University Press).

Rasmussen, B. (2004), 'Between Endless Needs and Limited Resources: The Gendered Construction of a Greedy Organization', *Gender, Work and Organization* 11:5, 506–25.

Reed, M.G. (2003), *Taking Stands: Gender and the Sustainability of Rural Communities* (UBC Press: Vancouver).

Reed, R. (1996), 'Entrepreneurialism and Paternalism in Australian Management: A Gender Critique of the "Self-Made" Man', in D.L. Collinson and J. Hearn (eds), 99–122.

Repassy, H. (1991), 'Changing Gender Roles in Hungarian Agriculture', *Journal of Rural Studies* 7:1/2, 23–9.

Riley, S. (2001), 'Feminism and Psychology. Maintaining Power: Male Constructions of "Feminists" and "Feminist Values"', *Feminism and Psychology* 11:1, 55–78.

Roberts, H. (ed.) (1981), *Doing Feminist Research* (London and New York: Routledge).

Roden, F.S. (2005), 'Becoming Butlerian: On the Discursive Limits (and Potentials) of Gender Trouble', in M.S. Breen and W.J. Blumenfeld (eds), 27–41.

Roper, M. (1996), '"Seduction and Succession": Circuits of Homosocial Desire in Management', in D.L. Collinson and J. Hearn (eds), 210–26.

Rose, G. (1993), *Feminism and Geography* (Cambridge: Policy Press).

Rosener, J.B. (1990), 'Ways Women Lead', *Harvard Business Review* November/December, 119–25.

Rosenfeld, R.A. (1985), *Farm Women: Work, Farm and Family in the United States* (Chapel Hill: The University of North Carolina Press).

Rutherford, S. (2001), 'Organizational Cultures, Women Managers and Exclusion', *Women in Management Review* 16:8, 371–82.

Sachs, C. (1983), *The Invisible Farmers: Women in Agricultural Production* (Totowa NJ: Rowman and Allenheld).

—— (1996), *Gendered Fields, Rural Women, Agriculture and Environment* (Boulder: Westview Press).

Samantra, R.K. (ed.) (1995), *Women in Agriculture: Emerging Issues, Problems and Prospects* (New Delhi: MD Publications).

Saugeres, L. (2002a), 'Of Tractors and Men: Masculinity, Technology and Power in a French Farming Community', *Sociologia Ruralis* 42:2, 143–59.

—— (2002b), 'She's Not Really a Woman, She's Half a Man: Gendered Discourse of Embodiment in a French Farming Community', *Women's Studies International Forum* 25:6, 641–50.

—— (2002c), 'The Cultural Representation of the Farming Landscape: Power, Masculinity, Nature', *Journal of Rural Studies* 18:4, 373–84.

Sawicki, J. (1991), *Disciplining Foucault: Feminism, Power and the Body* (New York: Routledge).

Schacht, S.P. (1997), 'Feminist Fieldwork in the Misogynistic Setting of the Rugby Pitch', *Journal of Contemporary Ethnography* 26:3, 338–63.

Scheurich, J.J. (2001), *Research Method in the Postmodern* (London: Routledge).

Schmitt, M. (1998), 'Gender Segregation at Vocational Schools – Women Farm Apprentices' Dilemma', *Sociologia Ruralis* 38:3, 303–317.

Schoenberger, E. (1991), 'The Corporate Interview as a Research Method in Economic Geography', *Professional Geographer* 43:2, 180–89.

Schwalbe, M. and Wolkomir, M. (2001), 'The Masculine Self as Problem and Resource in Interview Studies of Men', *Men and Masculinities* 4:1, 90–103.

—— (2003), 'Interviewing Men' in J.A. Holstein and J.F. Gubrium (eds), 55–72.

Scott, J. (1988), 'Deconstructing Equality Versus Difference: Or, the Uses of Poststructuralist Theory for Feminism', *Feminist Studies* 14:1, 33–50.

Scott, S. (1996), 'Drudges, Helpers and Team Players: Oral Historical Accounts of Farm Work in Appalachian Kentucky', *Rural Sociology* 61:2, 209–222.

Scutt, J.A. (1997), *The Incredible Woman Power and Sexual Politics Volume 2* (Melbourne: Artemis).

Sedgwick, E.K. (1985), *Between Men. English Literature and Male Homosocial Desire* (New York: Columbia University Press).

Sheppard, D.L. (1989), 'Organizations, Power and Sexuality: The Image and Self-Image of Women Managers', in J. Hearn, D.L. Sheppard, P. Tancred-Sheriff and G. Burrell (eds), 139–57.

Sheridan, A. (1994), 'Women in Agriculture: Where Are They?', in M.A. Franklin, L.M. Short and E.K. Teather (eds), 18–23.

Sheridan, A., Pini, B. and Conway, L. (2006), 'Modestly Staffed and Modestly Resourced: Understanding Women's Entrance to Regional Governance', *Rural Society* 16:3, 271–82.

Shortall, S. (1994), 'Farm Women's Groups: Feminist or Farming or Community Groups, or New Social Movements?', *Industrial and Labor Relations Review* 28:1, 279–91.

—— (1999), *Women and Farming: Property and Power* (London: Macmillan).

—— (2000), 'In and Out of the Milking Parlour: A Cross-National Comparison of Gender, the Dairy Industry and the State', *Women's studies International Forum* 23:2, 247–57.

—— (2001), 'Women in the Field: Women, Farming and Organizations', *Gender, Work and Organization* 8:2, 164–81.

—— (2006), 'Gender and Farming: An Overview', in B.B. Bock and S. Shortall (eds), 19–26.

Silvasti, T. (2003), 'Bending Borders of Gendered Labour Division on Farms: The Case of Finland', *Sociologia Ruralis* 43:2, 154–66.

Sinclair, A. (1995), 'Sexuality in Leadership', *International Review of Women and Leadership* 1:2, 25–38.

—— (1998), *Doing Leadership Differently* (Melbourne: Melbourne University Press).

—— (2000), 'Teaching Managers About Masculinities: Are You Kidding?' *Management Learning* 31:1, 83–101.

—— (2005), 'Body and Pedagogy', *Gender, Work and Organization* 112:1, 89–104.

Skelton, C. (2000), 'A Passion for Football: Dominant Masculinities and Primary Schooling', *Sport, Education and Society* 5:1, 5–18.

—— (2001), *Schooling the Boys: Masculinities and Primary Education* (Buckingham: Open University Press).

—— (2003), 'Male Primary Teachers and Perceptions of Masculinity', *Educational Review* 50:2, 195–209.

Smithson, J. and Stokoe, E.H. (2005), 'Discourses of Work-Life Balance: Negotiating "Genderblind" Terms in Organizations', *Gender, Work and Organization* 12:2, 147–68.

Smyth, A. (1992), 'A Political Postcard from a Peripheral Pre-postmodern State (of Mind) of How Alliteration and Parenthesis Can Knock You Down Dead in Women's Studies', *Women's Studies International Forum* 15:3, 331–7.

Sonser Breen, M. and Blumenfeld, W.J. (eds) (2005), Butler *Matters: Judith Butler's Impact on Feminist and Queer Studies* (Aldershot: Ashgate).

St Pierre, E.A. (2000), 'Poststructural Feminism in Education: An Overview', *Qualitative Studies in Education* 13:5, 477–515.

Stobke, L. (2005), 'Doing Machismo: Legitimating Speech Acts as a Selection Discourse', *Gender, Work and Organization* 12:2, 105–123.

Symes, D. (1991), 'Changing Gender Roles in Productionist and Post-productionist Capitalist Agriculture', *Journal of Rural Studies* 7:1, 85–90.

Symes, D. and Marsden, T. (1983), 'Complementary Roles and Asymmetrical Lives', *Sociologia Ruralis* 23:3/4, 229–42.

Taylor, A. (1995), 'Glass Ceilings and Stone Walls: Employment Equity for Women in Ontario School Boards', *Gender and Education* 7:2, 123–41.

Taylor, D. and Vintges, K. (eds) (2004), *Feminism and the Final Foucault* (Urbana and Chicago: University of Illinois Press).

Teather, E.K. (1992), 'Remote Rural Women's Ideologies, Spaces and Networks: The Example of the Country Women's Association of New South Wales', *The Australian and New Zealand Journal of Sociology* 28:3, 369–90.

—— (1994), 'Contesting Rurality: Country Women's Social and Political Networks', in S. Whatmore, T. Marsden and P. Lowe (eds), 31–49.

—— (1995), 'Origins of the New Farm Women's Movement in Canada, New Zealand and Australia', *Rural Society* 5:4, 3–12.

—— (1996a), 'Farm Women in Canada, New Zealand and Australia Redefine their Rurality', *Journal of Rural Studies* 12:1, 1–14.

—— (1996b), 'Mandate of the Country Women's Association of New South Wales', *Australian Journal of Social Issues* 31:1, 73–94.

—— (1996c), 'Rural Women's Self-Concepts and Aspirations as Members of Selected Voluntary Organisations in New Zealand, Australia and Canada', *New Zealand Geographer* 52:2, 35–45.

—— (1997), 'Voluntary Organizations as Agents in the Becoming of Place', *Canadian Geographer* 41:3, 226–34.

—— (1998), 'The Double Bind: Being Female and Being Rural: A Comparative Study of Australia, New Zealand and Canada', *Rural Society* 8:3, 209–222.

The London Feminist Salon Collective (2004), 'The Problematization of Agency in Postmodern Theory: As Feminist Educational Researchers, Where do We Go from Here?', *Gender and Education* 16:1, 25–33.

Thomas, R., Mills, A. and Mills, J.H. (eds) (2004), *Identity Politics at Work: Resisting Gender, Gendering Resistance* (New York: Routledge).

Trauger, A. (2004), 'Because They Can Do the Work: Women Farmers and Sustainable Agriculture', *Gender, Place and Culture* 11:2, 289–307.

Trethewey, A. (1999), 'Disciplined Bodies: Women's Embodied Identities at Work', *Organization Studies* 20:3, 423–50.

Van de Burg, M. and Endeveld, M. (eds) (1994), *Women on Family Farms: Gender Research, EC Policies and New Perspectives* (Wageningen: Wageningen University).

Van der Plas, L. and Fonte, M. (eds) (1994), *Rural Gender Studies in Europe* (Assen, The Netherlands: Van Gorcum).

Verstad, B. (1998), 'Cracking the Glass Ceiling: The Story of the Election Process in the Norwegian Farmers Union in 1997', *Sociologia Ruralis* 38:3, 409–426.

Voyce, M. (1993), 'The Farmer and His Wife', *Alternative Law Journal* 18:3, 121–5.

Wajcman, J. (1999), *Managing Like a Man: Women and Men in Corporate Management* (St Leonards: Allen and Unwin).

Wallace, C., Abbot, P. and Lankshear, G. (1996), 'Women Farmers in South-west England', *Journal of Gender Studies* 5:1, 49–62.

Wallace, C., Dunkerley, D., Cheal, B. and Warren, M. (1994), 'Young People and the Division of Labour in Farming Families', *The Sociological Review* 42:3, 501–530.

Ward, R. (1958), *The Australian Legend* (Oxford: Oxford University Press).

Weedon, C. (1987), *Feminist Practices and Poststructuralist Theory* (Oxford: Blackwell).

Wells, B. and Tanner, B. (1994), 'The Organisational Potential of Women in Agriculture to Sustain Rural Communities', *Journal of the Community Development Society* 25:2, 246–58.

Wells, N. (1998), 'Creating a Public Space for Women in US Agriculture: Empowerment, Organization and Social Change', *Sociologia Ruralis* 38:3, 371–90.

West, C. and Fenstermaker, S. (1993), 'Power, Inequality and the Accomplishment of Gender: An Ethnomethodological View', in P. England (ed.), 151–74.

West, C. and Zimmerman, D.H. (1987), 'Doing Gender', *Gender and Society* 1, 125–51.

—— (2002), 'Doing Gender' in S. Fenstermaker and C. West (eds), 2–23.

Wetherell, M. and Edley, N. (1999), 'Negotiating Hegemonic Masculinity: Imaginary Positions and Psycho-Discursive Practices', *Feminism and Psychology* 9:3, 335–56.

Whatmore, S. (1991), *Farming Women: Gender, Work and Family Enterprise* (Houndmills: Macmillan).

—— (1994), 'Theoretical Achievements and Challenges in European Rural Gender Studies', in M. Van de Burg and M. Endeveld (eds), 107–120.

Whatmore, S., Marsden, T. and Lowe, P. (eds) (1994), *Gender and Rurality* (London: David Fulton).

Whitehead, S. (1999a), 'From Paternalism to Entrepreneurialism: The Experience of Men Managers in UK Postcompulsory Education', *Discourse* 20:1, 57–72.

—— (1999b), 'Review Article: Hegemonic Masculinity Revisited', *Gender, Work and Organization* 6:1, 58–62.

—— (2002), *Men and Masculinities* (Cambridge: Polity).

Wicks, D. (2002), 'Institutional Bases of Identity Construction and Reproduction: The Case of Underground Coal Mining', *Gender, Work and Organization* 9:3, 308–335.

Wiegman, R. (2002), 'Unmaking: Men and Masculinity in Feminist Theory', in J.K. Gardiner (ed.), 31–59.

Wilson, M. (1995), 'Afterword: Perspectives and Difference: Sexualization, the Field and the Ethnographer', in D. Kulick and M. Wilson (eds), 251–75.

Winchester, H.P.M. (1996), 'Ethical Issues in Interviewing as a Research Method in Human Geography', *Australian Geographer* 2:1, 117–31.

Wood, G.J. and Newton, J. (2006), 'Childlessness and Women Managers: "Choice", Context and Discourses', *Gender, Work and Organization* 13:4, 338–58.

Woodward, R. (1998), 'It's a Man's Life: Soldiers, Masculinity and the Countryside', *Gender, Place and Culture* 5:3, 277–300.

—— (2000), 'Warrior Heroes and Little Green Men: Soldiers, Military Training and Construction of Rural Masculinities', *Rural Sociology* 65:4, 640–57.

Woodward, R. and Winter, P. (2006), 'Gender and the Limits to Diversity in the Contemporary British Army', *Gender, Work and Organization* 13:1, 45–76.

Yeoh, B.S.A., Teo, P. and Huang, S. (eds) (2002), *Gender Politics in the Asia-Pacific Region* (London: Routledge).

Zalewski, M. (2000), *Feminism After Postmodernism* (London: Routledge).

Zalewski, M. and Parpart, J. (eds) (1998), *The 'Man' Question in International Relations* (Boulder: Westview Press).

Index

farmers
  different from managers 78–9
  masculine identity 24–6, 34, 72–6
  physicality 30
  sexuality 28–9
  women 75–6
Farmers' Union
  authoritarianism 64–6
  battlefield imagery 73–4
  Chairman 59, 73, 78–81, 121
  Chief Executive Officer (CEO) 55–6, 82
  comparison with other organizations
    81–2
  electoral system 60–3, 118–19
  entrepreneurialism 66–8
  gender inequality 2
  gendered division of labour 57
  interviews 40–6, 117–18, 127
  management structure 39–40, 55–7,
    79–81, 120–1
  masculine identities 71–83, 120
  meetings 58–60
  paternalism 55–64, 68–9, 118–19
  professionalism 67–8
  resistance to change 121–2
  symbols and images 63–4
  women's networks 59, 64–6, 85 100,
    121–2
  women's place 72–7, 82–3
  Young Farmers' Group 66–8, 69, 119
farming organizations *see* agricultural
    organizations
Federated Women's Institutes of Ontario
    (FWIO) 86
Fellows, W. 29
feminist scholarship
  methodology 35–6
  rural agriculture 2–3
feminist theory
  gender identity 6–9
  and poststructuralism 4–6
Finney, M. 20
focus groups 65–6, 75, 127–8
Foucault, M. 4, 5–6, 114
France, farmer identities 25

Gardiner, J.K. 35
gender
  and agricultural management 124–5
  consciousness 103
  discourses 125

division of labour 57
management strategies 105–14
as performative 6–9
symbols and images 63–4
theories of 4–9
see also women
Gilbert, P. 20
globalization, and masculinity 19
Gramsci, A. 10
Gullifer, J. 30

Halford, S. 107
Harter, L.M. 32–3
Haugen, M.S. 25, 31–2, 43, 98, 101
Hearn, J. 1, 18, 51–5, 63, 65
hegemonic masculinity 10–13, 124
Herod, A. 47–8
heterosexuality, managerial masculinity 41–3
Hickey-Moody, A. 19
Hill, F. 117
homosexuality, farmers 29
'homosocial desire' 54, 60
Horn, R. 37
Howard, John 21
hunting, and masculinity 20

identity
  gender identity 6–9, 19–20
  masculine 24–6, 34, 71–83, 120
informalism, managerial masculinity 53–4
interviews
  Farmers' Union 40–6, 127
  gender dynamics 46–8, 117–18
  heterosexual men 41–3
  knowledgeable men 44–6
  male interviewer 48
  of men by women 36–9, 117–18
  powerful men 43–4
  women agricultural managers 102–3
Ireland
  agricultural masculinities 27
  rural masculinity 19–20

Jarnagin, S. 26
Jones, O. 21–2

Kanter, R.M. 114
Kenway, J. 19
Kerfoot, D. 59, 62, 64, 80
Knights, D. 54, 59, 62, 64, 80
Knoppers, A. 55

Printed in the United States
by Baker & Taylor Publisher Services